BLADES
ON ICE

A century of professional hockey

BLADES ON ICE

A century of professional hockey

CHRYS GOYENS | FRANK ORR

WITH

ALLAN TUROWETZ AND JEAN-LUC DUGUAY

TPE PUBLISHING

PUBLISHED BY
Team Power Enterprises Inc.
181 Whitehall Drive
Markham, Ontario
L3R 9T1

PROJECT DIRECTOR AND PUBLISHER
Allan Turowetz

TEXTS
Chrys Goyens, Frank Orr
with Allan Turowetz, Jean-Luc Duguay

PRODUCTION MANAGERS
Julie Desilets, Geneviève Desrosiers | GSM Design

PHOTO RESEARCH
Stu Hackel, Chrys Goyens

ART DIRECTION
Julie Desilets | GSM Design

GRAPHIC DESIGN AND COMPUTER GRAPHICS
GSM Design | Interiors, Visual Communication and Exhibition Inc.

PRINTING
Imprimerie Quebecor Graphique-Couleur

BINDING
Multi Reliure S.F. Inc.

CANADIAN CATALOGUING IN PUBLICATION DATA
Goyens, Chrys
Blades on Ice: A century of professional hockey
Issued also in French under title: Épopée sur glace : un siècle de hockey professionnel
Includes bibliographical references and index.

ISBN 0-9686220-0-3

1. National Hockey League – History.   2. Hockey – History.   3. Patrick family.
I. Orr, Frank, 1936-   II. Turowetz, Allan, 1948-   III. Team Power Enterprises.
IV. Title.   V. Title: Century of professional hockey.

GV847.8.N3G69 2000   796.962'64'09   C99-901623-7

Legal deposit, first quarter, 2000
National Library of Canada
Bibliothèque nationale du Québec
© Team Power Enterprises Inc.

PRINTED AND BOUND IN CANADA

CONTENTS

FOREWORD

A century of professional hockey.

Absorbing all of the meaning
and nuance of that short phrase makes humble men
of all of us who were fortunate enough to make our living
at this wonderful game.

A century of professional hockey.

This puts into context for me the enormity of accomplishment, and brings to mind memories, some long faded, of the colorful players and superstars who appeared in the National Hockey League, and other professional leagues, before I signed up for my rookie year in 1953. My heroes as a child.

Moreover, it evokes the wonderful talents that graced arenas during my time, which some call hockey's Golden Era, and the years of growth and development since my retirement in 1971.

Newsy, Howie, Eddie, Ace, the Reds, Hap, King... nicknames of a time long ago merge with those of my day... The Old Lamplighter, The Golden Jet, Moose, Jake the Snake, Gump, Punch, Boom Boom, Big M, Mr. Hockey and the Rocket.

And then we passed the torch to *Le Démon Blond*, The Great One, Nifty, Big Phil, Mario and friends... until, one day, they also moved on.

This book is all about the players who wore the many, many uniforms that filled North American arenas on winter nights for five generations. And about those who will come to share in the legacy of the greatest game.

Jean Béliveau

Jean Béliveau

I NTRODUCTION

The intergenerational debate forever rages...

Walter (Babe) Pratt's playing days were two decades behind him on this day in the early 1970s. The gregarious westerner's on-ice performances paled in comparison with his extracurricular shenanigans and quick wit that amused Broadway and probably added the final touch of snow to the silver mane on the head of the great Lester Patrick, Pratt's boss in New York.

Babe's son Tracy then was a regular with the Buffalo Sabres, along with the Vancouver Canucks in the class of '70 expansion that lifted the NHL population to fourteen teams. Pratt senior was hunkered down in Vancouver, an entertaining TV color man for the CBC and, later, a roving ambassador for the Canucks.

After a game-day morning "skate" at Pacific Coliseum, Pratt was swapping yarns with Frank Orr, co-author of this piece and a raconteur of note himself, when a small, elderly figure in a topcoat and Homburg hat, but wearing skates and holding a hockey stick, came on the ice for a skate. When asked who the skater was, Pratt replied: *"That's Cyclone."*

In the annals of hockey, the nickname was enough to identify Fred Taylor, the sport's first high-salaried (for the time) superstar. Pratt was asked the familiar question: If Cyclone played in the present NHL (1973), how many goals would he score per season?

That was really two questions in one. The first asked for an evaluation of the diminutive skaters who had played the game very early the century, at a time when hockey was like "rugby on ice" with no substitution. The second dealt with the NHL in the late part of the century, a crash-bang game played at high speed by large men well over two hundred pounds, who worked in 45-second shifts.

Would a tiny, five-foot, five-inch skater, barely one hundred and thirty-five pounds, have a chance in the modern game?

In reply to the how-many-for-Cyclone query, Pratt answered:

"Oh, sixteen or eighteen!"

"But Babe, he was one of the greatest players ever!" was the counter from the surprised questioner.

"Yeah, but he's eighty-nine years old," Pratt replied.

The point was made that professional ice hockey in the century has been several different games, but the athletes who played those games could have been top performers in any era.

Checking the photographs of those who were stars in the game's first quarter-century turns up shortcomings – photography's shortcomings. Those players were not small ice bugs who would be blown away by the draft of today's giant skaters.

They were victims of the art of taking pictures, at that time not the science it would become. The brothers Cleghorn (Sprague and Odie), Bad Joe Hall, Newsy Lalonde and the Johnsons (Moose and Ching), would not back up a step against the modern day gladiators in plastic composites, nylon and kevlar.

As photographers discovered zoom lenses, strobe lighting and hyper-fast film, hockey players captured in the camera's eye appeared bigger, faster and stronger. One reason for the change was that, in reality, they were bigger, faster and stronger. Color film added to the size and menace, TV lighting at modern rinks gave clarity to the action and definition to the players involved in that action.

Today, at century's end, new, multi-purpose entertainment centers have replaced arenas and stadiums. This game we know and love has travelled a long road in the twentieth century, accompanied by the writers and photographers whose job was to pass on the stories.

This book is dedicated to chronicling that century-long road. Our guides are the Patrick family, perhaps hockey's one consistent link for the entire one hundred years.

A Patrick was there every step of the way.

1901
19

Taking
To The
Ice

25

LESTER PATRICK of REHFREW CLUB

The Patrick Odyssey
Begins

South Durham and Carmel Hill.
Drummondville. Rich, arable land,
the kind that would produce hockey
talent with the names of Béliveau
and Perreault in future generations.
In rural Quebec during the late
nineteenth century, this fertile
farmland midway between Quebec
City and Montreal lay fallow,
in hockey terms at least.

Like thousands of other Irishmen who were forced to emigrate during the Potato Famine of the late 1840s, Thomas Patrick undertook the perilous trek to Canada in search of a new future for his wife and three children. Unlike thousands of his countrymen who died horribly of disease and starvation in transit, Patrick, a lawyer, made the transatlantic passage in relative comfort. He settled on a farm near that of his sister in South Durham, some sixty-five miles southeast of Montreal. Another seven children were born in Canada, among them a fifth son, Joseph, in 1857.

In 1881, the young, handsome Joseph left the family farm for nearby Drummondville to take a job as a clerk in a general store. Two years later, he married Grace Nelson, a schoolteacher. On the last day of the year 1883, Curtis Lester Patrick was born and, two years later, on December 21, 1885, Frank Alexis Patrick entered the world.

Like the fictional Henry clan of Herman Wouk's celebrated *The Winds of War*, the Patricks would find themselves at the confluence of several frozen streams of evolution. As a result, their family saga would closely parallel that of Canada and ice hockey in the twentieth century.

In 1887, Joseph Patrick became a partner in a general store in Carmel Hill, nine miles from Drummondville, just as the Intercolonial Railway was developing new lines between Montreal and Halifax. The store soon was supplying the ubiquitous railroad gangs on the line. When Joseph Patrick and his partner sold the store five years later, Patrick realized a profit of ten thousand dollars, a substantial sum in those days. He used half of it to enter the lumber business in Daveluyville, sixty miles southwest of Quebec City.

The Patricks were a typical Canadian family of the time. Although proud Methodists and English-speaking, the Patrick children were educated in local French-language (Roman Catholic) schools because no others were available. Good athletes at a young age, the boys played lacrosse and ran cross-country in the summer, and skated and snowshoed in the winter. They had no exposure to ice hockey. The fledgling game was still confined primarily to the English community of Montreal and environs, and had not made inroads into French Quebec, nor the rural areas of the province.

March 3, 1875

The earliest recorded hockey game is played, with McGill against the Victoria skating club, at the Victoria Rink in Montreal. The teams play with nine men a side, and a flat disk as a puck.

The game began with sticks and skates on frozen ponds.

In 1893, the year that Lord Stanley of Preston donated the Stanley Cup to the "champion of the Dominion", the Patrick family moved to Montreal. That year, the Montreal Amateur Athletic Association (MAAA) team bested Ottawa, the Crystals, Quebec and the Victorias to win the first-ever Cup, and players named Haviland Routh, Billy Barlow, Archie Hodgson and James Stewart became household heroes in Canada's metropolis. Lester Patrick, ten, and brother Frank, eight, were suitably impressed and soon were playing shinny on river ice opposite Nun's Island, southwest of the downtown core. When nature couldn't provide ice, the firemen in the Point St. Charles firehouse were cajoled into lending their hoses to freeze the vacant lot across the street from the Patrick home on Guy street.

Shinny, as Lester and Frank discovered, had but one rule: There were no rules. Knocked flat on your back, you were expected to get back up and rejoin the fray, doing your best to control whatever served as a puck with a combination of powerful skating, gymnastic balance and the stickhandling wizardry of a bandmaster. *"The best hockey school that ever existed,"* Lester Patrick would tell his New York Rangers fifty years later.

Within two years of the family's arrival in Montreal, the success of Joe Patrick's business dealings led to a move "uptown" to Westmount and to the boys meeting a new friend and neighbor, Arthur Howie Ross. The Patricks and Ross became inseparable, especially on the hockey rink, and soon were stalwarts on their high school team as well as "ringers" on regular call for action in neighborhood leagues all over the city.

> *"Shinny was the best hockey school that ever existed," Lester Patrick would tell his New York Rangers fifty years later*

December 27, 1897

In the only Stanley Cup challenge of the season, the defending champion Montreal Victorias turn back the Ottawa Capitals, 15-2, to retain their champion status.

The Montreal Gazette publishes the first formal rules of hockey, in an article entitled "Hockey on Ice".

February 27, 1877

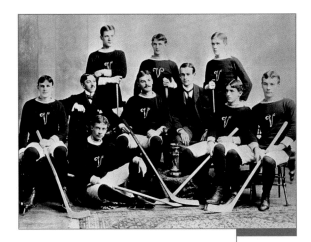

The Montreal Victorias in 1897

Montreal at this time was the capital of organized amateur, and then professional, ice hockey, for two reasons. The city's climate, shared with two other St. Lawrence Lowland cities, Ottawa and Quebec City, was uniformly cold in the winter, which allowed a lengthy season on outdoor or indoor natural ice. Second, the development of the railways, and the short distances between Montreal and Ottawa to the west, and Quebec to the northeast, made it convenient for quick day trips to either city. Teams could play games in the early evening and return home by rail late at night or early the next morning, allowing the players to return to their regular jobs. This meant that the best talents from the Ottawa Valley or the Montreal area could play top-level competitive hockey in their own backyard, before family, friends and co-workers. Southeastern Ontario centers like Kingston and Cornwall fell within this sphere of hockey influence.

In 1893, the Amateur Hockey Association of Canada was a five-team league comprising Quebec, Ottawa and three Montreal teams, the Crystals, Victorias and MAAA (Winged Wheelers). In 1896, the Shamrocks replaced the Crystals. During hockey's first two decades, most action circulated in and around the metropolis on the St. Lawrence, and although the league name would vary – Canadian Amateur Hockey League, Eastern Canada Amateur Hockey Association and others – most seasons it featured three or four teams from Montreal, as well as single entries from Quebec and Ottawa.

In the first decade of the twentieth century, Toronto was a hockey island unto itself, remote from the development centers of hockey in the eastern triangle and northwestern Ontario. Toronto's first Cup challenge, by the city's Wellingtons in 1902, saw the team drop a two-game series to the Winnipeg Victorias, 5-3, and 5-3, at Winnipeg. The Victorias would then lose to the Montreal Amateur Athletic Association's "Little Men of Iron" in a three-game set in the Manitoba capital.

*A game between the MAAA and the Victorias
at Montreal's Victoria Rink in 1892*

Hockey was developing in other parts of the country, as well. In February 1896, the Winnipeg Victorias travelled east and defeated the Montreal Victorias, 2-0, in a single challenge match to win the Stanley Cup. The Montreal team regained the trophy in December of that year with a 6-5 win in the Manitoba capital.

A thirteen-year-old Lester Patrick attended the 2-0 game with his father and was impressed mainly by the size of the crowd; one thousand, five hundred fans packed into the Victoria Arena.

When the new two thousand, five hundred-seat Montreal Arena was opened in Westmount in 1898, Lester Patrick was the visiting teams' stick boy, and a partner with Art Ross in a burgeoning scalping operation. The teenagers bought impressive numbers of reserved seat tickets for big games at thirty-five cents each and sold them for twice that and more as game time approached. At a championship game in 1899, Lester Patrick cleared the princely sum of fifteen dollars as a ticket entrepreneur.

Frank Patrick as a teenager

The Patricks and Ross made their marks on the ice, as well, and Lester was a star rover on the McGill University squad in 1902-03. He was good enough that the Montreal Shamrocks offered a tryout, but Joe Patrick demurred. The CAHL teams, the same as those in other leagues in Canada and the United States, were amateur in name only, and Lester would have lost his status as a "true" amateur in the university league had he succumbed to the Shamrocks' offer. That spring, however, Lester Patrick explained to his father that a university education was not high on his list of priorities.

Ottawa Silver Seven star Frank McGee records the first five-goal game in Stanley Cup history in an 11-2 win over the challenging Toronto Marlboros.

Hern, Glass, Stuart, Johnson and Marshall of Montreal Wanderers become the first pro players to compete for the Stanley Cup as defending champion Montreal downs the challenging New Glasgow (Nova Scotia) Cubs 10-3.

December 27, 1906

Amateur hockey evolved into professional hockey at the turn of the century with nary a missed beat. The typical sportsman of the Gay Nineties was nothing if not practical, whatever his class and means. Hard-nosed miners in Michigan's copper country, or those who extracted the rich silver lode of eastern Ontario, and their employers, supported teams of "hired guns" early in the new century. In Montreal, various large social clubs competed against each other in a variety of sporting events year-round, and that competition led to heavy wagering by club supporters from all walks of life.

Students at McGill University, the first participants in the development of the modern game, were not above a "sporting bet" for intra-mural or inter-scholastic competitions. The "gentlemen's wager" was all-pervasive, transcending class, wealth and position.

In hockey's earliest days, there often was more action in the stands than on the ice. The best way to guarantee victory and protect one's wager was to encourage the best talent to play for the favored club.

Thus, the money that circulated in the stands found its way to ice level, and it became a common practice for amateur teams to pay their top three or four performers.

A game at McGill in the 1890s

Taking to the Ice

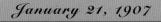

*Lester Patrick
as a teenager*

Even more interesting was how ice hockey policed itself in this matter. Moving down to ice level with the betting machine were "professional gentlemen", those who were charged in other organizations, such as The Jockey Club, with protecting the integrity of the wager. Among their number would be such notables as Léo Dandurand of the Montreal Canadiens, and his successor, Senator Donat Raymond, and Conn Smythe of the Toronto Maple Leafs. In fact, the powerhouse Leafs and Maple Leaf Gardens might not have seen the light of day in the early 1930s except for three judicious wagers placed and won (on hockey, the horses and college football) by Smythe.

Lester Patrick was exposed to the pecuniary aspects of amateur hockey at an early age, after informing his father that university was not for him. In the spring of 1903, the twenty-year-old followed Horace Greeley's advice and took the train to Calgary, with visions of the cowboy life dancing in his head.

In the Alberta town, all of Lester's dreams of the western life were dashed quickly. When he combined the low pay (twenty dollars per month), and long hours (sunrise to sunset) with his discomfort atop a horse, Lester elected to join the Canadian Pacific Railway as a chainman on a survey gang. When winter ended that activity for the year, he stopped off in Brandon, Manitoba, to visit with three Montreal friends who were playing hockey there. He was offered a "job" on the amateur team for his board and twenty-five dollars in expenses, and went on to play cover-point (a free-wheeling defenseman) on the team that won the Manitoba League. Lester's first exposure to the Stanley Cup as a player came when the Brandon team travelled to Ottawa to challenge the redoubtable Silver Seven, giving a good account of themselves before losing, 6-3, and, 9-3.

In 1904, the "Eastern Triangle" hockey scene was in turmoil. The previous season saw a split into two leagues, the CAHL of Quebec, Victorias, MAAA, Shamrocks and Ottawa, and the new Federal League of the Wanderers, Nationals, Cornwall and a second Ottawa team, the Capitals. Adding to the confusion, the defending Stanley Cup champions, the Silver Seven, resigned from the CAHL over the form of a Cup challenge. The league argued that its top team should defend the Cup, not the previous winner.

January 21, 1907

Kenora Thistles, with Art Ross on defense, win their only Stanley Cup championship, defeating the Wanderers, 8-6, at Montreal. ▶

Montreal Canadiens of the National Hockey Association play the first game in their history before five thousand fans at the Jubilee Rink in east-end Montreal. They beat Cobalt 7-6 in overtime.

January 5, 1910

The First Pro League

At the turn of the century, Doc Gibson discovered that copper was better than gold as a hockey metal. The result of this "discovery" was hockey's first professional team, the Portage Lake club of Houghton, Michigan, and the first professional league, the International Hockey League.

J.L. (Doc) Gibson

J.L. Gibson was a member of a team in Berlin (now Kitchener), Ont., that was tossed out of the Ontario Hockey Association in 1898 when the players received ten-dollar gold coins for their contributions in an important win, a violation of the amateur rules. Gibson became a dentist and took up practice in Houghton, a small city in northern Michigan, and an area where copper mining was big.

Homesick for hockey, and no stranger to a sporting wager, Gibson founded the Portage Lake team there and recruited Canadian amateur players for his club, turned them into professionals by paying them and dominated hockey in the area. Other teams, some backed by investors with mining interests, paid Canadian players to compete against Gibson's team. The result was the International league, which started in 1904 with Houghton, the Calumet-Larium Miners, the Indians of Sault Ste. Marie, MI., the Canadian Soo and two teams in Pittsburgh, which had one of only two artificial ice surfaces in existence.

Several young players destined to be major stars played in the league, including Newsy Lalonde (Canadian Soo), and the Houghton quartet of Cyclone Taylor, Riley Hern, Bruce Stuart and Joe Hall. The International League lasted for four seasons, folding when a recession hit the copper mining industry.

At season's end, Ottawa retained the championship of the Dominion by taking on all comers from all leagues, except the CAHL. A Winnipeg Rowing Club entry lost in three games, and then Toronto Marlboros, the Ontario Hockey Association champs, were dispatched, 6-3, and, 11-2.

The Stanley Cup trustees then decreed that a two-game series involving the Federal League champion Wanderers must be accepted. The teams played to a 5-5 tie in the first match, but the challengers refused overtime in a dispute with the referee. The trustees promptly ordered a new, two-game series to be played, both games in Ottawa, and the Wanderers refused, arguing that the tied game should be replayed in Montreal. The series never resumed and the Silver Seven completed their Cup challenge season with the two-game defeat of Lester Patrick's Brandon team.

Organizational chaos continued in the next season, and in 1905, the CAHL expanded to six teams, one from Quebec and five from Montreal: The Victorias, MAAA, Westmount, the Shamrocks and the Nationals. The Nationals folded after losing their first four games by a combined score of 42-6. Ottawa's J.P. Dickson kept his team out of the league, claiming the talent base was diluted by the new teams. He would reconsider only if the Victorias and Wanderers, Westmount and the MAAA, would merge into two competitive teams.

The Mighty Ottawas

The century's first quarter belonged to teams representing Ottawa, called the Silver Seven, in three consecutive Stanley Cup wins from 1903 to 1905, and the Senators in two later periods of pro hockey domination. In twenty-seven years, Ottawa teams won the Cup nine times, and many hockey historians argue that the number should be ten or more.

"There should have been plenty of good hockey players in Ottawa," said Frank (King) Clancy, who joined the Senators as an eighteen-year-old defenseman in 1921 and spent sixty-five years in and around the NHL. *"From late November to early April, it was so cold there wasn't much to do but skate and play hockey, and the Rideau Canal gave us a great spot to practise and play shinny."*

Led by Frank (One-Eye) McGee, Harry Westwick and goalie Bouse Hutton, the Silver Seven won three consecutive Cups, involving nine challenges. That included one of hockey's great folk tales, the twenty-three-day trip by the Dawson City Klondikers to lose to the Seven.

In 1906, sole credit for winning the Stanley Cup went to the Wanderers, who beat the Silver Seven, 12-10, on aggregate in their final series. However, Ottawa had already defended twice that year, against Queen's University and Smiths Falls.

With goalie Percy Lesueur as an anchor and such stars as Cyclone Taylor and Bruce Stuart, the Senators won the Cup in 1909 and 1911.

In eight seasons, from 1920 to 1927, the Senators won the Cup four times and were in three NHL finals with some of the best rosters ever assembled, coached by Pete Green. Goalies Clint Benedict and Alex Connell, Clancy, Lionel Hitchman, Eddie Gerard and George (Buck) Boucher on defense, forwards Frank Nighbor, Cy Denneny, Frank Finnigan, Jack Darragh and Punch Broadbent, were the stars of a superb team.

"We could beat you any way you wanted to play," Clancy said. *"We could score a few, we were great defensively, and if you wanted to play tough, we could handle that, too."*

Believed to be the first "flash" action photography of an indoor hockey game, Ottawa versus the Wanderers, 1905

The Ottawa Silver Seven,
arch-foes of the Montreal Wanderers

The Wanderers were refused admission because league president F. McRobie was not convinced that all of their players had amateur status. The team played a second Federal League season, joined by the Silver Seven. In reality, what existed was enough good teams for one league divided between two circuits, the Silver Seven and Wanderers in the Federal League, and the Victorias, MAAA and Quebec in the CAHL.

Making their CAHL debut that season with the mediocre Westmount team were defensemen Lester Patrick and Art Ross. Forward Frank Patrick, the McGill captain, played two games for the team during a break in the intercollegiate season.

Terrible goaltending was a Westmount woe, although goalie Fred Brophy caused a minor sensation in February when he rushed the length of the ice to score on Quebec's Paddy Moran. Despite Brophy's heroics, Quebec thrashed Westmount, 17-5, in a game that was a microcosm of Westmount's season. The team tied for fourth place with the Shamrocks, both with three wins and seven losses.

Ross scored ten goals, Lester Patrick had eight in eight games, and Frank counted four in his two games. Managers of other teams were happily awaiting the dissolution of the Westmount franchise to sign up the talented trio. Meanwhile, Ottawa repeated as Cup champs in 1905.

March 8, 1910

"Newsy" Lalonde scores six goals to lead the Renfrew Creamery Kings (also known as the "Millionaires") to a 17-2 win over Ottawa, in an NHA game. ▶

THE REDBANDS PREVAIL

Common sense ruled in the off-season and, on December 11, 1905, a new league – the Eastern Canadian Amateur Hockey Association – was born, featuring six teams: Ottawa, Quebec, MAAA, Shamrocks, Victorias and the Wanderers. Already a powerhouse, the Wanderers were bolstered considerably by the addition of Lester Patrick, Ernie (Moose) Johnson and Ernie Russell. They were thumped, 8-4, by the Silver Seven in their first meeting on January 13 in Ottawa, but three weeks later, with Lester Patrick and Pud Glass leading the way, the Redbands, as they were known, turned the tables on Ottawa, 5-3. At the end of the ten-game season, the teams were tied for first with 9-1 records.

Before the two had a playoff to decide a Cup winner, Ottawa accepted challenges from Queen's University and Smiths Falls, champions of the Federal League, and handily disposed of both, although Smiths Falls goaltender Percy Lesueur was a revelation.

The first game of the two-game, total-goal league series was played March 14 in Montreal, and the Wanderers clobbered the visitors 9-1, handing Ottawa its worst loss in memory. Ernie Russell and Glass led the way with four and three goals each, while Lester Patrick contributed a goal from the rover position.

Three nights later, fortunes were reversed before a frenzied crowd of five thousand that included Earl and Lady Grey, the Canadian Governor-General and his wife, at Dey's Arena in Ottawa. The Wanderers were lucky to escape from a 9-3 defeat with a 12-10 margin in total goals. Ottawa, in the fashion of the day, had "borrowed" Smiths Falls goalie Lesueur for the event and the strategy nearly paid off. In an emotional contest, Ottawa scored first, only to have Moose Johnson restore the nine-goal margin at 10-1. Ottawa then scored nine straight goals to tie the championship when the Wanderers inexplicably retreated into a defensive shell and made no effort to counter.

December 31, 1910

Montreal Canadiens goalie Georges Vézina ▶
plays the first of three hundred and sixty-seven
consecutive regular season and playoff games,
when Montreal loses its NHA season opener, 5-3
to the visiting Ottawa Senators. Vézina played every
game for the team for fifteen seasons.

Barney Stanley scores four goals
as the Vancouver Millionaires
win their only Stanley Cup
championship, with a 12-3 win
over the Ottawa Senators.

March 26, 1915

With the crowd in a frenzy, Lester Patrick took the game in hand. First, he broke away on a two-on-one with Johnson and beat Lesueur to restore the Redbands' lead. Then, with barely two minutes remaining on the clock, Patrick scored again on an end-to-end rush to seal the issue.

Montreal Canadiens win their first Stanley Cup, defeating the PCHA Portland Rosebuds 2-1, to take the final series in a fifth and deciding game.

March 30, 1916

The Wanderers received two "trophies" from the Governor-General. Earl Grey presented the Stanley Cup to the team at game's end. A short time earlier, during a scuffle along the boards, Moose Johnson's stick flew up and knocked the Governor-General's top hat from its normal perch. A quick-thinking Montreal fan, one of the thousand or so who had taken a raucous train trip to Ottawa, made off with the topper. The fan presented it to an overjoyed Johnson in the delirious Redbands' dressing room.

A year later, the Wanderers repeated as champions, going undefeated in their ten-game season. In the process, they managed to lose and regain the Stanley Cup within a period of eight weeks. In late December, just prior to the next ECAHA season, the Wanderers repelled a Stanley Cup challenge from New Glasgow, downing the Nova Scotians, 10-3, and, 7-2. In an unusual move, the Stanley Cup trustees decided that the Wanderers also would defend the Cup during the season against the strong Kenora (also called Rat Portage) Thistles of the Northwestern League. Kenora had given Ottawa all it could handle two years before and the Thistles had added two new players, one well-known to the Patricks, Art Ross. The Thistles also featured one of the best skaters in the history of the game, Tom Phillips, another CAHL veteran Art Hooper (MAAA) and American-born defender and rover, Si Griffis.

The Montreal Wanderers, or Redbands, in 1914

December 19, 1917

Seattle Metropolitans of the PCHA are the first U.S.-based team to win the Stanley Cup. Bernie Morris scores six times en route to a 9-1 triumph over the Montreal Canadiens.

The first two games in NHL history are played. Montreal Canadiens defeat Ottawa, 7-4, while the Wanderers outlast Toronto, 10-9.

March 25, 1917

[*The issue of professionalism came to a head at this time; it was no secret that several of the ECAHA teams were paying players, especially the stars*]

Phillips and Hooper scored the goals, and Ross and Griffis provided a stonewall defense, as the speedy Thistles stunned the Montreal crowds with 4-2, and, 8-6, victories and the Cup was on its way to northwestern Ontario. In March, after much wrangling with the Stanley Cup trustees, a two-game series was played in Kenora, and the Ross-less Thistles were defeated, 7-2, and then won 6-5, to lose the Stanley Cup, 12-8, on aggregate. Although the Wanderers ended 1906 and 1907 as Stanley Cup champions, they had been beaten in three of four games by Kenora.

The issue of professionalism came to a head at this time. It was no secret that Kenora and several of the ECAHA teams were paying players, especially the stars. The Wanderers were no different, as veterans Riley Hern in goal, Pud Glass, Moose Johnson and Jack Marshall split a pot of two thousand dollars.

Patrick was a classic amateur, earning a tidy seventy-five dollars a month from the Canadian (later Dominion) Rubber Company. Many of the "pros", however, did not have regular employment and played for two or three teams as ringers to earn a livelihood. Lester Patrick could afford his amateurism, many others could not and, finally, hockey began to acknowledge that fact. Prior to the 1907 season, it was decided that pros and amateurs could play side-by-side in the ECAHA, but teams had to file declarations listing the status of each player.

Just when Lester Patrick's hockey career was gaining momentum, it appeared to be over. While Lester played for the Wanderers, and Frank captained McGill University, their father sold his Montreal holdings and travelled to British Columbia to scout potentially lucrative timber concessions. He found his tract, and prepared to move the family home to Nelson, B.C., in the summer of 1907.

He asked Lester to accompany him, because Frank was entering his senior year at McGill. Lester had planned to remain for one more hockey season in the east at the request of his friend and teammate Hod Stuart. But, when Stuart lost his life in a tragic diving accident that summer, Lester decided to follow his family to British Columbia. Lester Patrick's move west would have lasting repercussions on the development of professional ice hockey, as well as on his personal life. In Nelson, he met the future Mrs. Patrick, a charming young woman from Nanaimo, B.C., who bore the same first name as Lester's sainted mother, Grace.

Joe Patrick and his eldest son developed their timber stand, bringing twenty French Canadian lumberjacks from Quebec to start the cutting. Meanwhile, Frank starred at McGill, and played for the Montreal Victorias as an amateur, keeping a close eye on developments in players and the game in the east. Lester set up a team in the Nelson city league to stay in shape, and soon someone came calling.

Joe Patrick *(top)* and wife Grace

(right) with Frank and his bride

Catherine, at the family home in

Victoria, on their wedding day.

Left The family logging camp

at Slocan, near Nelson, B.C.

Lester is in the middle, standing.

When the Wanderers were retrieving their Cup from Kenora the previous spring, the Alberta champions from Edmonton downed the Manitoba champs and issued a Stanley Cup challenge. The Albertans received the go-ahead to play a two-game, total-goal series just after Christmas and before the start of the 1909 ECAHA season, and set about recruiting a team. The western champions knew that they needed help against the Wanderers, who had lost only one player, Lester Patrick, and replaced him with a familiar talent, Art Ross.

Those Fabulous O'Briens

J. Ambrose O'Brien

M. J. O'Brien, silver magnate and dandy right down to his pearl-buttoned spats and of "stern regal bearing inclined to portliness," had a "problem". He had far more money than he knew what to do with.

His son, J. Ambrose, was not afflicted with that malady in any way. He talked O'Brien père into bankrolling the Upper Ottawa Valley League, which took in the silver mining town of Cobalt with the Valley centers of Renfrew and Pembroke. Renfrew, a dairy town an hour north of Ottawa, was O'Brien's team of choice, and his Creamery Kings won five consecutive league championships.

M. J. O'Brien specialized in silver, and the most famous prize in the land was a silver bowl which had been donated a decade earlier by Lord Stanley of Preston. The O'Briens aimed for the Cup when they applied for membership in the newly formed Canadian Hockey Association, which started after the Eastern Canada Amateur Hockey Association had split with the rambunctious Montreal Wanderers over home gate receipts for the Redbands, as the Montreal team was known.

When the CHA inexplicably turned down the O'Briens' bid, they had a ready-made ally in Sam Lichtenhein of the Wanderers. Within a month, the O'Briens' National Hockey Association was the dominant league and a merger took place. Six teams: Ottawa, Montreal Shamrocks, Renfrew, Wanderers, Haileybury and Cobalt were ready for action.

At this point J. Ambrose saw an opportunity to boost the gates for the two Montreal teams. He received the go-ahead to form a team representing French Montreal, called them the Canadiens, and seven teams were in the fold when the NHA began play. Meanwhile, the O'Briens had spared no expense in attracting All-Star quality hockey talent to their Renfrew club.

On January 15, 1910, the Renfrew Millionaires made their long-awaited NHA debut in Montreal against the Wanderers, and were thrashed, 7-2. While the Millionaires rebounded with a 9-4 shellacking of the Canadiens, they would never catch the Wanderers, finishing third behind the Ottawa Senators. That spring, the team barnstormed in New York and standing room-only crowds jammed the St. Nicholas Arena to watch the Patricks, Cyclone Taylor and the recently acquired Newsy Lalonde weave their magic against a combined team of Senators and Wanderers.

The following season, without the Patricks who had returned to their western logging interests, the Millionaires once again finished third in what proved to be their swan song. Swamped by two-year losses of close to fifty thousand dollars, the O'Briens decided to move on to other interests and an era had ended.

They had left a dual legacy, however. The Millionaires' trip to New York opened the eyes of the Patrick brothers to two things; the necessity of artificial ice plants for the development of pro hockey and the response to the sport by sophisticated American audiences. The second half of the legacy was the creation of the Canadiens, a franchise that would win more Stanley Cups (twenty-four) than any other.

Most of all, the O'Briens and their bankroll brought credibility to professional ice hockey at a time when franchises were born and died within weeks of each other.

The Haileybury Comets were one of the "reward-driven" teams that mining money bought.

Lester Patrick signed on with the Edmonton team for a hundred dollars in expenses and joined such experienced pros as goaltender Bert Lindsay (late of the International League), the fabulous Tom Phillips (Toronto Marlboros and the Ottawa Silver Seven), Didier Pitre, (International League, Nationals and Shamrocks), Steve Vair and Harold McNamara. In fact, the only player in the Edmonton line-up who had played for the team in a game prior to the Cup challenge was rover Fred Whitcroft, a member of the 1907 Kenora Thistles. It was old home week when Lester, the Happy Wanderer, returned to Montreal with his new team, to be greeted like a long, lost soul by his former teammates.

The Wanderers prevailed 13-10 in the challenge series, winning, 7-3, in the first contest, but losing, 7-6, in the second game when Edmonton returned regulars Harold Deeton (three goals) and Hay Millar (two goals) to their line-up. After the series, Lester had supper with Art Ross, and the conversation turned to hockey and money.

Ross inquired about Lester's stipend, and was told: *"Just expenses."*

"Why do you need to know," Lester retorted.

"Why?" snorted Ross. *"Do you know what kind of money we're getting now in the east to play hockey?"*

Lester knew because Frank Patrick was still playing there. Player salaries averaged six hundred dollars for a ten-game, ten-week season from New Year's Day through mid-March, at a time when a working man could comfortably raise a large family on a salary of fifty dollars a month. Ross had demanded one thousand, six hundred dollars and settled for one thousand, two hundred dollars for his season. He had also received a cash bonus of four hundred dollars to play against Edmonton. Ross also advised Lester that his Edmonton teammate Tom Phillips, who was injured halfway through the first game, received six hundred dollars in advance for his participation. Ironically, when Lester returned home to Nelson, steadfast Joe Patrick asked how much of the hundred dollars had been spent on expenses.

"Sixty-two dollars," Lester replied.

Joe Patrick made him return the thirty-eight dollars outstanding to the Edmonton club. Many years later, Lester mused: *"That must have been the first and last time in history that a hockey player ever returned any part of his expense money."*

Frank Patrick followed

big brother Lester

back east to play for

the Renfrew Millionaires.

He made two thousand

dollars for the season,

and Lester earned

three thousand.

January 31, 1920

Quebec Bulldogs' Joe Malone scores twice to become the NHL's all-time leading goal scorer, with fifty-nine, passing Cy Denneny. His two goals lead the Bulldogs to a 4-3 win over the Toronto Arenas.

Joe Malone sets an NHL record with seven goals in a 10-6 win over Toronto. ▶

The Quebec Bulldogs are transferred to Hamilton, Ontario, where they become known as the "Tigers". Percy Thompson is named the team's general manager.

January 7, 1920

November 2, 1920

The National Hockey Association

Sam Lichtenhein of Montreal Wanderers feuded with other owners in the Eastern Canadian Hockey Association in 1909, and they froze him out by forming a new league, the Canadian Hockey Association, with four teams: Ottawa, Shamrocks, Quebec and All-Montreal. The league also refused the application of J. Ambrose O'Brien of Renfrew.

Lichtenhein and O'Brien formed a new three-team league called the National Hockey Association, with Cobalt as the third team. Fabulous cash rewards were waved in the faces of pro hockey players and, as a result, the Creamery Kings became the Millionaires and players of the caliber of the Patrick brothers and Cyclone Taylor were in the fold.

The CHA and the NHA both opened the 1910 season, but a quick merger took place between the two leagues. Quebec dropped out, replaced by Haileybury, and six teams were ready to play hockey in the National Hockey Association.

J. Ambrose, ever on the lookout for lucrative rivalries, quickly spotted a major shortcoming. Everyone in pro hockey agreed that there were too many teams in Montreal, but a club representing the city's French-language majority was a necessity. O'Brien teamed up with T.C. Hare to launch a team stocked with French-speaking players. Two Ontario boys, Edouard (Newsy) Lalonde of Cornwall, and Didier Pitre of Sault Ste. Marie, were the first selections of the new Canadiens.

Cynical fans saw O'Brien's largesse as a simple attempt to hype the gate, but others hailed him as a visionary, especially when it was disclosed that the agreement had O'Brien turning over the team to French-Canadian interests the following year.

Lichtenhein's Wanderers were vindicated, winning the league championship with an 11-1 record to receive the Stanley Cup. On March 12, they accepted a one-game challenge from Berlin, the champions of the Ontario Professional League, winning, 7-3.

When Frank graduated from McGill, he joined the family lumber company in British Columbia. The brothers were the cornerstones of a plucky Nelson squad that challenged the Edmonton team in 1909, losing 6-5, and, 8-4, in a two-game series. The following winter, the lumber business was at a standstill and Lester talked Joe Patrick into allowing him to return east, where he signed with Renfrew as a professional player.

Lester demanded, and got, the princely sum of three thousand dollars for a twelve-game season, and mentioned that Frank was available for two thousand dollars. Renfrew wired back an agreement and the brothers were en route to a new hockey experience.

*Bert Lindsay was
a top goaltender
of his day.*

While Montreal Shamrocks president W.P. Lunny railed against the "lunacy and profligate spending" that would "ruin hockey", many top players deserted their teams to board the NHA gravy train. When Lester and Frank arrived in the Ottawa Valley, they were greeted by Renfrew's All-Star team of Creamery Kings, Fred (Cyclone) Taylor, goalie Lindsay, wingers Larry Gilmour and Bobby Rowe, center Herb Jordan and two former Edmonton teammates of Lester's, Millar and Whitcroft.

The two top eastern leagues merged and J. Ambrose O'Brien bankrolled a team to represent Montreal's French-speaking majority, the Canadiens.

The seven-team National Hockey Association, Canada's first truly professional league, was born, with three Montreal teams (Shamrocks, Wanderers and Canadiens), two in the Ottawa Valley (Ottawa, Renfrew), and two in northern Ontario mine country (Cobalt, Haileybury).

The Creamery Kings, re-baptized the Renfrew Millionaires, were known in the Ottawa Valley town as the Boarding House Gang because they shared lodgings in the same residence. The players were the focal point of Renfrew society, and the O'Brien family and Renfrew's upper crust were enthusiastic participants in the "social salon."

A time-worn hockey adage says that winning teams should spend more time practising than partying, a fact driven home with brutal clarity when "the best team money can buy" was hammered, 7-2, by the Wanderers in the season opener before a full house of four thousand rabid Montreal fans.

Team Captain Lester Patrick delivered the message to teammates and social butterflies alike, after the game. *"Unfortunately, the opening of the season interfered with our Renfrew social activities,"* he recalled. *"We couldn't please the O'Briens in the drawing room and in the arena, too."*

*Newsy Lalonde, Cyclone Taylor
and Frank Patrick in Renfrew*

The largest crowd ever to watch a hockey game, more than eleven thousand fans, jam the Vancouver Arena for the first game of the Stanley Cup final, as the Millionaires beat the Ottawa Senators, 2-1.

March 21, 1921

Interview

CYCLONE TAYLOR

In the eye of the cyclone

Fred (Cyclone) Taylor was the first quintessential professional hockey player and superstar, unashamedly going "where the game and the money was" during the first two decades of the twentieth century. Barely out of his teens, he played in the first all-professional league for Portage Lake in 1904, and later gravitated to the most famous pro team of that era, the Renfrew Millionaires, at the end of the decade.

Before, after and in-between, Cyclone would wear the sweater of the Ottawa Senators, the Vancouver Millionaires and any other team that needed a swift skater and dead-eye shot, for a price. Oddly enough, one of the prime attractions in luring Taylor to a team was the proximity of a Canadian government office. Like many hockey players of his day when the season was an abbreviated two- or three-months long, and no matter how much money he made, Taylor had a "day job." He was a federal civil servant, and would be on the government payroll until he retired at mid-century.

A player who had a lead role in the game's move from the pond to the arena, Cyclone was eighty-nine years old in 1973, and still went for the occasional skate in his overcoat and homburg hat, when he was interviewed in Vancouver.

YOUR GIVEN NAME IS FREDERICK WELLINGTON TAYLOR. DID YOUR PARENTS HAVE AN INTEREST IN HISTORY?

No, nothing like that. I was named after Frederick Wellington Thomas, the veterinarian in Tara, Ont., where I was born.

WHO GAVE YOU THE "CYCLONE" NICKNAME?

It happened after the first game I played in Ottawa against the Montreal Wanderers, the opening game in the new Ottawa Arena, which had seven thousand, one hundred seats. The Governor-General of Canada, Earl

Grey, was there that night – he donated the Grey Cup that goes to the champions of the Canadian Football League – and I scored four goals. The story goes that after the game, a reporter for the Ottawa Free Press, Malcolm Brice, was close enough to hear Earl Grey say: That new player, number four Taylor; he's a cyclone if I ever saw one. *The next day in the paper, Brice wrote that I had been called a tornado in Manitoba, a whirlwind in Michigan but, from now on, I would be Cyclone Taylor. He wrote about the Governor-General giving me that name, even though many people thought he might have used a little fiction in the story. I was just a country boy from a small town, and it was pretty impressive stuff.*

YOUR SKATING ABILITY WAS A BIG PART OF THE CYCLONE LEGEND. HOW DID YOU DEVELOP THAT?

I did move pretty well on a pair of skates, and the reason for that was some good teachers when I was a young lad. When I was five years old or so, we were living in the little village of Tara, and I tried skating on the town pond, wearing my sister's skates, called clamp skates because they clamped on your boots. The town barber, Jack Riggs, had been a speed skater and he taught a lot of kids in Tara to skate. We moved to Listowel, a bigger town, when I was seven, and there was a pond called the Piggery because it was near the slaughterhouse where they butchered hogs. Sometimes

Interview Cyclone Taylor

it didn't smell very good, but we skated for hours there. When I was sixteen and doing well in junior hockey, Norval Baptie, a famous speed skater, probably the best in the world, had a show he took to different towns. I raced against him a few times, and he taught me many tricks of skating, especially going backwards.

DIDN'T THE ROVER POSITION GIVE YOU A BETTER CHANCE TO USE YOUR SPEED?

I don't like to boast about myself but I was faster than most players in my time. Often, I had to slow down a little or I would be too far ahead of the play to work well with my teammates. Most of the time, I played the rover position, which meant I could go where I wanted on the ice. I developed a habit of skating across the ice to gain speed, then cutting towards the opposition net. We only had seven men plus a spare on a team so if the rover had to skate a lot and was a bit tired, he would switch spots with one of the points, as we called defensemen then, to get a rest for a minute or so.

HOW DID YOU GET FROM LISTOWEL TO PORTAGE LA PRAIRIE IN MANITOBA AS A TEENAGER TO START YOUR PRO CAREER?

I had to go there if I wanted to play. In 1903 when I was nineteen, Bill

Hewitt, whose son Foster was the famous hockey broadcaster, ran the Ontario Hockey Association. I was playing junior hockey in Listowel and working in the piano factory. Hewitt called and asked me to come to Toronto and play for the Marlboros, a senior team. I did not want to go to the big city and when I told Hewitt that, he said if I didn't play in Toronto, I wouldn't play that season. I didn't play because he had the clout to ban me. What Hewitt did was wrong and I could not forgive him for it. In 1904, I had to leave Ontario to play, and I went to Portage La Prairie to play senior hockey for room and board and twenty-five dollars a month spending money.

WHY DID YOU CHOOSE TO GO TO MICHIGAN LATER THAT SEASON?

I had an invitation from the Rat Portage (now Kenora) Thistles to go east with them to challenge for the Stanley Cup. But I also had an offer from the Portage Lake team in Houghton, MI, for four hundred dollars plus expenses for the rest of the season, and that's the offer I took. Copper mining in Michigan was big and so were the iron mines in Pittsburgh and Sault Ste. Marie. There was a fully professional six-team league, the International league, with two teams to Pittsburgh, the two Soos, Houghton and Calumet. I helped the team win that year and, in 1905-06 I was the top scorer and the team won again. But a recession hit the mining industry, and the league folded after the third season.

HOW MANY OFFERS DID YOU HAVE FOR THE NEXT SEASON?

Four from teams in the Eastern Canada Amateur league plus the Renfrew team in the Upper Ottawa Valley league. I had agreed to join the

Ottawa Senators, but I had a misunderstanding with the team and when the Renfrew team offered me more money, two thousand dollars, I explored it. But the Senators intercepted me and their offer of five hundred dollars plus a job as a clerk in the Canadian Civil Service got me back to Ottawa.

THERE WAS MUCH MORE TO THAT SEASON THAN YOUR NEW NICKNAME?

The Senators had a good team with such players as Bruce Stuart and Billy Gilmour, and we won the Stanley Cup in 1909.

WHY DID YOU LEAVE THAT SUCCESS TO GO TO RENFREW THE NEXT SEASON?

Money, pure and simple. The Renfrew Creamery Kings gave me a salary of five thousand, two hundred and fifty dollars for a two-month, twelve-game season. The O'Brien family had made big money in mining and wanted a team that could win the Stanley Cup. You must remember how much money five thousand, two hundred and fifty dollars was in 1908. My father was a salesman for a farm implement company and, if I remember right, he made ninety dollars a month as his top salary. The papers said I was the highest paid athlete in pro team sports. Ty Cobb had signed with the Detroit Tigers for six thousand, five hundred dollars for a baseball season that was seven months and one hundred and fifty-four games long.

DIDN'T THE PLAYERS HAVE THINGS THEIR WAY THEN WITH THE STRONG BIDDING FOR TALENT?

It was a great time for hockey players because the leagues were not very well structured, and we could jump all over the place, going where the money was the best. It wasn't like the 1920s on when a team could tie up your professional rights for life. We knew we were lucky. In the 1909-10 season, there were twenty-five pro teams right across Canada, all bidding for players. It was a little like the mid-1970s with the NHL and the WHA having twenty-eight teams and not enough good players. Back then, the players knew it wouldn't last. The costs of a competitive team were much more than the income produced by the small arenas. The players tried to get all they could before the owners got sick of losing money. For instance, one year there were five pro teams in Montreal, and they all lost money.

WHY COULDN'T THE O'BRIENS BUY A CHAMPIONSHIP FOR RENFREW?

In the two years I was there, we had very good talent but the Montreal Wanderers and then the Ottawa Senators were better teams. But my two years there was a great experience that enriched my life. Most of the players lived in one boarding house, and there were great hockey discussions at the dinner table and far into the night. Lester and Frank Patrick were the two smartest men about hockey I ever met and even at a young age, they had big visions. They talked about their ideas of rules and how hockey should be played, and how the modern game is played is the result of their innovations.

WHY DID YOU SIT OUT 1911-12 HOCKEY SEASON?

The other teams in the league had a draw for the Renfrew players, the Wanderers picked me but I wanted to play in Ottawa. I was working in the immigration department and wanted to stick with it. Ottawa and the Wanderers couldn't reach a deal so I sat out, but the Senators paid my salary of one thousand, two hundred dollars.

HOW DID YOU GET TO VANCOUVER?

At the end of the 1912 season, All-Star teams from the Pacific Coast league and the NHA played a three-game series in Vancouver, and I was to play for the NHA. I had a cut hand and couldn't play until the third game. But that trip convinced me to go out west and play in the new league the Patricks had created. The Toronto Tecumsehs had made a deal for me and offered me three thousand dollars for the 1912-13 season. However, I decided to go to Vancouver and a big reason was that I could transfer there in my immigration department job.

WAS IT A WISE DECISION?

In all ways. I played in a very good hockey league from 1913 to 1922 (one hundred and ninety-four goals in one hundred and eighty-six games). We had an extraordinary team in 1914-15 when we won the west and played the Ottawa Senators for the Stanley Cup. They figured they were bigger and tougher than we were, but we outscored them 26-8 in three games. We got two hundred dollars each for the Cup win. All seven regulars on the Vancouver team (goalie Hugh Lehman, Si Griffis, Mickey MacKay, Frank Patrick, Barney Stanley, Frank Nighbor and Taylor) were voted into the Hockey Hall of Fame, the only team in history that can say that.

YOU WERE ONE OF THE FEW WHO CORRECTLY FORECAST THE TROUBLE TEAM CANADA WOULD HAVE WITH THE RUSSIANS IN THE 1972 SUMMIT SERIES. HOW DID THAT HAPPEN?

In 1958, I paid my way as a fan to go to Russia with a senior team, the Kelowna Packers, for exhibition games against the Russians. I had a chance to study their player development program and talk to the great coach Anatoli Tarasov, and I realized they were on the right track. I watched their teams develop through the 1960s while Canadian hockey seemed to be standing still. When people here predicted a sweep by the Canadian team in 1972, I just said I didn't think it would be easy.

WHAT DO YOU LIKE, AND DISLIKE, ABOUT THE MODERN NHL (IN 1973)?

The players are big and fast and strong, but I don't think their basic skills are that strong. In my days, we played sixty minutes every game, and I liked that idea. I think any man between eighteen and thirty should be able to do that, the way players do in soccer.

DID YOU ACTUALLY SCORE A GOAL SKATING BACKWARDS AS HOCKEY LORE CLAIMS?

If I did, the puck must have hit me on the backside and gone into the net.

The Portage Lake club

The team rebounded with a 9-4 win over the freshmen Canadiens, a game in which Frank Patrick and Montreal's Newsy Lalonde managed to knock each other out with almost simultaneous blows to the head with their sticks. While the Renfrew faithful were upset by the incident, Frank politely invited Newsy back to the boarding house after the contest for a late snack and stitches.

The Wanderers won the league championship and the Stanley Cup that spring, with Ottawa as runner-up.

In a discussion with a team official after a tough 8-5 loss to Ottawa on February 12, Frank Patrick was asked what would put Renfrew over the top. His answer was two words: Newsy Lalonde. Less than a week later, the future Canadiens superstar had a regular berth at the boarding house, and Renfrew's offense shot forward. They destroyed Ottawa, 7-2, in their rematch but, unfortunately, Lalonde's arrival was too little, too late. Renfrew was doomed to finish third, and the Wanderers had their fourth Stanley Cup in five years.

The Renfrew Millionaires take in Manhattan.

Still, the hockey season wasn't over for the Millionaires. Two years earlier, Cyclone Taylor had accompanied his Ottawa team on a barnstorming visit to New York, where they played a two-game exhibition against the Wanderers. Taylor's dashing rushes had seduced Manhattan and sports promoters clamored for a return visit. This time, the Millionaires won a three-game set against a mixed team of Wanderers and Senators. New York, and the burgeoning fan base there, proved an education for Frank and Lester Patrick, and they would put the lessons learned during that week to good use in later years. The Millionaires stayed at the elegant Waldorf Astoria Hotel during their Manhattan sojourn, and another guest in the hotel was a sports promoter named Tex Rickard. Tex and the Patricks were destined to meet in the future.

A week later, the Patrick boys were back in Nelson, tending to the timber business, with Lester's statement that he was finished with ice hockey still ringing in the ears of dubious eastern friends. A lumber boom was on, and the Patricks did very well in the second half of 1910, when the only hockey played by Lester and Frank was with the local Nelson team. In January, 1911, the family sold its interest to an international company, and the two brothers found themselves with impressive cash reserves. Father Joe, nearing retirement age, had travelled about the West Coast and fell in love with Victoria, while Lester adored the attractive provincial capital for another reason: Miss Grace Linn had moved there that same year. On the other hand, Frank wanted a faster pace and found it in Vancouver.

Newsy Lalonde

One of the most fabled figures in Canadian sports history was not a big man at five-feet, nine-inches, and one hundred and sixty-five pounds, but Edouard (Newsy) Lalonde was a large factor in hockey's development from a game played on ponds to a spectator sport.

The son of a Cornwall, Ont., shoemaker, Lalonde acquired his nickname while working at a newspaper in his teens. In hockey and lacrosse, mention of the name "Newsy" caused a reaction of fear and awe.

On the ice, Lalonde was a rare combination of skill and toughness, rivalled only by Ted Lindsay, the superb winger of the Detroit Red Wings in the 1940s and '50s. Playing at center and rover in the seven-man days, Lalonde had an exceptional scoring touch, producing one hundred and twenty-four goals in ninety-nine games in the NHL, and a total of three hundred and fourteen goals in two hundred and twenty games in a career played in several major leagues.

But he is best remembered for his tough, hard play which led to violent clashes with such fabled sluggers as Bad Joe Hall and Sprague Cleghorn, incidents that often included stick-swinging at each other's heads.

Starting in 1905, at seventeen, Lalonde became a hockey itinerant for the next eight seasons in an era when players sold their talent to the highest bidder. He played for eleven different teams, including Sault Ste. Marie, Ont., in the first all-pro International League, and the fabled Renfrew Millionaires. He is best known for his ten seasons with the Montreal Canadiens, and was a big reason for that storied franchise's early success.

"I wasn't very big but I never backed up an inch," Lalonde said. *"I didn't start much trouble, but if anyone did me dirt, he got it right back."*

Lalonde often earned more money playing lacrosse than he did in hockey. In a 1950 poll, he was named the top Canadian lacrosse player of the first half century.

The 1916 Stanley Cup champion Canadiens

ALL-STAR TEAMS

1901

1ST TEAM ★ ★ ★ ★ ★ ★ ★ ★ ★ ★ ★ ★ ★ ★ ★ ★ ★ ★

Coach **Frank Patrick**
Executive **Lester Patrick**

Newsy Lalonde
Center

Jack Darragh
Right Wing

Cy Denneny
Left Wing

Moose Johnson
Defense

ERNIE JOHNSON

Cyclone Taylor
Rover

George Boucher
Defense

Georges Vézina
Goalie

1925 ALL-STAR TEAMS

2ND TEAM

Coach   Pete Green
Executive   J. Ambrose O'Brien

Didier Pitre
Right Wing

Joe Malone
Center

Frank Nighbor
Left Wing

Eddie Gerard
Defense

Frank McGee
Rover

Clint Benedict
Goalie

Sprague Cleghorn
Defense

37

Lads, We Hardly Knew Ye

Into every life, a little rain must fall. Pro hockey in the twentieth century was visited by its own tragedies over the years. The most well-known of these were Joe Hall's death to influenza at the 1918 Stanley Cup final in Seattle, Howie Morenz dying in hospital in March, 1937 after shattering his leg at the Forum, as well as Bill Masterton's untimely death in a January 1968, game between expansion cousins Minnesota North Stars and California Seals.

The first quarter of the century also featured great careers nipped in the bud, and two probably no greater than those of Bruce Ridpath and Alan Davidson.

Ridpath was a great right winger who starred in 1908 and 1909 with Toronto of the Ontario Professional Hockey League. Playing alongside former Renfrew Millionaire Newsy Lalonde, ex-Shamrock Bert Morrison and Wally Mercer, he took part in a Stanley Cup challenge against the Wanderers on March 14, 1908. The Toronto team had won the OPHL championship with a 10-2 won-lost record, represented a decidedly

Bruce Ridpath

inferior league, and that challenged the three-year champions who included such luminaries as Art Ross and Walter Smaill on defense, Pud Glass, Ernie Russell and Moose Johnson up front, and Riley Hern in goal. Still, the champions from the new league gave a good account of themselves — Ridpath proved to be the fastest skater on the ice and managed a goal (Lalonde had two) in a 6-4 loss to the heavily favored Redbands.

Ridpath played another season with Toronto, scoring eighteen goals in eleven games, before he joined the Ottawa Senators in the NHA, winning a Stanley Cup in 1911.

And then the flashing speed came to a crashing halt. Ridpath was struck down by a car in the streets of Toronto on November 2, 1911, and never played hockey again.

Alan (Scotty) Davidson was a solid forward with strong skating and a powerful shot who led the Kingston Frontenac juniors to consecutive OHA championships in 1910 and 1911, before turning professional with the NHA's Toronto franchise in 1913.

Davidson scored forty-two goals in forty games over two seasons, winning the Stanley Cup with the Blueshirts in 1914. The Kingston, Ont., native then enlisted when World War I broke out in August and eventually lost his life in Belgium on June 6, 1915.

A third player was showing promise in hockey's early days when he was struck down and died as the result of a hockey game.

Owen (Bud) McCourt played a couple games with his hometown Cornwall team as a nineteen year old in the 1904 Federal League season, scoring a goal, and adding another seven scores in eleven games over the next two seasons. By the 1907 season, he was a regular with the team and had scored sixteen goals, including a league-record seven against Morrisburg on February 22, and was tied for the league lead.

On March 6, McCourt became embroiled with Ottawa's Art Throop and a general melee resulted. Somewhere in the middle of the fight, a stick struck McCourt's head and he was led dazed and bleeding from the ice. He lost consciousness in the dressing room and was rushed to Cornwall's Hôtel-Dieu hospital. McCourt, twenty-two, died the following morning and a coroner's inquest was convened immediately. This led to a charge of manslaughter against Ottawa's Charles Masson. Eyewitness accounts were inconclusive, however, and Masson was acquitted on April 12.

Cornwall withdrew from the league and Ottawa, rightly or wrongly, was awarded the championship. The league never played another game.

The family discussed ways to invest the profits from their previous business, and at the first of those talks the idea was firmly planted to move to the West Coast, start a new hockey league, and build Canada's first artificial ice rinks. No pro hockey league could survive in the temperate Lower Mainland climate on natural ice, as was the case in the frigid east.

The Renfrew Millionaires' tour of New York City, and the three games played on artificial ice at the St. Nicholas Arena, would pay dividends for dozens of professional hockey players for the next fifteen years.

Frank Patrick suggested a family-owned West Coast league, and presented a business plan to his older brother and father during a family brainstorming session. When it came time to vote on the proposal, it was carried, 2-1, with Lester's being the negative vote. Although Lester

The Denman Street Arena in Vancouver,
and the 1912 edition of the Vancouver Millionaires

would in some ways rue the decision to take such a financial gamble several years later, he proceeded with the project at "Patrick speed" in other words, once a decision was taken, everyone worked to produce results. Blueprints were drawn up quickly for arenas in Victoria and Vancouver, and the family sought franchise holders for the Vancouver suburb of New Westminster, as well as Edmonton and Calgary.

When news of the venture worked its way east, outrage mingled with derision was the reaction, and the doomsayers in Montreal and Ottawa convinced the Edmonton and Calgary investors to back out. The Patricks would not be deterred, and groundbreaking for the construction of a ten thousand, five hundred-seat (Vancouver) and four thousand-seat (Victoria) facilities with artificial ice took place in April 1911.

Always practical, Lester had used his honeymoon trip to the east a month earlier to study artificial ice technology and meet with the players of the Wanderers and the Senators, who were on a barnstorming tour of New York and Boston. When Lester returned home, he had commitments from Johnson, Jimmy Gardner, Harry Hyland and Walter Smaill of the Wanderers, as well as two top goaltenders of the era, Lindsay and Hugh Lehman. Others in the western odyssey included Phillips, Tom Dunderdale, Rowe, Fred Harris and Griffis.

Hugh Lehman

November 1, 1921

Léo Dandurand, Joseph Cattarinich and Louis Letourneau purchase the Montreal Canadiens from George Kennedy's estate, for the price of eleven thousand dollars.

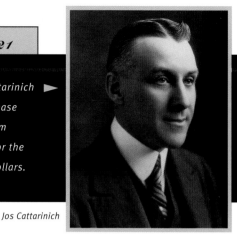

Jos Cattarinich

Canadiens beat Hamilton 5-4 in Montreal, in the first penalty-free game in NHL history.

January 31, 1923

On December 7, 1911, the Pacific Coast Hockey Association, comprising the Vancouver Millionaires, Victoria Senators and New Westminster Royals, came into being, at the Hotel Vancouver. On January 3, 1912, the first professional ice hockey game played west of Ontario or Michigan took place at Victoria, when Lester Patrick's Senators (renamed the Aristocrats a year later) in colorful red, white and blue uniforms, played the black-and-gold Royals.

Victoria's line-up had Lindsay in goal, with Lester Patrick and Smaill on defense, Dunderdale at rover and a forward line of Don Smith, Skinner Poulin and Rowe. The Royals included goalie Lehman, Archie McLean and Johnson on defense, Hyland at rover and a forward trio of Ken Mallen, Gardner and Ran McDonald. Some two thousand, three hundred curious fans saw Lester Patrick score pro hockey's first goal "west of the Mississippi", and then Moose Johnson took over, scoring twice as the Royals won 8-3. Two nights later, Frank Patrick's Vancouver Millionaires defeated the Royals by the same score, with their star-studded line-up of Griffis and Patrick on defense, Newsy Lalonde at rover and a top forward line of Phillips, Harris and Sibby Nichols.

New Westminster won the league's first championship with a 9-6 won-loss record, ahead of Vancouver (7-8) and Victoria (7-9) in the unbalanced schedule. Lalonde was one of the several stars lured back east after that season, but many more went west, including Cyclone Taylor, in the PCHA's second season and a serious professional league was born.

The Quebec Bulldogs won consecutive Stanley Cups in 1912 and '13 in the expanded National Hockey Association. The six-team league included two Toronto entries, Toronto and the Tecumsehs (called the Ontarios a year later), as pro hockey also grew in the east. In 1914, Toronto won the Stanley Cup in a two-game, total-goal series over the Canadiens, and then met PCHA champion Victoria in an exhibition challenge, as the Aristocrats had failed to file an official challenge with the Stanley Cup trustees.

Flying Frank Frederickson, Hockey's Renaissance Man

A game of professional hockey or two had to seem like peace and quiet for Frank Frederickson. If players and fans figured they had found something hot with this fast sport played on sharp blades, it was definitely Slumber City for this elegant Icelandic-Canadian.

No other member of the early pro leagues, the PCHA, NHA or NHL, was a bona fide World War I fighter pilot, roaming the skies over France in pursuit of the fabled Red Baron, flying alongside Captain Eddy Rickenbacker. No other skater had a warship torpedoed out from under him by German U-boats as Frank did in 1914.

Frank Frederickson (fourth from left) made a nostalgic trip back to the airport in Reykjavik in the 1960s.

Nor could they lay claim to potential as a classical violinist, or had they captained the first Canadian team to win a gold medal at the Olympic Games.

Thus, when the war ended, hockey managers were eager to sign the affable Manitoban with the size (five-feet, eleven-inches tall, weighing one hundred and seventy-five pounds) and exquisite skill as a playmaker.

The son of Icelandic immigrants, Frederickson spoke no English until he enrolled in elementary school in Winnipeg at six years of age. Taunted by schoolyard bullies, he responded by becoming one of the foremost athletes of his day, but continued serious violin studies at his mother's behest.

Frederickson attended the University of Manitoba, then left as a sophomore when war broke out. When he reached England, he transferred from the Royal Canadian Army to the Royal Flying Corps, and was sent to Egypt to train. On his way back to England, the HMS Leasowe was torpedoed and sunk. Frederickson refused to abandon the stricken ship until he had rescued his beloved violin from his cabin.

When the war ended, he assembled a private hockey team, the Falcons, which beat the Manitoba league champs and then defeated the Toronto Eatons to win the Allan Cup as Canadian senior champions. Frederickson returned to Europe in 1920 to lead the Canadian team at the Olympic Games demonstration winter sports section. Victories over Czechoslovakia, Sweden and the United States gave Canada the gold medal.

Lester Patrick was one of the many hockey managers awaiting Frederickson on his return, but to no avail. The talented aviator signed a five-year contract for an aerial survey and a feasibility study on air services for Iceland. When the project's funds ran out after a year, Frederickson returned to Canada, married his sweetheart Bea, a classical pianist trained at the Toronto Conservatory, and listened to hockey offers.

Bea and Frank Frederickson were conducting musical soirees at the Fort Garry Hotel in Winnipeg when Patrick signed him to a two-year contract for two thousand, five hundred dollars, to play for the Victoria Cougars of the PCHA.

In his first game on New Year's Day, 1921, he outscored superstar Cyclone Taylor 2-0 in a 5-3 win over Vancouver. In 1923, he topped the PCHA in scoring with forty-one goals in thirty games. With Hap Holmes in goal, and Frank Foyston and Jack Walker on a line with him, Frederickson led the Cougars to the Stanley Cup title in 1925, defeating Howie Morenz and the Montreal Canadiens in the final.

When the PCHA folded, Frederickson moved to Detroit of the NHL and wound down his career with Pittsburgh and Boston, a member of Boston's first Stanley Cup winners in 1929. A knee injury forced his retirement in 1931.

Frank Frederickson as cover boy

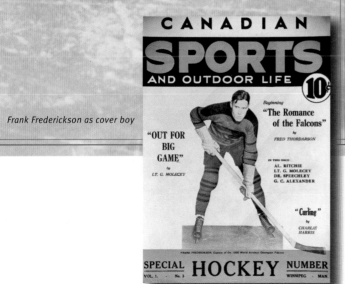

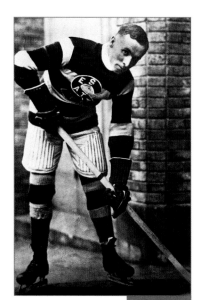

Frank Foyston (top) and Jack Walker in their PCHA days

Toronto won all three games, 5-2, 6-5 and 2-1, with the second played under western rules (seven players and forward passing in the neutral zone). Within two years, most of the Toronto stars, notably Cully Wilson, Jack Walker, Frank Foyston and goalie Hap Holmes, were playing in the west.

The strength of the western league had been established by 1915 when the Stanley Cup trustees ruled that the PCHA could challenge for the Cup, with two thousand, five hundred dollars guaranteed to the winner in the best-of-five series. They also ruled that future Cup series would alternate between west and east.

Vancouver made its first official Cup challenge that year, playing at home. The Millionaires had an All-Star roster with such stars as Frank Patrick, Taylor, Frank Nighbor, Mickey MacKay, Barney Stanley and goalie Lehman. When star defenceman Griffis was injured, Vancouver tried to replace him with Lester Patrick of Victoria, but Ottawa declined. In the first Stanley Cup game west of the Rockies, the Millionaires delighted seven thousand home fans with a 6-2 victory in the opener. The second game, played under eastern six-man rules, was an 8-3 Vancouver win. The Ottawa team was defenseless in the third game, Stanley's four goals leading a 12-3 romp over the Senators.

March 28, 1922

Babe Dye scores four goals to lead Toronto St. Patricks past Vancouver Millionaires 5-1 in game five of the finals, winning the 1922 Stanley Cup.

Art Ross is appointed first manager of the Boston Bruins, on the day the team is granted its NHL franchise.

October 11, 1924

The next eastern power was the Montreal Canadiens. Led by several players with PCHA experience, Lalonde, Didier Pitre and Poulin, they won the Cup, 3-2, in a best-of-five series over the visiting Portland Rosebuds, who had replaced the New Westminster Royals. A year later, the PCHA expansion Seattle Metropolitans were home to the defending champion Canadiens, losing the opener 8-4, then outscoring the easterners, 19-3, to sweep the next three games. The Toronto connection of Foyston, Wilson and Holmes led the way for the first U.S. team to win the Stanley Cup.

The NHL increases the regular season schedule to thirty from twenty-four games per team.

November 3, 1924

The teams met again in Seattle under tragic circumstances two years later. With the series tied at two wins and a tie each, several Canadiens, including defender "Bad" Joe Hall, team captain Lalonde and team manager George Kennedy, were felled by the Asiatic flu, a raging pandemic that would kill more than twenty-five million persons around the world. Too many players were missing and the final game, scheduled for April 1, was never played. It was the only time in Stanley Cup history that the trophy was not awarded. On April 5, Hall, a rugged performer for many years with three Montreal teams and the Bulldogs, died in a Seattle hospital.

In 1917, four NHA clubs met in Montreal and formed the National Hockey League

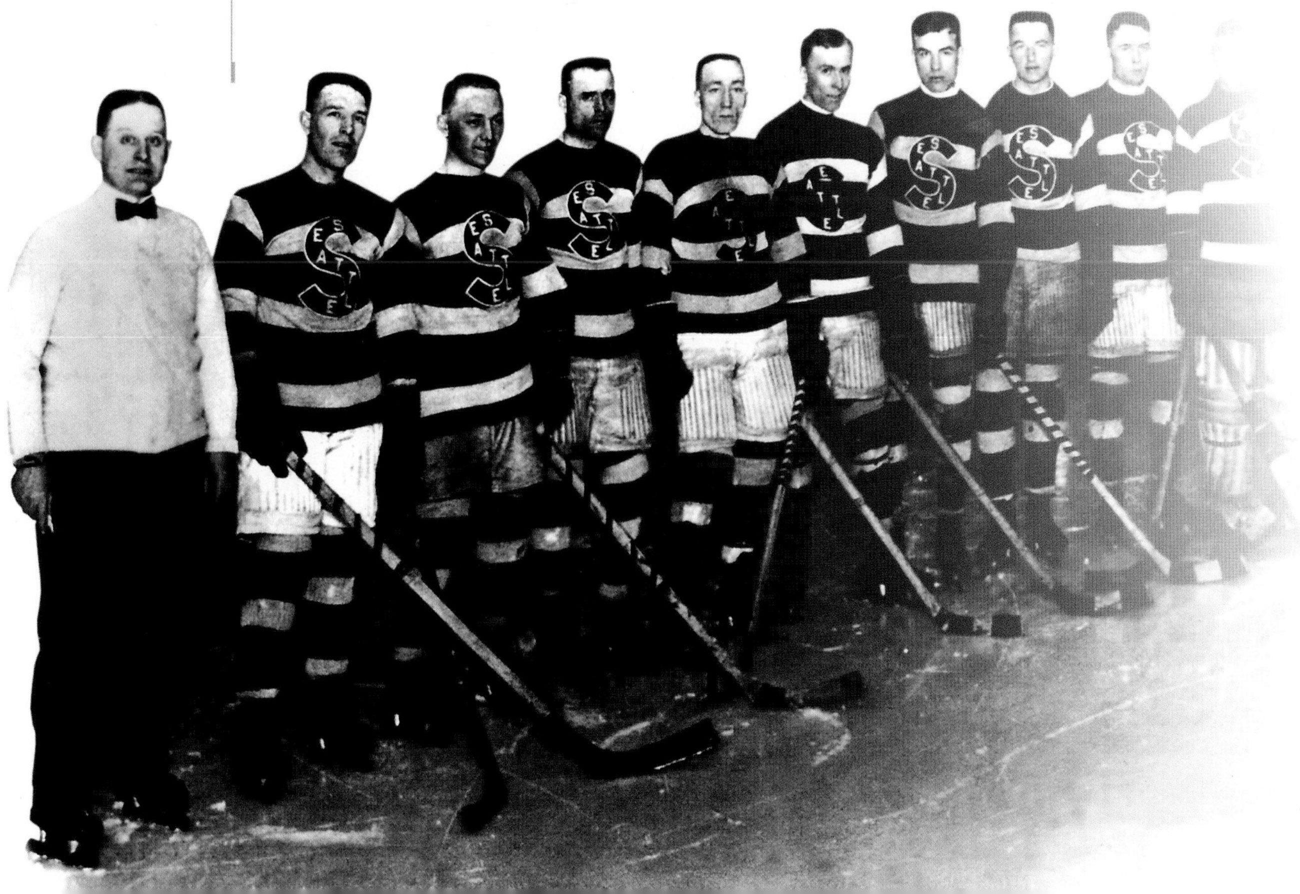

The Stanley Cup champion Seattle Metropolitans in 1917

Birth of the National Hockey League

One man was a large inspiration in the founding of the National Hockey League and not because of his big vision on the game's future.

Owner of the Toronto franchise in the National Hockey Association, Eddie Livingstone waged what seemed a never-ending battle against the other owners, hassling them with debates on the rules, lawsuits and injunctions and threatening to form a rival league.

To solve the "Livingstone problem," the other teams, Ottawa Senators, Quebec Bulldogs, Montreal Canadiens and Montreal Wanderers plus a new Toronto entry, the Arenas, met in Montreal's Windsor Hotel in November, 1917, to form the NHL with newspaperman Frank Calder as its first president.

"We didn't throw Eddie Livingstone out because he's still got his franchise in the NHA," said one owner. *"His only problem is that he's playing in a one-team league."*

"We should thank Eddie," said George Kennedy of the Canadiens. *"He solidified our new league because we were all sick of him."*

The new league got off to a rocky start. The Quebec team lacked the resources to open the season. Six games into the schedule, the Wanderers left hockey forever when their home rink burned to the ground, leaving the league with three teams.

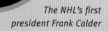

The NHL's first president Frank Calder

Despite assorted legal challenges from Livingstone, the new owners of the Toronto team built a strong club that beat the Canadiens in the first NHL final and won the Stanley Cup against the Vancouver Millionaires.

The Toronto Blueshirts (right)
Toronto's Mutual Street
Arena (background)

> *All pro hockey was in a fragile state*
> *at this time and the Patricks knew it,*
> *recognizing that the sport's growth*
> *would happen in the eastern United States*

The Montreal Forum has its official
opening, and the Canadiens beat the
Toronto St. Patricks 7-1, before a
crowd of nine thousand fans. Billy
Boucher has three goals to lead
the scoring.

The Canadiens team that lost to Seattle in 1917 was the last to represent the
National Hockey Association. That year, four NHA clubs (Montreal Canadiens, Quebec
Bulldogs, Ottawa Senators and Montreal Wanderers) plus a new Toronto team, the Arenas,
met in Montreal and formed the National Hockey League. The Bulldogs dropped out
before the season, and the Wanderers folded after a fire on New Year's Day in 1918 burned
down the Montreal (Westmount) Arena, destroying their equipment.

All pro hockey was in a fragile state at this time and the Patricks knew it. Although the PCHA
was popular, there wasn't a large enough fan base to support teams in Portland and Seattle for the
long run. In 1914, Frank and Lester had enthralled Californians with plans for a facility in San
Francisco, an arena and sports complex billed by the local media as the eighth wonder of the world.
However, World War I scuttled those plans and the long-term future of the sport on the West Coast.

The Patricks recognized that the sport's growth would happen in the eastern United States,
in the high population areas such as New York and Boston. In 1922, the PCHA abandoned the rover,
moving to the six-man game, and played an interlocking schedule with the Western Canada Hockey
League (Edmonton, Regina, Calgary and Saskatoon) for three seasons until the leagues merged in 1924.

Goalies Jake Forbes of the Hamilton Tigers
and Alex Connell of the Ottawa Senators
play in the first 0-0 tie in NHL history.
It was the first scoreless game in eight
seasons of NHL play.

Victoria Cougars of the WCHL beat
the Canadiens 6-1 to become the last
non-NHL team to win the Stanley Cup.
Victoria wins the best-of-five series
3-1 over Montreal.

The Quebec Bulldogs returned to the NHL for the 1919-20 season, then moved to Hamilton as the Tigers. The Tigers finished first in the 1924-25 campaign, but the players refused to participate in the playoffs unless they received a bonus for the lengthened season schedule. The team was suspended, and transferred to the United States where they began play in 1925-26 as the New York Americans, joining Boston and Pittsburgh as the NHL's first U.S. teams. The Adams family owned the Boston franchise and Art Ross was manager, a job he held for thirty years.

In 1924, the league added a second Montreal franchise, called the Maroons as of their second season, conditional on the construction of a new arena. The impressive building, called The Forum, had artificial ice and some nine thousand seats for hockey-mad English Montrealers. Lester Patrick's big building dream had moved east, a dozen years after construction of his Vancouver facility.

Ironically, the Canadiens inaugurated the Forum, beating the Toronto St. Patricks 7-1, because a fire at their home rink, the Mount Royal Arena, had left them without a venue. Jack Adams, who had built his reputation with Frank Patrick's Vancouver team and would become a legendary coach and general manager in Detroit, scored the visitors' only goal.

November 28, 1925

Playing in his three hundred and twenty-eighth consecutive regular season contest for the Canadiens, goaltender Georges Vézina collapses during a game against Pittsburgh. Suffering from tuberculosis, he dies four months later.

As the first quarter of the twentieth century waned, a hockey revival was under way in the east, fuelled by the move to the U.S., but the pro game was in trouble in the west.

But, the Patrick influence would continue as they played a pivotal role in the U.S. expansion of the NHL and in stocking new NHL teams there in the Roaring Twenties.

The Tigers Strike

When the Quebec Bulldogs failed in that city, the team moved to Hamilton, the steel city on Lake Ontario, and began play as the Tigers in the 1921 NHL season.

By 1925, they were the toast of the league, edging out their neighboring Toronto rivals to capture first place in the regular season. With Vernon (Jake) Forbes in nets, and Billy Burch and the Green brothers, Redvers (Red) and Wilfrid (Shorty) leading the way, the team was favored for the Stanley Cup.

The Tigers (19-10-1) had a bye for the post-season round, while Toronto (19-11) and the third-place Canadiens (17-11-2) were to play off for the right to meet the Tigers in the league final.

Hamilton was a blue-collar, union-shop kind of town and the Tigers reflected their adopted home. In March 1925, the Tiger players told the league they would not play any further games unless they received additional compensation. Many of the players had signed two-year contracts prior to the twenty-four game season in 1924, and when the league increased the schedule to thirty games with expansion Boston and Montreal added, salaries for the Hamilton players were not adjusted to match the increase.

When the league refused to yield on the issue, Toronto and the Canadiens played the league final. The Hamilton players all were fined, and the franchise was moved to New York, where it became the Americans.

There would be no strikes in the Big Apple. Veteran hockey executive Tommy Gorman was appointed governor for the team, and Colonel John S. Hammond of Madison Square Garden Corporation was president, but the real owner was William V. Dwyer, the biggest bootlegger in the northeast during Prohibition.

Redvers (Red) and Wilfrid (Shorty) Green

Big Bill, like many of his counterparts in a cash-only business, had invested his profits in many legitimate endeavors, including ocean tankers, trucks and warehousing, New York nightclubs, a Miami casino and several racetracks.

The Tigers had missed a golden opportunity to win pro hockey's greatest honor. They never got close to the Cup as members of the New York Americans.

The Hamilton Tigers in 1925

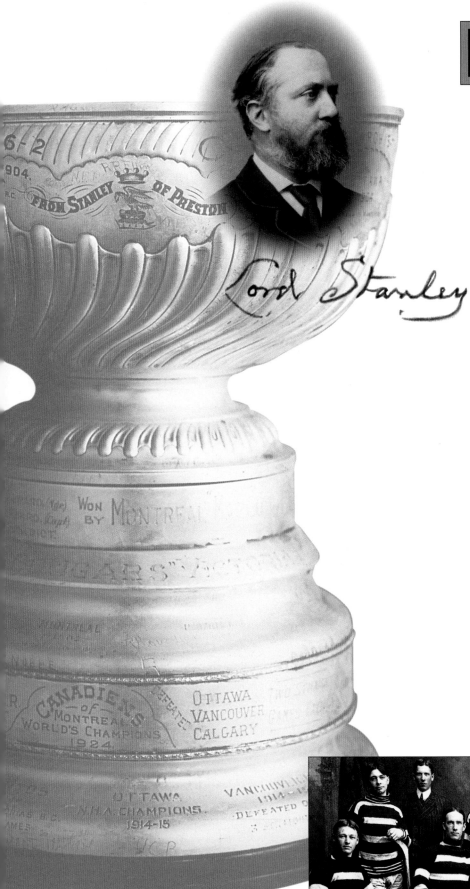

STANLEY CUP

1900-01	WINNIPEG VICTORIAS
1901-02	MONTREAL AAA
1902-03	OTTAWA SILVER SEVEN
1903-04	OTTAWA SILVER SEVEN
1904-05	OTTAWA SILVER SEVEN
1905-06	MONTREAL WANDERERS
1906-07	KENORA THISTLES /
	MONTREAL WANDERERS
1907-08	MONTREAL WANDERERS
1908-09	OTTAWA SENATORS
1909-10	MONTREAL WANDERERS
1910-11	OTTAWA SENATORS
1911-12	QUEBEC BULLDOGS
1912-13	QUEBEC BULLDOGS
1913-14	TORONTO BLUESHIRTS
1914-15	VANCOUVER MILLIONAIRES
1915-16	MONTREAL CANADIENS
1916-17	SEATTLE METROPOLITANS
1917-18	TORONTO ARENAS
1918-19	*NO CUP AWARDED*
1919-20	OTTAWA SENATORS
1920-21	OTTAWA SENATORS
1921-22	TORONTO ST. PATRICKS
1922-23	OTTAWA SENATORS
1923-24	MONTREAL CANADIENS
1924-25	VICTORIA COUGARS

1905
OTTAWA SILVER SEVEN

1925

VICTORIA COUGARS

1907

KENORA THISTLES
MONTREAL WANDERERS

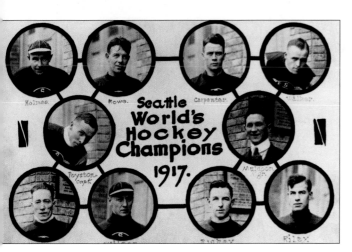

1918

TORONTO ARENAS

1917

SEATTLE METROPOLITANS

II Second Quarter

1926
19
19

GROWING THE SPORT

The Patricks
The Big Apple and Points East

When the National Hockey League expanded
to the United States in the mid-twenties, the
Patricks appeared to be adversaries of the
eastern professional hockey establishment.
But the brothers and their West Coast-based
repository of talent really held the key
to long-term success for the NHL
south of the border.

The Patricks had two major assets: experience in marketing the sport in the U.S., and a bank of playing talent to stock the new teams and make them competitive immediately. The first major league hockey team with a U.S. home base was the Portland Rosebuds, created when the New Westminster Royals were transferred to Oregon, in January, 1914. When the National Hockey Association made a protracted attempt to repatriate Cyclone Taylor from Frank Patrick's Stanley Cup champion Vancouver team in 1916, the Patricks retaliated by devastating the 1914 Cup-winning Toronto Blueshirts, luring Frank Foyston, Hap Holmes, Jack Walker and Cully Wilson west to stock the expansion Seattle Metropolitans.

Most of those players, plus many others from the PCHA and the Western Hockey League, would stock the new NHL's U.S. teams, under a plan devised by Frank Patrick. Already home to several Hall-of-Fame players, the PCHA linked up with the remaining teams of the Western league, and other future superstars came under the Patrick umbrella – including Eddie Shore, Art Gagne and Duke Keats (Edmonton), Archie Briden, Red Dutton and Harry Oliver (Calgary), Bill and Bun Cook, Corbett Denneny and Leo Reise of Saskatoon.

The bold NHL plan to move into the U.S. underwent several unexpected "accelerations." The league created two expansion franchises in 1924 to place teams in Boston and New York. Art Ross secured an owner, Charles Adams, in Boston, but New York wasn't ready. Sports promoter George Lewis (Tex) Rickard took an option on a new team for Manhattan in the 1926 season.

Gordon (Duke) Keats moved from Edmonton to Boston and then Detroit in 1927.

The National Hockey League grants franchises to two new teams: Chicago Blackhawks and Detroit Cougars, raising the league total to ten teams.

Chicago Blackhawks

Montreal Canadiens donate the "Vézina Memorial Trophy" to the NHL in memory of Georges Vézina. The trophy is to be presented annually to the goaltender with the best goals-against average.

May 14, 1927

Eddie Shore's Midnight Ride

Only Eddie Shore could have outdone Paul Revere.

Long after the icon of the American Revolution had been laid to rest, the man they called the Edmonton Express had an overnight journey because, of all things, he missed a train.

On January 2, 1929, Boston's star defenseman was stuck in hopelessly snarled downtown traffic in stormy Boston, and missed his train to Montreal where the Bruins would play the Maroons the next day. When Shore pulled up at the station, he managed to secure the services of a luxury sedan complete with chauffeur, from a well-heeled Bruins' supporter.

They struck out for Vermont and points north, with the weather getting worse with each mile. When the chauffeur quit, Shore took over the driving, and when the windshield wipers went, he drove with his hand on the outside of the windshield, to melt a spot he could see through.

The car skidded off the road several times, only to be wrestled back onto the tarmac by the intrepid duo. Just inside the Quebec border, and in the dark of wintry night,

the car went into another ditch and Shore walked through waist-deep snow to a farmhouse, where he convinced the local farmer to bring a team of horses to rescue the vehicle.

At 6 p.m. Thursday, January 3, Shore and company pulled up to the hotel that the Bruins were just leaving to go to the Forum. His hands were frozen hooks, shaped by twenty-eight hours around a steering wheel, his eyes were bloodshot, he had not slept.

Art Ross took one look at The Franchise and said, *"Check in and get some sleep. Our train home doesn't leave until tomorrow morning."*

"Not on your life," Shore croaked. *"I'm here. I'm playing."*

After a catnap in the equipment room at the Forum, Shore went out and played his customary forty minutes against the physically punishing Maroons in a 1-0 Boston victory.

One more thing.

Shore scored the goal.

Art Ross used his extensive
hockey connections in both countries
to sign players

That made room for a second Montreal franchise. The team, which became known as the Maroons in its second year, arrived for the 1924-25 season with its brand new Forum, an eastern arena to rival those in Victoria and Vancouver. Four teams fought for the league title that season, with the Hamilton Tigers, formerly the Quebec Bulldogs (19-10-1), edging out the Toronto St. Patricks (19-11), the defending Cup champion Canadiens (17-11-2) and the Ottawa Senators (17-12-1). However, when playoff time came, the Tigers went on strike over contract issues, the team was suspended and moved at season's end to New York where they became the Americans. Also joining the league for 1925-26 was a new Pittsburgh Pirates franchise. A second (Tex Rickard's) team in New York and teams in Chicago and Detroit, were accepted into the NHL for the 1926-27 season.

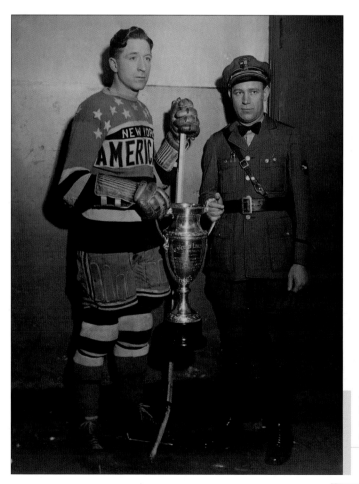

Mervyn (Red) Dutton was a star defenseman
with the Montreal Maroons and the New York
Americans before becoming president of the
NHL in 1943.

Art Ross used his extensive hockey connections in both countries to sign players, but the embryonic Bruins would struggle for the first two seasons, as did Montreal and Pittsburgh in their first campaigns. With three more teams joining the league, Ross was concerned about a talent shortage, and approached his childhood friends.

To his immense relief, the visionary Patricks had a plan, which also represented an opportunity for the family to recoup most of its investment in hockey. While it was patently obvious that the western league was on its last legs, Lester Patrick had to get one last detail out of the way; winning the Stanley Cup with his Victoria Cougars. It wasn't to be, as the Maroons

NHL Nomads

One team started as the Bulldogs, became the Tigers, then turned into the Americans. The Senators became the Eagles, and the Pirates tried to extend NHL life as the Quakers.

While Boston, Chicago, Detroit and the Rangers would survive and eventually thrive, the Great Depression and World War II led to the folding of four NHL teams, despite attempts to revive three of them by moving them to new cities.

The Quebec Bulldogs had won the Stanley Cup in 1912 and 1913, led by the great star Joe Malone. The team was a member of the NHL when the league was formed in 1917, but financial problems prevented an entry until the 1919-20 season. When the Bulldogs won only four games, the franchise was sold to interests in Hamilton, Ont.

Named the Tigers after a prolific senior amateur team from the area, the Hamilton club missed the playoffs for four seasons, then finished first in 1924-25. However, the Tiger players refused to participate in the playoffs unless they received an additional two hundred dollars in salary to compensate for extra games being added to the regular season.

The Tigers were sold to famed New York bootlegger Bill Dwyer, renamed the Americans, and were the first NHL club to play in Madison Square Garden. The team lasted for sixteen years, making the playoffs five times while playing second fiddle to the Rangers.

After one season under the Brooklyn Americans label, the club folded.

Pittsburgh, where hockey had flourished from 1904 on, seemed a natural site for an NHL team, and the Pirates entered the league in 1925. But a big recession in the steel industry hit the club's crowds, and in 1930 the team shifted across state to Philadelphia, existing as the Quakers for one year before folding.

The depression also took its toll on the illustrious Ottawa Senators and in 1934 the team was moved to St. Louis and called the Eagles.

Despite the presence of two young players who became great stars, Syd Howe and Bill Cowley, the team folded after one year in Missouri. Attempts to resurrect the moribund Senators in subsequent years met with failure.

The saddest case may have been that of the Montreal Maroons, the team the fabled Forum was built for, and the only one of the "nomads" to win Stanley Cups in the city in which it would eventually fold.

When the Montreal Canadiens were formed in 1910, they were founded with the express intent of attracting the loyalty of the city's French-speaking hockey fans, what with a variety of teams like the Wanderers, Shamrocks and Victorias cater to the English-speaking community. A fire ended the Wanderers franchise in 1918, and efforts abounded to replace that team in the NHL. Tom Duggan received the league's go-ahead in 1924, the Forum was built and the team that would be named the Maroons in its second season, began play. By year two, the Maroons were a powerhouse and won the first of their two Stanley Cups. With the S Line of Nels Stewart, Hooley Smith and Babe Siebert leading the way, the physical Maroons waged war with the Canadiens for fourteen seasons, gaining a loyal following in Canada's metropolis.

Their last game, a 6-3 loss to the Canadiens, took place at the Forum on St. Patrick's Day, 1938.

The Mad Major

Frederic McLaughlin was wealthy, a Harvard grad, a top polo player, a U.S. army battalion commander in World War I, husband of dancer and Hollywood actress Irene Castle and owner of the Chicago Blackhawks.

"Where hockey was concerned, Major McLaughlin was the strangest bird and, yes, perhaps the biggest nut I met in my entire life," said Conn Smythe, owner of the Toronto Maple Leafs, who had many legendary boardroom battles with the heir to a coffee fortune.

When the NHL expanded into the U.S. in 1926, McLaughlin was talked into buying the original Chicago franchise by Tex Rickard, the legendary New York promoter. During World War I, he had served in the U.S. Army's Blackhawk Division and used that name for the team. For many years, the two-word spelling was used, then in 1990, research revealed that the army division had employed one word, Blackhawk.

Wife Irene, who had designed the Blackhawk sweater with the Indian head crest, did not keep her job long. When she divorced the Major in 1937, she claimed their large house in suburban Chicago was so cold that her three dogs had to wear sweaters.

A hands-on owner for much of his eighteen years with the team, McLaughlin set records with eighteen coaching changes, involving thirteen men. One Hawk coach for a few weeks was Godfrey Matheson, a Winnipeg native, who met McLaughlin on a train from Minneapolis to Chicago and impressed the Major with his hockey ideas. He was hired on the spot, and lasted for two practices.

Despite the Major's eccentricities, the Blackhawks won the Stanley Cup in 1934 and 1938. Veteran Ottawa coach/manager Tommy Gorman led the 1934 Hawks to the Cup and, after the team's victory party, packed up his car and drove to Montreal never to return (where he won the Cup a year later with the Maroons).

McLaughlin then professed to the NHL that he wanted a team stocked with only U.S. players. While some general managers laughed him out of league meetings, he won the 1938 Stanley Cup with a team featuring eight U.S.-raised players. That team was coached by Bostonian Bill Stewart who, in typical McLaughlin style, was fired early the next season.

McLaughlin demanded that Stewart coach the team during games from the balcony where he could see the play better. The latter declined saying he did not want to be a "puppet master."

Stewart lost little sleep over the incident, returning to his career as a major league baseball umpire the following spring.

The Mad Major was famous for his feuds with several of his NHL peers, the most prominent featuring James Norris, a fellow Chicagoan. A former Montrealer, Norris ran the Norris Grain Company and a variety of other enterprises out of the Loop, and had attempted to secure the Chicago franchise for himself. When McLaughlin shut him out, Norris fielded a team in the American Association. Later, when Norris bought the bankrupt Chicago Stadium, the Major moved his team to a suburban arena.

Norris eventually bought the Detroit franchise and won Stanley Cups in 1936 and '37, and the family eventually purchased the Hawks after McLaughlin's death.

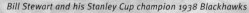
Bill Stewart and his Stanley Cup champion 1938 Blackhawks

November 15, 1927

Boston's Dit Clapper scores his first NHL goal
in the Bruins' season opener, a 1-1 tie against
the Chicago Blackhawks.

won the best-of-five series in the first of many Stanley Cup finals to take place at the Forum. His consolation was Victoria's share of the gate at the splendid new hockey palace. The trip was valuable for another reason: It provided first-hand evidence that the western league's days were numbered.

"Frank, some of these Maroons are making close to ten thousand dollars a year, and the owners are throwing their money around like confetti," Lester told his brother one night during the playoffs. What amazed him was the sight of Nels Stewart clutching a wad of bills "big enough to choke a horse," a thousand-dollar bonus for the Montreal star's performance that was pressed into his hand by a team supporter who had casually strolled into the Maroons' dressing room, while an incredulous Lester looked on.

The top salary for western league players that season was about four thousand dollars, making it difficult for the Patricks and other WHL owners to keep their players much past 1927, in the face of offers of fifteen thousand dollars a season circulating in hockey's eastern circles. The western teams could go one more season, and then witness an exodus as their players' contracts expired, or they could move quickly and get value for their assets. Saskatoon had already given Maroons' director Tom Duggan an option of sixty thousand dollars to purchase the team's assets; the Patricks asked for three hundred thousand dollars for the remaining five teams in the league.

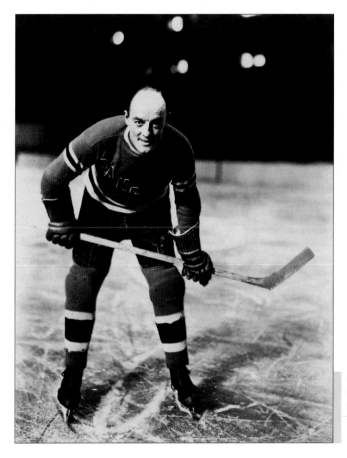

Ivan (Ching) Johnson was the
cornerstone of the Rangers defense
for more than a decade.

Bun Cook was one of the most feared snipers in the NHL, patrolling the wing alongside his brother Bill and center Frank Boucher.

Art Ross returned to Boston and convinced Charles Adams to underwrite the deal, despite opposition from the president of Madison Square Garden, Colonel John S. Hammond. Hammond flatly refused a one hundred thousand-dollar deal for a list of fourteen players prepared by Lester. He had engaged Toronto's Conn Smythe to put together a team, which included defensemen Taffy Abel and Ivan (Ching) Johnson, and was convinced that it could be done cheaper. As it turned out, the Hall-of-Fame trio of Bill and Bun Cook and Frank Boucher, all originally going to the Maroons, were either sold to the Rangers by Tom Duggan or signed by Smythe. Both sides maintained their version as true, to the grave.

Credit or blame aside, the Rangers had a competitive team from the first drop of the puck at Madison Square Garden on November 16, 1926, and the Detroit Cougars and Chicago Blackhawks would be close. The Motor City franchise acquired Frank Frederickson, Frank Foyston, Jack Walker, Clem Loughlin and Art Duncan as coach from the Cup-finalist Victoria Cougars, while Portland's Dick Irvin, Mickey MacKay, George Hay and Rabbit McVeigh were the cornerstone of the Chicago franchise.

Bankrollers of the deal, Boston did very well with the venerable Eddie Shore and his Edmonton teammates Duke Keats, Perk Galbraith, Harry Oliver and Harry Meeking joining him. Leo Reise and Laurie Scott joined the New York Amerks, while Art Gagne, Herb Gardiner and Amby Moran were assigned to the Canadiens. Jack Adams rejoined the Ottawa Senators, Red Dutton became a presence on the Maroons blue line, and Jack Arbour was signed by Pittsburgh.

Their league dissolved, players distributed and investment retrieved: What future did ice hockey hold for the Patricks?

November 22, 1927

The Olympia in Detroit plays host to its first NHL game, as Ottawa defeats the Cougars 2-1, before fourteen thousand fans.

Boston Garden opens its doors to hockey for the first time. In the inaugural game, Montreal's George Hainsworth records his first of twenty-two shutouts in forty-four games that season, 1-0 over the Bruins, before an estimated crowd of sixteen thousand.

November 20, 1928

An answer was not long in coming. Montreal's Duggan, a friend and fellow horseman, was the man who had given Tex Rickard a taste of professional ice hockey when he invited him to a game at the Forum in 1925. After returning home, Rickard made sure that Madison Square Garden II, which was going up on Eighth Avenue between Forty-Ninth and Fiftieth streets, would include an ice plant. Rickard then convinced his crony, Col. Hammond, to acquire the franchise rights for the new team (as he had done with another friend, Major Frederic McLaughlin, in Chicago).

During the sale of the western league assets, Frank and Lester spent a pleasant evening at the Windsor Hotel with Tex Rickard. The Patricks explained how they had shared the dream of placing a major league franchise in the Big Apple since their 1910 visit to Manhattan with the Renfrew Millionaires. Tex was impressed with their successes in Portland and Seattle, which included the first Stanley Cup awarded to an American team.

Dick Irvin and many of his Portland teammates became Blackhawks in 1926.

Howie Morenz and the Flying Frenchmen

It certainly wasn't an auspicious beginning.

As the rest of the Montreal Canadiens skated through their paces on the first day of training camp in Grimsby, Ont., on December 4, 1923, the muscular young man stood hat in hand before managing director Léo Dandurand, tearfully begging to be released. Doubting he was good enough to make it, and fearful of the loss of his amateur status and his job in the Stratford, Ont., railyards, William Howard Morenz implored Dandurand to take back his eight hundred and fifty-dollar signing bonus and release him.

Johnny Gagnon

"*Monsieur Léo*" demurred and the man who would become known as The Stratford Streak reported for his first scrimmage. Within a day, rinkside observers commented that the line of Morenz and wingers Aurel Joliat and Billy Boucher was the fastest that the *bleu-blanc-rouge* had ever seen. The Flying Frenchmen were born.

The 1923-24 season would end with tears of joy for Morenz, as his four goals in the two-game, total-goal series against Calgary would lead the Canadiens to the Stanley Cup with 6-1 and 3-1 victories. Morenz was the Canadiens' top scorer for his first eight seasons in the league, 1924-32, and he led the Habs to another pair of Cups in 1929-30 and 1930-31. The Flying Frenchmen represented the league's marquee franchise in that era, especially when it came to selling the game in the United States. After New York sports promoter Tex Rickard took in a Morenz performance at the Forum in 1924, he returned to Manhattan

Aurel Joliat mourns the departure of a teammate and friend.

and approved plans for an ice plant to be included in the construction of the new Madison Square Garden.

Small, five-feet, seven-inches, one hundred and fifty-five pounds, Morenz was hard as nails and would routinely take a pounding from such punishing opponents as Boston's Eddie Shore and Dit Clapper, Red Horner of Toronto, Maroons' Nels Stewart, Hooley Smith and Red Dutton, and Earl Seibert of the Blackhawks, to name a few. He was widely respected throughout the NHL for quietly bouncing back with nary a complaint.

His legs slowing, Morenz was traded to Chicago in 1933-34, and then on to the Rangers, before rejoining the Canadiens for the 1936-37 season.

The Stratford Streak's demise was as dramatic as any Morenz end-to-end rush during his career. On January 28, 1937, in a game at the Forum, Morenz was skating in the Chicago zone when he was nudged into the boards. Somehow his skate blade got caught in a crack in the boards, just as Seibert lined him up for a body-check. The collision resulted in a severely broken leg and Morenz was taken to hospital. He was still there five weeks later when a blood clot lodged near his heart and he died of a pulmonary embolism.

His body lay in state at the Forum for two days while thousands of Montrealers filed past, and some fifteen thousand attended his funeral. Later that year, the Canadiens retired Morenz's number seven to honor him and in December, 1950, a cross-Canada poll of sports editors selected him as hockey's best player of the first half of the twentieth century.

The deal finally done, the Patricks returned west to spend time with their families, which included Lester's sons Lynn and Murray, Frank's son, Joe, and daughters Gloria and Frances, to contemplate future business opportunities. Their league might be gone, but they had two large, modern arenas to operate.

February 20, 1930

Montreal Maroons' goalie Clint Benedict is the first goalie to wear a mask in an NHL game, in a 3-3 tie against the New York Americans. Benedict wore the mask temporarily, during an injury.

In mid-October of 1926, Col. Hammond offered Lester Patrick the coaching job with the New York Rangers at a fabulous salary of eighteen thousand dollars. It was patently obvious that the offer really came from Rickard, because Frank Patrick had feuded openly with Hammond during the sale of the western league assets. Rickard appreciated the job that Conn Smythe had done in assembling the Rangers, but felt Smythe was not a Manhattan type of entrepreneur. Elegant, well-spoken and now silver-haired, Lester was the man to fill the seats at Madison Square.

More urbane than Smythe, Patrick's PCHA experience also placed him miles ahead of his Toronto counterpart in credibility, although Smythe would go on to forge a golden career of his own. Ranger player Murray (Muzz) Murdoch recalled Patrick's first pep talk to the team prior to its inaugural game: "*Gentlemen, when we start playing in the National Hockey League, you're going to win some games, and you're going to lose some. I just want to stress this: If you lose more than you win, you won't be around.*"

With New York Mayor Jimmy Walker and a substantial percentage of the city's glitterati in attendance, the Rangers won their Madison Square Garden opener, 1-0, on a goal by Bun Cook. The team ended its first season with a record of 25-13-6, to capture the American Division title, third overall behind Ottawa and the Canadiens. A year later, the Rangers won the Stanley Cup.

A Hall-of-Fame hockey player who knew Lester Patrick's prowess on and off the ice was Francis (King) Clancy, Smythe's right-hand man in Toronto and a lifelong Leaf.

February 28, 1929

Chicago Blackhawks are shut out for the eighth straight game, an NHL record, when Rangers' goalie John Roach and Hawks' Chuck Gardiner duel to a scoreless tie, in Chicago.

ALL-STAR TEAMS

1ST TEAM ★ ★ ★ ★ ★ ★ ★ ★ ★ ★ ★ ★ ★ ★ ★

Coach   **Hap Day**
Executive **Jack Adams**

Maurice Richard
Right Wing

Ted Lindsay
Left Wing

Howie Morenz
Center

Eddie Shore
Defense

Turk Broda
Goalie

Earl Seibert
Defense

ALL-STAR TEAMS

★ ★ ★ ★ ★ ★ ★ ★ ★ ★ ★ ★ ★ ★ ★ ★ ★ ★ **2ᴺᴰ TEAM**

Coach   **Dick Irvin**
Executive **Conn Smythe**

Milt Schmidt
Center

Charlie Conacher
Right Wing

Aurel Joliat
Left Wing

Dit Clapper
Defense

Tiny Thompson
Goalie

King Clancy
Defense

"*Lester was one of the finest people I have ever met,*" he said. "*A real class person and he raised two fine sons. He fit the New York scene just like a glove. He'd walk to his place behind the bench all immaculately dressed, silver-haired, and with that elegant bearing – he just oozed class. It was written all over him, and the Garden fans loved him for it. In his special way, he was one of them.*"

Smythe bore no grudge. He took his severance pay from the Rangers, made a few lucrative wagers, and parlayed his increased fortune into ownership of the Toronto hockey club, construction of Maple Leaf Gardens, and a Hall-of-Fame career in the NHL. Lester Patrick's western Canadian connections served his new team well. A Patrick pipeline from Manitoba (and points west) to Manhattan would deliver much fine talent: Walter (Babe) Pratt, Bryan Hextall, Alex Shibicky, Neil and Mac Colville, Art Coulter, Cecil Dillon, Ott Heller, Muzz Murdoch and Dave Kerr, to the Rangers, the backbone of three Cup championships in a dozen years.

Two other strapping young players, Lester's sons, Lynn and Murray (Muzz), also would join the Rangers, to give the Patrick family NHL connection an on-ice presence, as well.

Concerned with the growth of the game in the U.S., Lester built a strong New York farm system, basing many of those teams along the Eastern Seaboard. It helped create a fan base, while getting Americans interested in the sport as players.

Art Coulter was captain of the 1940 Stanley Cup champion Rangers and a four-time selection to the NHL's second All-Star team.

Jolly Jack Adams and Motor City Juggernaut

Through much of Jack Adams' thirty-five years at the helm of Detroit's NHL team, including nineteen seasons in double duty as general manager and coach, he was often called Jolly Jack. But near the end of his career, after he led the quick squashing of the players' attempt to form an association/union, Adams was called much less flattering names.

What cannot be debated is Adams' outstanding record as the builder and coach of strong hockey teams. The team was called the Cougars and Falcons during Adams' early years at the helm, with the name changed to Red Wings when James Norris bought the team in 1932.

Norris claimed that Adams was on "pro-bation" as manager-coach, and if the team's fortunes did not take an upturn quickly, he would be out of a job. With shrewd trades and the development of players, Adams turned around the fortunes of the team, winning the Stanley Cup crown in 1936 and 1937. During Adams' time with the team, the Wings finished in first place twelve times, including a record seven consecutive pennants, and had seven Cup triumphs.

Add two Cup titles (with Toronto and Ottawa) in Adams' playing career, and his name is on the Cup nine times.

"It wasn't hard for me to be a hockey manager after spending all the time I did with Frank Patrick in Vancouver," Adams acknowledged, remembering his days as a leader of the Millionaires of the PCHA.

"He was the best hockey man of his day. Playing for him and working with him was a learning experience beyond compare."

The lessons took, according to Adams's peers.

"Jack Adams was as shrewd a judge of hockey talent as the NHL ever had," said Frank Selke, the NHL's legendary executive with the Maple Leafs and Montreal Canadiens. *"He made many trades, and I doubt if you can make a strong case that anyone got the better of him in any deal."*

Adams always claimed that his smartest move was signing a teenager from Saskatchewan named Gordie Howe around whom the brilliant Wings of the late 1940s and '50s were built. Howe's NHL career lasted twenty-six years, and alongside such teammates as Ted Lindsay, Sid Abel, Red Kelly, Marcel Pronovost, Bob Goldham, Terry Sawchuk and the Wilson brothers, he made the Red Wings a Cup challenger, year-in, year-out.

They all had one thing in common: The man they called Jolly Jack brought them together.

October 10, 1930

Toronto Maple Leafs announce the acquisition of King Clancy from Ottawa, in exchange for Art Smith, Eric Pettinger and thirty-five thousand dollars, a record price paid for any hockey player.

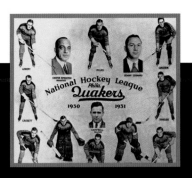

Philadelphia plays host to its first NHL game as the Quakers, formerly the Pittsburgh Pirates, are shut out 3-0 by the New York Rangers. The Quakers would drop out of the league after posting a 4-36-4 record.

Critical to the growth of the Rangers was Lester Patrick's rapid elevation as a Manhattan presence. Success on and off the ice was necessary to compete for the entertainment dollar with the Murderers Row (the legendary New York Yankees of 1927) of Ruth and Gehrig, John McGraw's perennial champion Giants, Gene Tunney and Jack Dempsey fighting for boxing's heavyweight supremacy, and George M. Cohan, Cole Porter, Rogers and Hart, Kern and Hammerstein, and the Gershwins lighting up Broadway with such classics as *Funny Face, A Connecticut Yankee, An American in Paris* and *The Front Page*.

Some of the hottest songs around had a "Rangers' theme", including *My Blue Heaven, Blue Skies* and *Makin' Whoopee*. The time was right for a Silver Fox and his Blueshirts to make a noise in the "Golden Age" of the Big Apple. If New York could be successful, the rest of the league, especially the new American-based franchises, could bask in the afterglow.

While the team publicists tried to make up stories that would get the notice of the competitive New York dailies – one even suggested a staged kidnapping of the Cook brothers – the Silver Fox found a way to make his own headlines without any subterfuge. What helped the legend grow for the Manhattan faithful was that the story began when the Blueshirts were banished from New York to the wilds of icy Montreal.

[
The time was right for a Silver Fox and his Blueshirts to make noise in the Golden Age of the Big Apple
]

The irony of the Rangers winning Stanley Cups in 1928, 1933 and 1940, is that all three victories came on the road, even though some of those games normally should have been played in New York.

At fault was Madison Square Garden economics. Each spring, the Barnum & Bailey circus came to town for a lucrative two-week stay. When the Rangers were in playoffs, that might provide two or three capacity crowds, but that would consequently cancel the elephants and the clowns. Having discovered they were the building's poor cousins, the Rangers took to the road, playing their entire 1928 final in Montreal, four of five 1933 final games, and three of five 1940 final games, in Toronto. They would not win a Stanley Cup on Madison Square Garden ice, until 1994.

In 1928, the Rangers journeyed to the Forum to play the physical Maroons, a team that won the Cup in 1926, its second season. The visitors were blanked, 2-0, by Clint Benedict to open the best-of-five series and were locked in a scoreless middle period in the second game when a deflected shot by Nels Stewart caught goalie Lorne Chabot under the eye, opening a vicious, game-ending cut. In that era, teams did not carry spare goalies, and the home team generally made available a back-up. Montreal suggested a minor league goalie, but Patrick knew Ottawa's Alex Connell was in the stands and asked for permission to use him.

After a long argument, Patrick retreated to the Rangers dressing room and emerged wearing Chabot's equipment. Stunned silence greeted him as he skated to the net, although the rink quickly revived when the Maroons began buzzing the New York cage. *"Make them shoot! Make them shoot!"* Patrick hollered as defensemen Ching Johnson and Taffy Abel and their teammates threw themselves in front of pucks with abandon, desperately hoping that the Maroons couldn't hear their goalie. Bill Cook put the Rangers up, 1-0, early in the third period, but Stewart managed to equalize, forcing overtime. Seven-and-a-half minutes into extra time, Frank Boucher deflected a puck past Benedict, giving the Blueshirts a 2-1 victory.

January 3, 1931

Montreal Maroons forward Nels Stewart scores goals four seconds apart in the third period (8:24 and 8:28), in a 5-3 win over Boston, to set an NHL record for the fastest two goals by one player.

Those wonderful early days of parity

Wonderful talents, colorful characters, memorable player combinations and larger-than-life coaches and managers... all of these factors combined to sell hockey in the newly expanded National Hockey League in the late 1920s, but especially during the hard times of the Great Depression of the 1930s.

The biggest sales point, however, was as much a cause as an effect of all of the above, and perhaps the most important when it came to selling the sport to new franchises – league parity.

In the third decade of the century, professional hockey in the NHL had its best distribution of post-season honors as seven different teams won the Stanley Cup between 1930 and 1939. Only one of these teams, the Maroons (1935 Stanley Cup), would not survive the decade, but the remaining group would go on to be known as the Original Six and drive hockey through its first Golden Age of 1942-67.

The Canadiens (1930, '31), Blackhawks (1934, '38), and Red Wings (1936,'37) were the decade's double winners, with the Leafs (1932), Rangers (1933) and the Bruins (1939) rounding out the decade's success story.

What that meant in player terms was that just about every star of the era took his turn in hoisting Lord Stanley's silver bowl, including Howie Morenz, Eddie Shore, Frank Boucher and the Cook brothers, Marty Barry, Joe Primeau, Lorne Chabot and Chuck Gardiner.

Chicago management 1934

Any team that played in the decade and did not win the Cup at least once would not survive. That included the Pittsburgh Pirates and New York Americans. Pittsburgh barely made it into the decade, transferring its franchise to Philadelphia where the team would see action as the Quakers for a single season before disappearing after the 1930-31 campaign. The Americans, like Montreal's Maroons, proved to be the odd man out in a two-team city, giving up the ghost at the end of the 1941 season as the NHL went off to War. The Maroons, two-time winners of the Cup, (1926, 35), had wrapped it up in 1938.

The only other decade with such an equitable distribution of league silverware? The 1990s, with eight different Cup champions.

The 1935 Montreal Maroons

The 1939 Boston Bruins

Conn Smythe and the Barn on Carleton Street

The year was 1931, the time of the Great Depression, and when Conn Smythe announced that he was building a large hockey arena in downtown Toronto, most figured he had taken leave of his senses. Raising money for such a project in an almost non-existent economy was viewed as impossible.

But Smythe, a Canadian Army major who served in two world wars, was a scrapper who defied popular opinion much of his life. With his associate Frank Selke a very valuable aide, Smythe built Maple Leaf Gardens from scratch in five months for one-and-a-half million dollars.

Pivotal in the construction was the effort of Selke, a former business manager of the electricians' union, in convincing the workers to take stock in the new building as part of their salaries.

"In those hard times, construction work was hard to find, and it wasn't difficult to convince the trades unions that 80 per cent of a salary was better than no salary," Selke said.

"When the unions took our offer, the bankers got in on the act, loosening up a little money for us to go ahead," Smythe said. *"The contractors took some shares, too, instead of cash or we never would have made it."*

Smythe had operated successful amateur teams in Toronto in the early 1920s, then was hired as manager to build the first New York Rangers team. Smythe did an amazing job, acquiring thirty-one players, including goalie Lorne Chabot, defensemen Ching Johnson and Taffy Abel, forwards Bill and Bun Cook, Frank Boucher and Murray Murdoch for thirty-one thousand dollars. But just before the Rangers' first game, Smythe was fired and replaced by Lester Patrick.

Smythe vowed to build a better team in Toronto when he later bought the Toronto St. Patricks and renamed them the Maple Leafs. One of his first actions was to purchase Francis (King) Clancy from the Ottawa Senators, and surround him with quality young players seasoned in junior hockey by Frank Selke. It wasn't long before Conn Smythe was on top of the world, with a Stanley Cup replica in his trophy case in his office in his own Maple Leaf Gardens, a hockey showpiece.

He would rule the team with an iron fist and a flair for the theatrical into the 1960s, and was famous for his feuds with the likes of Boston's Art Ross and Detroit's Jack Adams. The Leafs were Conn's team through and through, and he bled royal blue until he died.

The Rangers won the series in five games, and the Silver Fox and his team were greeted by Mayor Jimmy Walker on the steps of City Hall later that April.

How tough was it to compete in the Big Apple, and how valuable were Patrick's heroics? Earlier that year, Mayor Walker held a famous New York tickertape parade for Charles Lindbergh upon his return from his epic flight to Paris. A few months later, Hizzoner feted Babe Ruth as the first major leaguer to hit sixty home runs in a season. New York was a tough town to crack, but with Lester's coaching and marquee players like the Cook brothers and Frank Boucher, the Rangers grabbed an important and respected piece of the New York sports pie.

It was important for the survival of the National Hockey League in the United States that its anchor was dropped in New York. The 1920s saw the arrival of a new universal communications device called radio. By the 1930s, network radio had changed the lifestyles and habits of Americans all across the U.S., and New York was where network radio was based. All of the major entertainment stars played a role in "the radio business" as North America struggled through the post-Crash era and the Great Depression.

Lester Patrick became part of the Big Apple's fabric, and the man who coined the phrase on his radio program, Walter Winchell, recognized that fact and gave the Rangers the occasional mention. At the height of his popularity, Winchell reached forty million Americans.

While Lester blended quickly into the NHL landscape, it took brother Frank several years to return east. While Lester's wife and children remained in Victoria for his first Rangers' season, Lester's business interests shifted east and his family joined him in Manhattan. On November 11, 1929, the Victoria Arena mysteriously burned to the ground. A building that had cost more than one hundred thousand dollars to build was insured for less than half that amount.

June 1, 1931

Work begins on Toronto's new arena, Maple Leaf Gardens. The building opens one hundred and sixty-five days later, on November 12, 1931.

February 14, 1931

In an historic first, three assists are awarded on one NHL goal! Toronto's Charlie Conacher scores, with assists given to King Clancy, Joe Primeau and Busher Jackson, in the Maple Leafs' 1-1 tie against Detroit.

The fire affected Frank, who was pursuing western business interests and prospecting for gold and silver in the British Columbia Interior. Frank was also president and general manager of the new Pacific Coast league, a four-team minor league with a franchise in Victoria and his own Vancouver Lions. By 1933, Frank's business fortunes were sagging when NHL President Frank Calder came calling. The league had created a new post of managing director to oversee its officials and he offered it to Frank.

Frank quickly was thrown into one of the most controversial incidents in NHL history.

During a game in Boston between Toronto and the Bruins, superstar Eddie Shore had his hands full with the Leafs, especially the feisty King Clancy who delighted in needling Shore non-stop. With the Bruins in a two-man advantage and increasingly frustrated by Toronto's strong penalty-killing, Shore headed up the ice with the puck, only to be tripped by Clancy, who turned toward the Bruins goal with the puck. Toronto forward Irvine (Ace) Bailey took Clancy's spot at the blue line, next to defenseman Red Horner.

Shore skated behind Bailey, thinking he was Clancy, and struck him with such force that Bailey flew into the air and landed head-first on the ice, where he lay unmoving in a pool of blood. Perhaps stunned by what he had done, Shore stood quietly by as Horner knocked him unconscious with a single punch. When his head struck the ice, it made a second pool of blood on the ice.

November 12, 1931

The first NHL game played at the Maple Leaf Gardens is won 2-1 by Chicago. Mush March scores the first goal, two-and-a-half minutes into the first game.

Chicago beats Detroit 1-0 in overtime of game four of the final to win the Stanley Cup. Chuck Gardiner turns in the shutout, and Mush March scores the winner at 30:05 of overtime to give the Hawks their first Cup in their eighth season in the NHL.

April 10, 1934

Toronto's Harvey (Busher) Jackson is the first NHL player to score a hat trick in one period. He finishes with four goals in the third period to lead the Leafs to 5-2 win over the St. Louis Eagles.

Francis (King) Clancy

recently purchased from Ottawa

by Conn Smythe,

is welcomed to the Maple Leafs

by coach Art Duncan.

*Bailey and Shore shook hands
and the incident was closed*

Art Ross and Conn Smythe went to war in the press, and talk of vigilante vengeance rose in both cities. Frank Patrick was assigned to rule on the matter. Bailey slipped into a coma in Boston hospital and Shore recovered from his injuries, as Frank deliberated. He handed a six-game suspension to Horner, and deliberately took his time with the Shore decision, while pressure to act mounted.

Ten days later, after two delicate brain surgeries, Bailey was out of danger, and shortly thereafter, Patrick levied a sixteen-day suspension against the Boston defenseman. Later that spring, a special benefit game was held in Toronto for Bailey, and, just prior to the opening face-off of what was the NHL's first All-Star game, Bailey and Shore shook hands and the incident was closed.

That summer, Art Ross decided to concentrate on management duties and offered the Bruins' coaching job to Frank Patrick, who moved his family to Boston in time for the 1934-35 season. Frank hit it off well with the Adams, Charles and his son Weston who would soon take over the team. He guided the Bruins to a first-place finish in the American Division that winter with the second best record in the league, before dropping the playoff semi-final to Toronto. Joe Patrick Jr., Frank's son, eventually enrolled at Harvard where he became the Crimson hockey team's top scorer.

Frank Patrick's

coaching career in the NHL

was a far too short

two seasons with Boston,

from 1934 to 1936.

Boston GM Art Ross

February 22, 1936

Canadiens rookie Toe Blake scores his first career NHL goal, the only goal in the game against the visiting New York Americans.

A year later, the honeymoon ended. There were rumors that Frank, originally a teetotalling Methodist, was drinking, and Art Ross began to interfere, feeling his coach was too friendly with the players. The Bruins finished in a tie for second place in the American Division during an NHL season of parity. The Maroons and the Maple Leafs were atop the Canadian Division, with fifty-four and fifty-two points respectively, while Detroit took the American Division with fifty-six points, six ahead of the Bruins, Blackhawks and Rangers. Only the New York Americans and the Montreal Canadiens were out of contention.

The Bruins faced the Leafs in a two-game, total-goal, quarter-final and won the first game at home, 3-0. They scored the first goal in Toronto before the Maple Leafs erupted for eight straight to win the playoff. The next day, a Boston newspaper alleged that Frank Patrick was drinking on the day of the game and was unable to handle the team. Several days later Art Ross announced that he would return to the coaching job for the next season, and Frank was out.

The Rocket's Red Glare

Red Storey, banqueteer emeritus and hockey's *raconteur par excellence*, credits Maurice Richard with a scientific discovery well ahead of its time.

"*I don't know who invented the laser, but the Rocket was using it in the 1940s,*" the former NHL referee fondly recalls.

"*He'd come down the ice with the puck on his stick and these laser beams flashing on the target, and I know some referees and linesmen who were tempted to jump over the boards and run away. Imagine what was going through the minds of the defensemen and goalie who had to play this guy.*"

If the eyes are the window of one's soul, the Rocket's soul was equal parts determination, intensity and pure passion. Once his laser-guided tracking system fixed on a target, the puck was sure to end up in the net.

American literary giant William Faulkner took in a Rangers-Canadiens game at Madison Square Garden on special assignment for the fledgling *Sports Illustrated* magazine in the mid-1950s. He was fascinated by the Rocket who stood out with the "*passionate, glittering, fatal, alien quality of snakes.*" The Nobel Prize author and Southerner knew his metaphors.

The soul of the *bleu-blanc-rouge* for eighteen seasons, Richard led a moribund franchise out of the doldrums of the 1930s and 1940s, capturing eight Stanley Cup championships, including a record five straight, and eight NHL regular-season titles.

The Rocket forged hockey history at every turn. He raised emotions and *routinely* brought entire crowds to their feet, earning the admiration and respect of teammates and opponents alike. The spectacular goals and crowd-lifting plays were legion – the first NHL player ever to score fifty goals in a season, Richard set the record in only fifty games in 1944-45.

An idol of his people, Richard's importance to Montreal was amply demonstrated when his season-ending suspension for striking a linesman in March 1955, touched off a riot that spread like wildfire through downtown Montreal.

But it was on the ice rink that Richard became a household name with hockey fans around the world. On October 19, 1957, the Rocket became the first player in the history of the NHL to score five hundred regular-season goals, beating goalie Glenn Hall of the Chicago Blackhawks.

His explosiveness was evidenced in twenty-six career hat tricks. On December 28, 1944, he scored five goals and added three assists against Harry Lumley in a 9-1 Canadiens' romp over the Detroit Red Wings at the Forum, after spending the day toting heavy furniture and moving house.

During the playoffs, the Rocket was even more spectacular with eighty-two goals in one hundred and thirty-three playoff games. He scored seven hat tricks, including a game with five goals and three others in which he netted four. He also was the go-to man in overtime, scoring six extra time game-winners. At his retirement, he had accumulated five hundred and forty-four goals and four hundred and twenty-one assists, for a total of nine hundred and sixty-five points in nine hundred and seventy-eight regular-season games. A ferocious player, Richard also totalled one thousand, two hundred and eighty-five minutes in penalties.

On October 6, 1960, the Canadiens retired sweater number "9" in honor of Maurice Richard, in a ceremony at center ice at the Forum. Several months later, Maurice Richard was inducted into the Hockey Hall of Fame.

Maurice Richard Career Highlights

August 4, 1921

Maurice Richard is born in Montreal.

October 31, 1942

Rookie Maurice Richard plays his first NHL game with the Montreal Canadiens. He wears number "15", and picks up his first NHL point (an assist) thirty-six seconds into the game, a 3-2 win for the Canadiens over the Bruins, at the Forum.

November 8, 1942

He scores his first-ever NHL goal against Steve Buzinski of the Rangers in a 10-4 Montreal win at the Forum.

December 27, 1942

Maurice Richard breaks his ankle and ends his first NHL season, with a record of five goals and six assists in sixteen games.

March 23, 1944

He becomes the first player of the modern era to score five goals in a play-off game, scoring all of his team's goals in a 5-1 win over Toronto at the Forum.

April 6, 1944

Maurice Richard scores the first of his NHL-record three Stanley Cup final hat tricks, in a 3-1 win over Chicago. The win is the second of four straight by the Canadiens over the Blackhawks.

December 28, 1944

Maurice Richard is the first player in NHL history to score eight points in a game. He scores five goals and three assists as the Canadiens beat Detroit, 9-1.

February 25, 1945

The Rocket sets an NHL record with his forty-fifth goal of the year, in a 5-2 Canadiens win over Toronto, breaking the NHL single season mark of forty-four set by Joe Malone in 1917-18.

March 18, 1945

In the final game of the 1944-45 season, a 4-2 Montreal win at Boston, Maurice Richard becomes the first player in NHL history to score fifty goals in a season. Richard scores his fifty goals in just fifty games.

March 29, 1945

He scores four goals, including three goals and an assist in the final period, as the Canadiens win 10-3 over the visiting Maple Leafs, in the fifth game of the semi-finals. Richard is the first player in NHL history to get three playoff hat tricks.

April 2, 1946

Maurice Richard extends his playoff record goal-scoring streak to eight games as the Canadiens win 3-2 over the visiting Boston Bruins, in game two of the Stanley Cup final.

March 23, 1947

The Canadiens end the season with a 3-2 win in Boston. The Rocket ends up with forty-five goals, and finishes second in NHL scoring to Max Bentley. He later receives the Hart Trophy as the league's Most Valuable Player.

January 15, 1949

The Rocket scores a hat trick and reaches the two hundred-goal level in a 7-1 win over Chicago at the Forum.

October 29, 1951

The Rocket scores twice in a 6-1 win over the Rangers, witnessed by Her Royal Highness Princess Elizabeth, and HRH Prince Philip, the Duke of Edinburgh. However, he is overshadowed by defensive forward Floyd Curry who scores three goals.

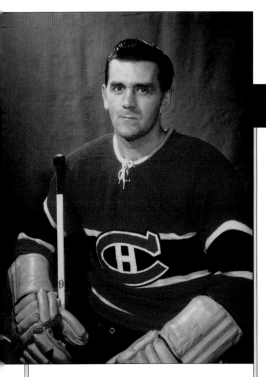

November 8, 1952

He scores his three hundred and twenty-fifth goal, surpassing the NHL record for career goals held by Nels Stewart. It comes in a 6-4 win over the Blackhawks in Montreal, on the tenth anniversary of Richard's first NHL goal.

October 10, 1953

Maurice Richard is the first player in NHL history to score three hundred and fifty goals, as the Canadiens defeat Detroit 4-1 at the Forum.

December 18, 1954

The Rocket scores his four hundredth career goal, an NHL first, when the Canadiens defeat the Blackhawks 4-2 in Chicago.

March 13, 1955

Maurice Richard gets involved in a vicious stick-swinging incident with former teammate Hal Laycoe of the Bruins, and strikes linesman Cliff Thompson in the melee. He receives a major penalty and a misconduct and it is believed that further sanctions will follow when the league assesses the incident.

March 17, 1955

A riot erupts in the streets of Montreal, as fans protest NHL President Clarence Campbell's suspension of Maurice Richard the day before. The Canadiens forfeit the game to the Red Wings after a tear gas canister empties the Forum late in the first period of the game.

President Campbell

October 15, 1955

Henri Richard, fourteen years younger than the Rocket, plays his first game for the Canadiens and scores his first NHL goal, in a 4-1 win over the Rangers.

April 10, 1956

The Canadiens defeat the Red Wings 3-1 at the Forum, to win the Stanley Cup in five games. It is the first of five straight Maurice Richard will receive as team captain.

October 9, 1956

The Rocket scores Montreal's only goal in the league's annual All-Star Game, a 1-1 tie with the All-Stars.

October 19, 1957

Maurice Richard is the NHL first player to score five hundred career goals; the goal comes in his eight hundred and sixty-third career game as the Canadiens beat Chicago, 3-1.

April 12, 1960

Maurice Richard circles the net and scores on a backhand shot against Toronto goalie Johnny Bower, as the Canadiens defeat the Leafs 5-2 at Maple Leaf Gardens, in game three of the final. It turns out to be the Rocket's last goal in NHL competition, as the Canadiens would sweep the Leafs two nights later.

September 15, 1960

Maurice Richard scores four goals during a morning intra-squad game at the Canadiens training camp. In the afternoon, the Canadiens stage a press conference and the Rocket announces his retirement, after eighteen seasons. He leaves the game with five hundred and forty-four goals, and eighty-two playoff goals, both league records.

June 25, 1998

The NHL Board of Governors announces that a new trophy is to be awarded each year (starting in 1999) to the league's leading goal-scorer; the new award is called the Maurice Richard Trophy.

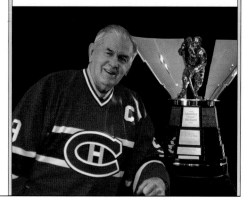

The 'Norris House League'

James Norris Sr.

James Norris was a one-man rescue operation for the fledgling National Hockey League, single-handedly resurrecting the Red Wings and Blackhawks, while buffering the Rangers at a time when U.S.-based franchises were expiring at an alarming rate.

Big Jim, a garrulous six-feet, two-inches and almost two hundred and seventy-five pounds of hard-nosed businessman who could still whip young pups half his age in squash in his fifties, was a man who brooked no nonsense, and even less negativity when he plunged headlong into a project.

Born in Ontario in 1879, he grew up a Montrealer and an athlete of note, competing for the Montreal Amateur Athletic Association in hockey, lacrosse, squash and tennis. He moved the family's Norris Grain Co. to Chicago in 1907, where the charged world of grain futures and trading was made-to-measure for him. By the 1920s, the Norris Grain Co. was the biggest guy on the block, with a fleet of some forty Great Lakes tankers and vast holdings worth some two hundred million dollars.

The Olympia

His MAAA days had taught him the value of sports, and, as the Depression took its toll, James Norris showed an understanding of his social responsibility rare in tycoons of his day. He bought up the Olympia Stadium in Detroit, and the Chicago Stadium, both teetering on the brink of bankruptcy, and injected a large amount of money in Madison Square Garden to keep that storied building afloat.

He turned to his son, James D. *"We have got to find a lot of regular work for a great many boxers, skaters, wrestlers, circus hands, and athletes of all types. If we don't give fans happy nights to forget their troubles, we are sunk and so is this country."* James D. Norris became czar of boxing as president of the International Boxing Club in the 1950s and raced a string of expensive thoroughbreds. When his father died in 1952, James D. became owner of the Blackhawks and the Red Wings in the NHL and owned a major piece of the Madison Square Garden Corporation which owned the Rangers. At one point, columnist Jim Coleman suggested that NHL stood for Norris House League.

Norris had applied for an NHL franchise in 1928, several years before his 1935 bail-out of the Chicago Stadium, but Blackhawks' owner Major Frederic McLaughlin thwarted him. As a result, Norris founded the Chicago Shamrocks of the rival American Hockey Association and shut the Hawks out of the Stadium. The two feuded for years, and the senior Norris finally joined his adversary in the NHL when he bought the struggling Detroit franchise in 1933.

James D. took over management of the Red Wings franchise, serving as the team's governor between 1934-46 before passing on the reins to sister Marguerite Norris Riker, and later, younger brother Bruce. And, although the Norrises did a competent job of building up Detroit, which became a league powerhouse in the late 1940s and early '50s, James Norris Sr. was frustrated by his attempts to own the team in what he considered his "hometown."

When McLaughlin died in 1944, a syndicate of businessmen ostensibly led by team president and GM Bill Tobin, owned the Blackhawks. However, much of that money came from the Norris-owned Stadium Corporation. In 1952, a group of independent businessmen including James D. Norris, and Arthur Wirtz, finally acquired the Blackhawks.

For their efforts in allowing the National Hockey League to survive in the United States through troubled times, James Norris Sr., James D. Norris and Bruce Norris, all were admitted to the Hockey Hall of Fame in the Builders' category.

The MAAA Winged Wheelers

If that wasn't enough grief for the family, a fire that began in an adjacent shipyard building engulfed the Vancouver Arena that summer, and the last Patrick connection to hockey on the West Coast went down in flames.

March 8, 1937

Montreal's Howie Morenz dies six weeks after suffering a broken leg during a game against Chicago. Three days later, a funeral service is held at the Forum and more than fifteen thousand people pay their respects.

Although Frank would not return to the NHL for several years, there continued to be multiple Patricks in the league. Lester Patrick extended an invitation to the Rangers' 1934 training camp in Winnipeg to a husky six-footer who had excelled with the Montreal Royals of the Quebec junior league. The kid, Lynn Patrick, was a dedicated Maple Leafs fan, thanks to the regular broadcasts by Foster Hewitt that he had listened to while growing up in Victoria.

Lester's eldest son was in Winnipeg against Lester's better judgment. The Silver Fox had no choice because the boy was recommended by his scouts. Conn Smythe warned that Toronto would take him if the Rangers didn't.

The Rangers had the first NHL camp to include amateurs in full tryouts, and the harvest was impressive: Babe Pratt, the Colville brothers, Alex Shibicky, Don Metz, Bert Gardiner and others. The Rangers needed new talent because the Cooks, Frank Boucher and Muzz Murdoch were slowing down and Ching Johnson talked of retirement.

Bill and Bun Cook recommended that a reluctant Lester sign Lynn, who played well with nine goals and thirteen assists, even though some press pundits harped on nepotism within the club. Lynn's six-feet, one-inch, one-hundred-and-ninety-pound frame, helped a team that had ceased to play a physical game on many nights, and he quickly won over the demanding Madison Square Garden crowd. Lynn led the Rangers in scoring twice, and earned selections to the first and second All-Star teams. His best season came in 1940-41 when he scored thirty-two goals in forty-seven games.

March 24, 1936

Mud Bruneteau scores the only goal of the game as Detroit beats the Maroons 1-0 at 116:30 of overtime – five hours and fifty-one minutes after the opening face-off, in the longest game in NHL history. Goalie Norm Smith made ninety-two saves for the Red Wings.

March 17, 1938

The Canadiens defeat the Maroons 6-3 in a penalty-free contest, the last-ever game between the two teams. The Maroons dropped out of the NHL at season's end.

Younger brother Murray, nicknamed Muzz, excelled in many sports as he was growing up, and his favorite appeared to be boxing. Lester first learned of his second son's pugilistic prowess when Muzz asked for a loan to go to the Canadian amateur championships in Edmonton.

"Why do you want to spend all of that money just to watch a bunch of amateurs," Dad asked.

"I don't want to watch them; I want to fight them," was the terse reply.

Lester accompanied Muzz to the championships and was surprised to find his son in the heavyweight final against defending champ Tommy Osborne. Osborne's name was already inscribed on the back of the gold medal and he knocked Patrick down twice in the first round. Muzz returned the favor in the second round, with Osborne staying down, and Muzz was Canadian heavyweight champion.

When the family returned to New York, Muzz played hockey with the Brooklyn Crescents, a top-rated amateur team that was part of the Rangers pipeline, and boxed locally in the CYO amateur tournament. Professional boxing managers were impressed, and Muzz had the option of going pro. A deviated septum ended that, and he focused on hockey after an operation to correct the problem.

Muzz Patrick played defense with the Crescents (renamed the New York Rovers), and later with the Philadelphia Ramblers, and was called up to the Blueshirts in 1939, where he immediately became popular with the fans and the press.

The Rangers youth movement paid off for Lester Patrick. Hextall, Shibicky, the Colvilles, Pratt and his two sons joined veterans Ott Heller, Clint Smith, Dutch Hiller, Alf Pike, Phil Watson and goalie Dave Kerr. Patrick appointed his former captain, Frank Boucher, to coach the team, and the Rangers finished second behind the Stanley Cup champion Bruins in a season that included a nineteen-game undefeated string. The confident young team fell behind Boston, 2-1, in their best-of-seven quarter-final before storming back with three straight wins.

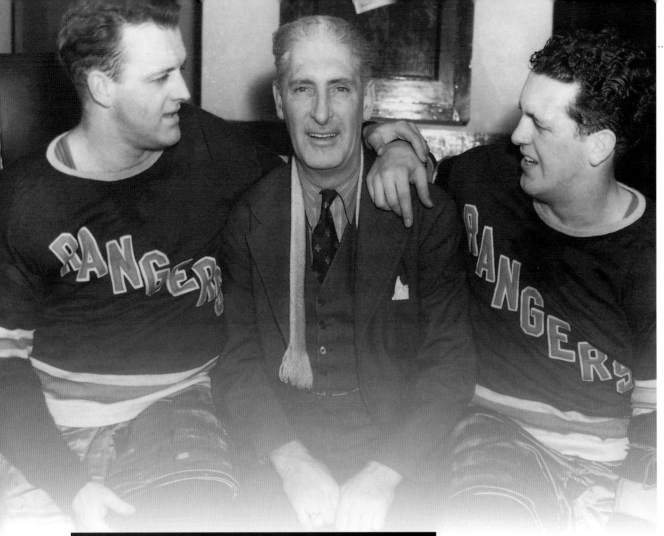

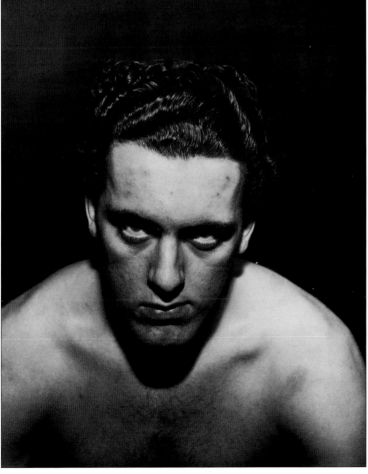

Top **Proud papa Lester Patrick**

celebrates a Stanley Cup victory

with sons Lynn *(left)* **and Muzz.**

Left **Muzz Patrick was the Canadian**

amateur heavyweight boxing

champion before joining the Rangers.

The top-scoring line in the NHL in 1941-42:

Bryan Hextall (fifty-six points),

Phil Watson (fifty-two points)

and Lynn Patrick (fifty-four points).

Patrick also topped all goal scorers

with thirty-two.

The Cup final opened at Madison Square Garden on April 2, 1940, with the visiting Maple Leafs agreeing to play on consecutive nights because the omnipresent circus was in town. Kerr was brilliant in goal and Alf Pike was the hero at 15:30 of overtime in a 2-1 New York victory. On the next night, in Boston, Bryan Hextall's hat trick overcame an early 2-0 Toronto lead and led to a 6-2 victory.

April 2, 1939

Boston's Mel Hill scores after forty-eight minutes of overtime to lead the Bruins to a 2-1 playoff win over the Rangers in game seven of the Stanley Cup semi-final. It was Hill's third overtime goal in the series against New York.

In Toronto, the Leafs rebounded with 2-1 and 3-0 victories, and things looked grim as the Blueshirts played what should have been a home game on foreign ice. They won, 2-1, on Muzz Patrick's goal at the 11:43 mark of the second overtime period, then won the Cup, 3-2, in game six when Hextall scored off a Phil Watson pass, after two minutes of extra time.

The Silver Fox took great delight in posing with the Stanley Cup and his two sons, the first time three members of a single family had their names inscribed on the trophy.

The delight ended there for the Rangers. Although the rich mix of youngsters and veterans would finish first overall in the 1941-42 regular season, they fell to Toronto in the Cup semi-final and then saw much of the team march off to war later that spring. The Rangers never recovered from World War II. Their best young players on military duty, the Rangers hit depths never experienced before in the NHL. A record of twenty-eight wins, ninety-nine losses and twenty-three ties over the three war seasons was the NHL's worst, and Lester Patrick and Frank Boucher suffered the most.

November 20, 1938

Boston's Tiny Thompson is the first goaltender in NHL history to record two hundred and fifty victories, in the Bruins' 4-1 win over the visiting Red Wings.

For the first time in history, the members of one line (Milt Schmidt, Woody Dumart and Bobby Bauer of the Kraut Line) finish 1-2-3 in NHL scoring. Boston scored five goals in the third period to beat Montreal, 7-2, to capture the NHL regular-season title.

March 17, 1940

When Lynn, Muzz and the other soldiers had returned for the 1945-46 season, Lester and Boucher were at loggerheads, much the same as Frank Patrick and Art Ross had been in Boston. Both sons barely lasted that season; Lynn played thirty-eight games, Muzz twenty-four, before they headed in different directions, Muzz as a player-coach in the American Association, and Lynn to coach the Rangers' farm team in New Haven.

Frustrated and tired after nearly a half century in hockey, Lester Patrick had enough, too. He resigned on February 22, 1946, and for the first time in twenty years, no member of the Patrick family was in the NHL.

After his Boston experience, Frank Patrick had waited four years for his next opportunity in the league. In 1940, Senator Donat Raymond hired him as the Montreal Canadiens' business manager to assist general manager Tommy Gorman and newly hired coach Dick Irvin. The Habs were emerging from the worst period in team history, thirteen years without the Stanley Cup (1931-44) and Raymond wanted as much hockey acumen around the club as possible.

Brothers Doug (left)
and Max Bentley in 1948

A Foliate Trio

When World War II ended in 1945, the Toronto Maple Leafs had much depth in NHL players from two sources – the sixteen players who had been in the armed services, and the large group of talented youngsters discovered by Frank Selke, who had filled the role of general manager when owner, Major Conn Smythe, was away at war.

The Leafs won the Stanley Cup championship in 1945 with a patchwork roster of veterans and youngsters. But in the 1945-46 season, the Leafs missed the playoffs, and Selke was fired after a dispute with Smythe. He then joined the Montreal Canadiens to build that organization to dynasty status.

The Leafs broke in nine NHL rookies in 1946-47 season – only five players from the 1945 champs were on the roster – and under the strong hand of coach Hap Day, the team embarked on three consecutive Cup victories, the first team in NHL history to "three-peat."

Goalie Turk Broda, defenseman Wally Stanowski, forwards Syl Apps, Harry Watson, Don and Nick Metz supplied the veteran anchors for a strong group of youngsters – forwards Ted Kennedy, a four-season veteran at twenty-one, Howie Meeker, twenty-one, Joe Klukay, twenty-four, Vic Lynn, twenty-one, and Bill Ezinicki, twenty-one, defensemen Jim Thomson, eighteen, Gus Mortson, twenty, Garth Boesch, twenty-six and Bill Barilko, twenty.

After the team beat the Canadiens in a tough six-game final in 1947, Smythe felt another top center was needed if the Leafs were to hold off the rebuilding Canadiens and a strong club in Detroit built around Gordie Howe.

The Leafs made perhaps the biggest NHL deal to that point when they acquired center Max Bentley and Cy Thomas from the Chicago Blackhawks for five players – Gus Bodnar, Bob Goldham, Ernie Dickens, Gaye Stewart and Bud Poile. Bentley, who had starred for Chicago for many years alongside his brother Doug, had won back-to-back scoring titles and was a master stickhandler who was especially strong on the power-play.

The usually taciturn Clarence Campbell gave the deal his presidential stamp: *"It's the biggest trade in the NHL for a long, long time and only goes to emphasize the worth of a player like Bentley."*

Bentley, Kennedy and Apps gave the Leafs superb pivots and when team captain Apps retired after another Cup win in 1948, the Leafs traded defenseman Wally Stanowski to the Rangers for Cal Gardner to fill the hole.

On April 16, 1949, history was made at Toronto when the Leafs defeated Detroit 3-1 in game four of the Stanley Cup final. It was the team's second straight sweep of the Wings in the final, and the Leafs' third Cup in a row.

A year later, the Leafs were first-round casualties in the playoffs. But, with the basic roster intact from the three wins, they won a fourth crown in 1951, with a goal by defenseman Bill Barilko winning the final against Montreal in five games. That summer, Barilko died in a northern Ontario plane crash, and the Leafs plummeted, too, the team a disaster through the 1950s.

The War Years

World War II would have little effect on the National Hockey League teams in that first season after the Dominion of Canada declared war on Germany in September, 1939. That all changed dramatically when Pearl Harbor was bombed December 7, 1941.

With the disbanding of the New York Americans at the end of the 1941-42 season, only six teams remained in the league. That meant a maximum of one hundred and twenty players drew regular NHL paychecks. By 1942, eighty of these were in uniform.

Hockey was hit hard by conscription (the draft) in Canada and the U.S. The Rangers unit of player-coach Frank Boucher, Alf Pike, Alex Shibicky and the Colville brothers played for the Ottawa Commandos, while the Patricks and Art Coulter entered service in the United States.

Boston was equally decimated. Goalie Frank Brimsek joined the U.S. Navy and several other players enlisted in various services. The Kraut Line of Schmidt, Dumart and Bauer, and teammate Roy Conacher enlisted in the Royal Canadian Air Force and played for the RCAF Flyers in Ottawa.

Toronto lost stars like goalie Turk Broda, defenseman Bob Goldham, Billy Taylor and the Metz brothers, but those gaps were filled with the acquisition of Babe Pratt from the Rangers, Mel (Sudden Death) Hill

from the disbanding Americans as well as a youth movement that included Gaye Stewart, Bud Poile, Jack Hamilton and Ted (Teeder) Kennedy.

Detroit and Chicago had their share of defections and, although it was popular for Toronto to complain that Montreal had an unusually high number of deferments, the Canadiens saw the Reardon brothers, Frankie Eddolls and Kenny Mosdell report for service, and defenseman Doug Harvey serve in the Royal Canadian Navy before joining the team as a twenty-four-year-old rookie at war's end.

Overtime was shelved for the duration of the war so that teams could get to trains on time during the tightly controlled schedules of the period

If losing all the players to military service was a hardship, reintegrating the returning servicemen in 1946 was as big a problem. General managers and coaches trying to fit in rising talents who were too young for military service between 1942-45, with returning veterans six or seven years older who experienced very different lives during the conflict, were faced with a rare generation gap.

It would not be until the 1947-48 season that the NHL would finally emerge into its post-War era.

It was an impossible situation for Gorman, a veteran hockey manager who had delivered Stanley Cups with three teams (Ottawa Senators, Chicago Blackhawks, and Montreal Maroons) and who would be the only man in NHL history to share in Cup championships with four teams. Gorman protected his turf, and Frank found himself on the outside looking in, although he had signed the talented Butch Bouchard, Elmer Lach and Kenny Reardon. Patrick resigned in January, 1941, to take a senior position with a Montreal company heavily involved in war production.

Lester and Frank were gone, but their legacy to the sport will never be forgotten. Simply put, their legacy was the game itself.

Coach Dick Irvin of the Canadiens with son Dick Irvin Jr., who would serve as a sports broadcaster in Montreal for almost forty years.

January 29, 1942

Syd Howe Night turns out to be perhaps the best "night" a player ever had. After playing a gift piano at center ice for the fans in Olympia, he scores both goals in a 2-0 Red Wings win over Chicago. John Mowers got his seventh career shutout.

Chicago's Reg Bentley scores a goal, with assists from brothers Max and Doug, in a 3-3 Blackhawks' tie at New York. It is the first goal in NHL history with three points from the same family!

January 3, 1943

Interview

FRANK SELKE

Q&A

Canada Day, 1983

WHEN DID YOU FIRST GET INVOLVED WITH HOCKEY?

I was 14 and it was back home in Berlin, which changed its name to Kitchener during the World War 1. It was park hockey and I put together teams back then because there were few structured leagues or hockey associations to speak of. My first real good team was the Berlin Union Jacks, which today might sound funny. I was 19 and this collection of Polish- and German-Canadian blue-collar boys had an unbeaten season all the way to the 1913-14 Ontario provincial championship. Back then the best teams came from the best neighborhoods where they could afford to play the game in their leisure time. We were the tough kids from the wrong side of the tracks, and proud of it.

WHAT WAS THE NEXT STEP?

I served in the Royal Canadian Army for three years during World War I, and they asked me to set up some hockey for the troops, and so I did. This gave me some experience in dealing with adult hockey players.

YOU MOVED TO TORONTO AFTER THAT?

Yes. I apprenticed as an electrician and, after the war, I moved to Toronto and went to work as an electrician at the University of Toronto. There I

coached the U of T Schools (high school) team that won the Ontario junior championship in 1918. Six years later, I became coach of the Toronto Marlboros, a feeder team for the St. Patricks.

WHO WERE SOME OF YOUR FIRST STARS?

Go down a list of Hall-of-Fame players who passed through the Maple Leafs. The Kid Line of Joe Primeau, Busher Jackson and Charlie Conacher all played for me. Red Horner was my grocery boy... he'd stop over for milk and my wife Mary's homemade cookies before he played organized hockey. Alex Levinsky and Bob Gracie also played for those powerhouse Marlboros.

The Kid Line

WHEN DID YOU MOVE INTO THE PRO RANKS?

When Conn Smythe took over the Maple Leafs in 1927, he hired me as his assistant.

WHAT WAS YOUR MOST IMPORTANT CONTRIBUTION TO YOUR NEW TEAM?

There were two. I convinced Conn Smythe to drop a lot of older, non-producing Leafs and replace them

with Marlboros, and I got the unions onside when we built Maple Leaf Gardens.

HOW DID YOU GET THE UNIONS ONSIDE?

We were under the gun to build the Gardens over the summer of 1931 so that it would be ready for the hockey season, and money was very tight. In fact, it looked like we might not make it. I was a card-carrying member of the electricians union and I went to my union brothers and convinced them to take twenty per cent of their salaries in Gardens' stock. They agreed to that, and Conn Smythe was able to turn around and get the banks to do the same thing. The rest is history, and nobody complained later about the dividends on that stock.

HOW DID YOU END UP IN MONTREAL?

I had the inevitable falling out with Conn Smythe. He had a very strong personality and ironclad opinions on everything. He eventually decided that I had been given too much credit for winning the Stanley Cup in 1945, while he was serving overseas during World War II, and a rift developed. When Senator Donat Raymond came to get me for the Canadiens, I didn't hesitate.

WHAT KIND OF TEAM DID YOU JOIN IN MONTREAL?

Overall, an organization that was in disarray, even though the veteran team had just won the Stanley Cup. I began work on August 1, 1946, and I'll never forget that first afternoon at the Montreal Forum. The place was filthy and the stench of poorly managed urinals knocked you down when you opened the front door. I had come from the working class and I would not stand for sloppiness at any level. The fans deserved to sit in comfort and enjoy a high quality of entertainment, so my first task was to invest more than one hundred thousand dollars in a new plumbing system and undertake major renovations in the building.

WHAT WAS SPECIAL ABOUT THAT DECISION?

Strangely enough, it was the first, real independent decision I had ever taken in professional hockey. I didn't have to look to someone for approval because Senator Raymond had given me carte blanche.

WHAT WAS YOUR NEXT DECISION?

We had to build the organization from the ground up, adding farm or feeder teams from across the country. But, most importantly, because the 1946 Stanley Cup Canadiens had only five French-Canadian players, we had to develop the pool of players in our own backyard, Quebec. Sam Pollock, who was a talented organizer from the west end of Montreal, and Kenny Reardon, who retired from the team after the 1949-50 season and was from Saskatchewan, were the two men in charge.

HOW WELL DID THIS NEW SYSTEM WORK?

Within four years, we had sponsored teams in British Columbia, Alberta, Manitoba, Ontario and Quebec, and scouts beating the bushes in the Maritimes. We had ten teams in the Winnipeg area and we paid for the whole amateur system in Regina. And at one point we were paying three hundred thousand dollars a year in amateur development sin Edmonton.

WEREN'T THOSE HIGHLY EXPENSIVE PROPOSITIONS: THREE HUNDRED THOUSAND DOLLARS IN THOSE DAYS WAS A STEEP PRICE TO PAY?

All we were interested in was developing good players and that we did. It paid for itself because we were able to sell about a quarter million dollars worth of quality players every season. In other words, once the system was in high gear, the other five NHL clubs were paying for it. It was very convenient for some other organizations to save their seed money and they came to depend on us to beat the bushes for quality players for them.

Frank Selke, Jean Béliveau and Dick Irvin in 1953.

BUT THIS MEANT THAT YOU WOULD HAVE FIRST CHOICE OF A WHOLE POOL OF TALENT, DIDN'T IT?

That meant, of course, that they bought players who were a level below our best, and that we knew everything there was to know about those players. This would eventually work out to our advantage.

A LOT OF PEOPLE WHO HAVE CONFERRED SAINTHOOD ON YOU MIGHT NOT REALIZE THAT YOU DIDN'T WIN A STANLEY CUP IN YOUR SIX FIRST SEASONS IN MONTREAL. DID THAT BOTHER YOU?

No, because the Cups were coming. We lost to the Leafs in 1951, and they deserved to win that one, and a superior Detroit team defeated us in 1952. A year later, we won, and after losing in game seven overtime in 1954, and without the suspended Rocket Richard in seven games in 1955, we won five straight. With very few exceptions, Bert Olmstead and Marcel Bonin among them, these players were all homegrown.

HOW DID YOU RATE PLAYERS? WHAT WAS FRANK SELKE'S RECIPE FOR SUCCESS?

I believe that each successful pro hockey player must go through a four-stage system in his professionalization, if you will. Number one is awakening of interest in a professional career. That is followed by the crystallization (resolve) of the interest, and then, consolidation and commitment to career. Number four is a review of that commitment. By this stage, the player would be fully committed to going as far as he could in professional hockey, and aware of the sacrifices and work it would take.

WHAT WAS THAT "SPECIAL SOMETHING" THAT MADE THE MONTREAL CANADIENS THE JUGGERNAUT THAT WOULD BE FOR A QUARTER-CENTURY?

We saw three essentials; a strong hockey background, a deep commitment to winning or an equally strong aversion to losing, and the self-motivation necessary for the player to sublimate his needs to the team's. The team then embraced the players as an extended family would. We were successful because we treated players like a family, and did many things socially that involved their families.

Among the members of the Renfrew Millionaires were (clockwise from the top) Bert Lindsay, Frank Patrick, Bobby Rowe, Newsy Lalonde, Jack (Hay) Millar, Cyclone Taylor, and Lester Patrick (center).

Back **in 1908**, Renfrew teammates Cyclone Taylor and Frank Patrick were sitting around the team's boarding-house, when Patrick complimented Taylor on his performance the previous evening. There was a proviso, however.

"*You got away with murder,*" Patrick said.

Taylor was nonplussed. He had scored two goals, set up another pair in a victory.

"*You did what you do every time you think you need a breather, and when the heat's on,*" Patrick retorted. "*You stopped play by flipping the puck into the stands. Five times last night by my count.*"

"*So, what's wrong with that?*" Taylor retorted. In those days, players put in a full sixty minutes, and "*skating breathers*" were common when teams had one or no substitutes.

"*Nothing, according to the rules,*" Frank countered. "*But it's wrong. It's cheating. Hockey is supposed to be played with the puck on the ice, and not in the stands.*"

"*Frank, you know I always play by the rules,*" Taylor responded indignantly.

"*True. I think I'll propose one to stop that little trick of yours.*"

If Frank Patrick suggested a rule change, it usually came about. The younger Patrick was without a doubt the single most-influential "game guru" in the sport's first half century, with brother Lester a close second.

Frank and Lester discussed adjustments to hockey over breakfast or in arena corridors late at night after the final siren. Because they owned the Pacific Coast Hockey Association, what the Patricks said, happened. Occasionally, father Joe suggested an innovation. Just prior to the first PCHA game **in 1912**, Joe Patrick was reading the latest issue of *London Illustrated* magazine when he noticed a picture of a cross-country race in England. All of the runners wore numbers on their backs. Many times in poorly lighted rinks, players often skated away into anonymity, the farther they were from center ice, Joe was certain that numbered sweaters was the answer, and numbered jerseys were worn by the New Westminster Royals and the Victoria Aristocrats in the first PCHA game. Within three years, sweater numbers had spread throughout the hockey world.

In 1912, the hockey goalie was little more than an immobile post. By rule, he had to stay on his feet at all times, in much the same manner as his counterpart in field hockey.

"*It doesn't make sense,*" Lester argued. "*A goalkeeper should be allowed to make any move he wants, just like the rest of us. He should be allowed to make the most of his physical abilities.*" Within months, acrobatic goalies were an entertaining and exciting part of the game. Unfortunately, it would take sixteen years for this innovation to catch on back east.

Another detriment to an entertaining and smooth flow of hockey was the rule derived from rugby that prohibited forward passing outside of the offensive zone. An attacking player could make only lateral passes to his mates joining the rush. As a result, games often ground to a halt under the many offside whistles. In an exhibition game between Victoria and Quebec, Lester Patrick counted fifteen offside whistles in the first five minutes, and Lester had no quibble with the referee, his close friend, Art Ross, who was just following the rules.

Lester and Frank fixed that situation with the creation of two blue lines to divide the rink into three zones, and allowing forward passing in the newly created central, or neutral, zone. In the first year of application, the blue lines were eighty feet out from the end boards. After a year, they were moved ten feet closer to the end boards, sixty feet in front of the goals.

In 1918, Frank Patrick came up with another innovation that most observers would argue is the most important part of the professional game to this day. In 1918, the defending Cup champion Seattle Metropolitans were the best team in the PCHA and ran away with the league right from the beginning of the season. As a result, attendance sagged in the other cities.

February 3, 1944

Detroit's Syd Howe scores six goals (in a 12-2 win over the New York Rangers) to set a modern record for goals in one game by a player.

Blackhawks' Mike Karakas and Maple Leafs' Paul Bibeault duel to the only scoreless, penalty-free game in NHL history. The game, officiated by referee Bill Chadwick, takes only 1:55 to play.

February 20, 1944

September 4, 1946

Clarence Campbell becomes president
of the National Hockey League,
replacing Red Dutton, who presided
over the NHL from 1943 to 1946.

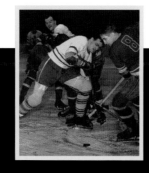

Playing in the final regular season game of his
NHL career, Syl Apps scores three times to give
him two hundred and one career goals. The
milestone comes in a 5-2 Toronto win in Detroit.

March 21, 1948

"What we need is a second chance for teams that, for whatever reason, have fallen too far behind to make a race of it," Frank said. *"It's not right, for example, that a team strong enough to make a challenge should be ruled out of early-season contention by injuries."* The solution was post-season playoffs between the top two teams, with the winner advancing to inter-league championships.

In 1921, Frank and Catherine Patrick were holidaying in England with Joe and Grace Patrick, and the quartet took in a polo match with some ten thousand Englishmen. When the referee signalled a penalty shot, the proverbial lightbulb was illuminated for Frank.

The Patricks invented the assist, thereby celebrating the talents of the playmaker, and they speeded up the game, especially in the face-off circle, by allowing players to kick the puck into play, but not for goals. As hockey got faster and teams began using two forward lines and four defense-men, they invented changing "on the fly", or line substitutions in mid-play. Prior to that, teams could only substitute on a whistle.

Lester Patrick, the Silver Fox, was renowned for his play, management and contribution to hockey's evolution at all levels. Brother Frank got less ink and public recognition, but he single-handedly contributed some twenty or more rule changes that would become part of modern hockey.

As the century reached its halfway point, professional ice hockey was a maturing game that was building a faithful following in Canada and the northeastern United States. The time was coming for the game to move south and west. Again.

This time, Frank and Lester wouldn't be there to help.

On Lester Patrick Night

at Madison Square Garden in 1947,

the Rangers' "first unit" of Bun Cook,

Ching Johnson, Bill Cook,

Lester, Taffy Abel and Frank Boucher,

got together to discuss old times.

Toronto Maple Leafs become the first NHL team to win three straight Stanley Cups, with a 5-1 win over Detroit in game four of the Stanley Cup final.

Clarence Campbell

Carl Voss

King Clancy

Refereeing was a developing art in the 1930s and '40s,

and some of the more practical performers were former players.

King Clancy, always at the center of controversy as a player,

was often in a similar situation as a referee *(below right).*

Other players who served some time as on-ice officials

after their careers had ended included Cy Denneny, Babe Dye,

Frank Foyston, Odie Cleghorn, Harry Cameron, Aurel Joliat

and Sylvio Mantha. Carl Voss, *(below left)*

who played for eight different teams

over twelve years, including the St. Louis Eagles,

became the league's referee-in-chief in the 1950 and '60s.

Another group of former players also coached

and refereed at some time in their careers.

This number included Art Duncan, Hap Day and Bill Stewart,

whose "day job" was that of umpire in major league baseball.

Both Day and Stewart won Stanley Cups as coaches,

as well as serving in the ranks of league officials.

Some referees moved up in the league.

Clarence Campbell, *(upper left)* who officiated in the 1930s,

went on to become a special prosecutor at the Nuremberg Trials

after World War II, and then returned to North America

to serve as NHL president from 1946-47 to 1977-78.

STANLEY CUP

1925-26	MONTREAL MAROONS
1926-27	OTTAWA SENATORS
1927-28	NEW YORK RANGERS
1928-29	BOSTON BRUINS
1929-30	MONTREAL CANADIENS
1930-31	MONTREAL CANADIENS
1931-32	TORONTO MAPLE LEAFS
1932-33	NEW YORK RANGERS
1933-34	CHICAGO BLACKHAWKS
1934-35	MONTREAL MAROONS
1935-36	DETROIT RED WINGS
1936-37	DETROIT RED WINGS
1937-38	CHICAGO BLACKHAWKS
1938-39	BOSTON BRUINS
1939-40	NEW YORK RANGERS
1940-41	BOSTON BRUINS
1941-42	TORONTO MAPLE LEAFS
1942-43	DETROIT RED WINGS
1943-44	MONTREAL CANADIENS
1944-45	TORONTO MAPLE LEAFS
1945-46	MONTREAL CANADIENS
1946-47	TORONTO MAPLE LEAFS
1947-48	TORONTO MAPLE LEAFS
1948-49	TORONTO MAPLE LEAFS
1949-50	DETROIT RED WINGS

1937

DETROIT RED WINGS

WINNERS

1931
MONTREAL CANADIENS

1933
NEW YORK RANGERS

1927
OTTAWA SENATORS

1939
BOSTON BRUINS

1949
TORONTO MAPLE LEAFS

1951
19

ХОККЕЙ
СССР·КАНАДА

ST. LOUIS
BLUES

ST. LOUIS
BLUES
35

A Real Major League

The Patricks
and a Quarter Century of Change

Lester Patrick appointed former Ranger captain
Frank Boucher as New York coach in 1939,
and when Frank moved up to GM of the Rangers,
he named Lynn Patrick coach of the team in 1949.

Art Ross had hired, and then replaced, Frank
Patrick as Boston Bruins coach in the
mid-1930s. Art later named Frank's nephew,
Lynn, as a successor to George Boucher,
Frank's brother, as Boston coach in 1950-51.

Murray (Muzz) Patrick and Frank Boucher shared coaching duties with the Rangers in 1953-54 and, when Boucher retired as Rangers GM in 1955, he named Muzz as his successor.

Concurrently, members of the Norris family were involved with the Chicago Blackhawks and the Detroit Red Wings.

In other words, the National Hockey League of the 1950s was emerging in the modern, post-war era, but it still remained a Family Compact, if not a downright incestuous private club. Yet, the four U.S.-based teams competed ferociously on the ice. Rangers-Bruins and Hawks-Wings were rivalries as strong as Canadiens-Maple Leafs north of the border, no matter how many siblings, nieces, nephews and cousins cohabited in the executive boxes upstairs. By the end of this, pro hockey's third quarter century, however, the "family" NHL would be replaced by the "corporate" NHL that rules the current era.

Lynn Patrick took the Rangers to a Cup final in his short two-year term as coach.

Lynn Patrick's Rangers were a force to contend with.

When Lester Patrick left the Rangers in 1946, the team was on a definite downswing, and Frank Boucher soon realized that the double duties of coach and general manager were too taxing for him. The team had finished fifth with fifty points, five short of the last playoff spot, and had been unable to replace the Patrick brothers, Ott Heller and Alex Shibicky, who had retired together after the previous season.

The Rangers new season started under a heavy cloud when four members of the team defied a club policy instituted many years earlier by Lester Patrick. Most of the Rangers were Canadians, and preferred driving their cars to Montreal, and then south to Lake Placid each year for training camp. Patrick had made the trip from Montreal to Manhattan and knew that the highways through the Adirondacks were dangerous, especially for drivers on long trips. He decreed that the players would take the train to camp, sending their vehicles to New York by freight, and picking them up after camp when the team returned to the city.

In October 1948, team stars Buddy O'Connor and Edgar Laprade were among four players injured in a training camp car accident and, as a result, the team was shorthanded when the season started. While Boucher attempted to secure replacements, Lynn Patrick was promoted from New Haven to coach the team. He guided the Rangers into the playoffs ahead of the aging Canadiens and the Blueshirts played well, but lost the best-of-seven series, 4-2, to the powerful Red Wings. A year later, with goalie Chuck Rayner leading the way, the Rangers made it to the final – more precisely, to overtime of the seventh game of the final – before Detroit's Pete Babando broke their hearts.

March 23, 1952

Chicago's Bill Mosienko sets an NHL record for fastest three goals by one player: twenty-one seconds in a 7-6 win over the Rangers at New York.

Montreal Canadiens defeat Detroit 2-1 at the Forum, in the first hockey game televised on the CBC.

October 11, 1952

The many "looks"

of Gordie Howe,

whose pro hockey career

spanned five decades.

Mr. Hockey

9

The career was unique in professional sports, thirty-two years of big league combat, and to the end, a heavy-duty regular who warred in the trenches.

Many feel Gordie Howe was the greatest player in hockey history, in a battle with Bobby Orr and Wayne Gretzky for that honor, longevity and durability conferring upon him the Number One rating. A combination of skill and toughness, his elbows as famous as his feats with a hockey stick, Howe stands alone.

"A very few might be Howe's equal in skill and instinct for the game, some as tough, but no player – there's no one even close – was able to do as many things so well that long, and that makes him one of a kind," said King Clancy, who spent sixty-five years in and around pro hockey as an NHL player, referee and executive.

Incredibly, this career that spread over five decades almost didn't happen. On March 28, 1950, three days short of his twenty-second birthday, Howe was in pursuit of the puck with teammate Black Jack Stewart and Toronto's Teeder Kennedy, in the first game of the best-of-seven semi-final. Somehow Kennedy and Howe collided, with Stewart landing atop both, and Howe suffered a deep cut near his eye, a fractured nose and cheekbone, as well as a fractured skull.

An emergency ninety-minute operation relieved the pressure on his brain, and it was touch-and-go until he emerged from critical condition late the following day. The Wings went on to defeat Toronto and then New York in the final, and Howe's first appearance in front of the Olympia faithful was on crutches, when the Stanley Cup was presented to his teammates, on April 23.

Howe's longevity spanned generations of NHL play. He spent the first fifteen years of his career competing against, and chasing the exploits of another right winger, Maurice Richard. And, in the end, Howe's amazing achievements would be eclipsed by Wayne Gretzky, a player born five months after Richard retired in September, 1960.

In one thousand, seven hundred and sixty-seven NHL games, Howe turned in eight hundred and one goals and one thousand and forty-nine assists for a total of one thousand, eight hundred and fifty points, and added one hundred and sixty points in one hundred and fifty-seven playoff games. With his six seasons in the World Hockey Association factored in, his prodigious scoring record was one thousand, two hundred and seventy-five goals and two thousand, three hundred and fifty-eight points.

That astonishing record included twelve selections to the NHL's first All-Star team, and another nine to the second All-Star team at right wing,

six Art Ross trophies as the league scoring champion, and another half dozen Hart Trophy awards as the NHL's Most Valuable Player. In 1967, Howe received the Lester Patrick award, "for outstanding service to hockey in the United States."

A self-effacing man whose humor was primarily self-deprecating, on the ice Howe was a devastating physical force, using exceptional natural upper body strength to turn his elbows into pile drivers. A few opponents considered Howe to be a "dirty" player, which he denied.

"I very seldom started anything but if someone did dirt to me when it was unnecessary, I gave it back, or if a guy was picking on one of my smaller teammates, I straightened him out," Howe said. Number 9 rarely had to drop the gloves, and his one-punch knockout of Rangers policeman Lou Fontinato underscored that point for friend and foe alike.

Few played the game with the economy of Howe, who seldom wasted a stride.

"I guess I was good at figuring out where the puck was going to be and then taking the shortest route to get there," he said.

From Floral, Sask., Howe attended a New York Rangers training camp when he was fourteen and was sent home as too young. The Wings snapped him up a year later, the major sales point being a team jacket, and at seventeen Howe played a minor pro season before embarking on his extraordinary NHL career.

His wrists sore with arthritis, Howe retired from the Wings in 1971. But when sons Marty and Mark showed much skill with Toronto Marlboro juniors, Howe jumped at the chance to join them with the Houston Aeros of the WHA. The team won two championships in four years, and then the three Howes shifted to the Hartford Whalers of the WHA. Gordie played his last NHL season when the Whalers joined the NHL in 1979.

"The highlight of my hockey career?" Howe said. *"That's easy. Being able to play on the same team as my boys was an incredible experience."*

Gordie Howe Career Highlights

March 31, 1928

Gordie Howe is born in Floral, Saskatchewan.

November 1, 1945

Gordie Howe signs his first professional hockey contract, with the Omaha Knights of the United States Hockey League, at age seventeen.

October 16, 1946

Eighteen-year-old Gordie Howe scores his first NHL goal in his first game, as Detroit ties Toronto, 3-3. Howe wears uniform number 17 and also has two fights.

October 29, 1947

Gordie wears uniform number 9 for the first time in his NHL career during a 5-2 Red Wings win at Chicago.

November 3, 1948

Gordie Howe makes the first of his NHL record twenty-three All-Star appearances, helping the All-Stars to a 3-1 win over Stanley Cup champion Toronto Maple Leafs.

December 25, 1956

Gordie Howe scores his twelfth career hat trick and adds three assists, as the Red Wings beat the Rangers 8-1 at the Olympia. It would be the biggest single-game scoring output of Howe's twenty-six-year NHL career.

November 28, 1957

He picks up an assist during Detroit's 3-3 tie against Toronto to become the NHL's all-time assist leader, with the four hundred and ninth of his career breaking the previous record set by Montreal's Elmer Lach.

January 16, 1960

Gordie scores a goal and an assist in his eight hundred and eighty-eighth career game to become the NHL's all-time leading scorer, with nine hundred and forty-seven points; surpassing Montreal's Maurice Richard, as the Red Wings beat Chicago 3-1 in Detroit.

May 6, 1960

Gordie Howe is named winner of the Hart Memorial Trophy as the NHL's MVP for a record fifth time.

November 27, 1960

Gordie Howe becomes the first NHL player to score one thousand career points. The milestone comes in his nine hundred and thirty-eighth NHL game, a 2-0 win over Toronto.

November 26, 1961

He is the first player in NHL history to play in one thousand regular season games, in a 4-1 Red Wings loss at Chicago.

May 10, 1963

Gordie Howe is named winner of the Hart Memorial Trophy as the NHL's MVP, for the sixth time in twelve seasons.

November 10, 1963

He becomes the NHL's all-time leading goal scorer, moving past Maurice Richard with his five hundred and forty-fifth goal in Detroit's 3-0 win over Montreal.

April 5, 1964

Gordie Howe becomes the highest career point scorer in Stanley Cup playoff history when his goal (in a 3-2 loss at Chicago) gives him one hundred and twenty-seven career playoff points in one hundred and twenty-two games.

October 19, 1966

Mr. Hockey undertakes his twenty-first consecutive season in the NHL, breaking the previous record of twenty years he shared with Dit Clapper and Bill Gadsby. Howe picks up an assist in the game, a 6-2 loss at Boston.

December 4, 1968

Gordie Howe beats Pittsburgh's Les Binkley for his seven hundredth career NHL goal, in a 7-2 Red Wings win,

becoming the first NHL player to reach this plateau.

March 30, 1969

Gordie Howe becomes the third player in NHL history to score one hundred points in a season. His one hundredth point (a goal) comes in a 9-5 Red Wings loss to Chicago.

October 29, 1970

He is the first player in NHL history to record one thousand career assists, when he picks up two helpers (along with a goal) in a 5-3 Red Wings victory over Boston at the Olympia.

February 18, 1971

Gordie Howe scores his twentieth goal of the season in 5-3 win over the Minnesota North Stars, in Detroit. It is the twenty-second consecutive season Howe has reached the twenty-goal mark, an NHL record.

June 7, 1972

Gordie Howe is elected to the Hockey Hall of Fame. He would return seven years later to play again in the NHL.

June 5, 1973

The WHA Houston Aeros draft Gordie, Marty and Mark Howe.

December 7, 1977

New England's Gordie Howe scores his one thousandth professional goal (NHL and WHA inclusive) in a WHA game against Birmingham.

April 21, 1978

In a WHA game at Edmonton, Gordie Howe scores on his first shift, just minutes after finding out that he has become a grandfather! The arrival of Travis, the baby son of Mark and Ginger Howe, makes Gordie the first playing grandpa in pro hockey history.

October 13, 1979

Hartford's Gordie Howe scores his first NHL goal since 1971, number seven hundred and eighty-seven of his NHL career. It helps the Whalers to a 3-3 tie at Pittsburgh, the team's first-ever point in the NHL.

March 9, 1980

NHL history is made when Gordie skates on a line with sons Mark and Marty for a shift midway through a 1-1 tie in Boston.

April 6, 1980

Hartford's fifty-two-year-old Gordie Howe scores his eight hundred and first (and final) NHL goal, as the Whalers defeat the visiting Red Wings, 5-3.

April 11, 1980

Gordie Howe and Bobby Hull appear in their final NHL games, as the Hartford Whalers lose to Montreal in the playoffs. Yvon Lambert scores at 0:29 of overtime for the 4-3 Canadiens' win.

Four months later, Lynn Patrick was coaching in Boston, to everyone's surprise, including his. Unlike his father and brother, Lynn was ill-at-ease in New York and made his discomfort known to Frank Boucher during the 1949-50 season. He told Neil Colville, the former teammate who had replaced him as coach in New Haven, and assistant Phil Watson, that they should both apply for his position, because he wouldn't return "even if we win the Stanley Cup."

"The plain and simple truth was that I just didn't want to live in New York City any more. I had a happy marriage and three young children to think about, and I just didn't feel that New York was a good family environment. I wanted to get the kids into a different atmosphere with more space, more fresh air. It would have been tough to explain that sort of stuff to the New York writers, let alone Frank Boucher."

Having returned home to Victoria two years earlier, Lester Patrick was working with the minor league Cougars, and he travelled east seeking players that spring. He met Lynn in Montreal, where the Rangers were leading the Canadiens, 3-1, in their playoff. Lynn explained his distress in New York and volunteered to coach the Cougars the following season, an offer his father accepted after a long conversation. They agreed to keep the matter between themselves until after the playoffs.

Lynn coached the Rangers to the brink of a championship, with the New York home games being played in Toronto because of the circus in Madison Square Garden. At the end of the season, he announced his resignation and that he was returning to Vancouver Island to coach the minor league Cougars. Victoria hockey fans were happily anticipating the arrival of their new, highly regarded coach. Back east, the NHL was in shock: A member of the Patrick family, builders of the game, was leaving the Big Apple to return to a small, provincial backwater.

Lynn had moved his wife and children into the family home on Lyndon Avenue in Victoria, when Art Ross telephoned from Boston. Rumors had circulated for several months that the Boston job was open, but Lynn did not feel he was a contender.

December 27, 1952

Glenn Hall plays his first NHL game, a 2-2 Red Wings tie against Montreal. ▶

Jean Béliveau signs his first contract with the Montreal Canadiens, and is assigned uniform number 4, (after wearing numbers 17, 20 and 12) during previous tryouts with the Canadiens).

October 3, 1953

May 10, 1954

Detroit's Red Kelly is named the first
winner of the Norris Trophy (awarded
annually to the NHL's top defenseman).

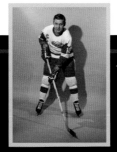

◄ Alex Delvecchio scores twice as the Red
Wings beat the Rocket-less Canadiens 3-1
in game seven, becoming the 1955 Stanley
Cup champions.

April 14, 1955

"*I wouldn't have taken the job with Lester if I really thought I was in line for the Boston job,*" he explained. "*Right up to the time Art called me, I had no desire to take another post in the east. After all, I'd left a pretty good one. But Art was persuasive, and he made me a great salary offer – twelve thousand dollars, which was big money then – and I accepted right there over the phone. Lester understood. I think he was expecting something like this to happen.*"

The narrative of this book, as represented by the Patrick family odyssey, rests on the fact that the members of this storied hockey dynasty either initiated, shared in or witnessed the great feats of the game throughout the century.

To Lynn's chagrin, one of those historical moments personally witnessed was what he later called "the most sensational goal in hockey history" and it came against his Bruins. It took place in the 1952 Boston-Montreal semi-final, and the artisan of this spectacular event was none other than Rocket Richard.

Chuck Rayner vs Detroit's "Terrible" Ted Lindsay

! LES CANADIENS SONT LÀ !

Ken Dryden (above)

and Henri Richard

in characteristic poses.

Les Canadiens sont là

Maurice Richard and Gordie Howe in action

The top franchise in pro hockey's first century is the Montreal Canadiens. Twenty-four Stanley Cup championship banners that bedecked the fabled Forum, and now the Molson Centre, bear eloquent witness to this fact.

At the half-century mark, the argument would have been a lively one, what with the Canadiens, Toronto, Detroit and Ottawa the prime candidates. The domination by the Habs in this second half of the century, especially in the first three decades (1950s, '60s, '70s) of that period, makes any such discussion moot.

Various accomplishments by the *bleu-blanc-rouge*, team and individual, include:

- The only team in professional hockey's top echelons to win a Cup in each decade it competed (1916, 1924, 1930, 1944, 1953, 1965, 1971, 1986, 1993)

- The only team to win five straight Cups (1956-60)

- The only team to win four straight Cups twice (1950s, 1976-79)

- The only team to win six Cups in a decade (twice, 1950s and 1970s)

- The only team with players to have won as many as eleven Cups (Henri Richard), ten Cups (Jean Béliveau, Yvan Cournoyer) or nine Cups (Claude Provost)

- The only team with goalies to have won as many as six Cups (Jacques Plante, Ken Dryden)

- The only goalie to win five straight Vézina trophies (Jacques Plante)

- The only team in the modern era to go through a regular season (seventy-plus games with fewer than ten losses (1976-7, 60 wins, 8 losses, 12 ties)

One enduring myth, promoted enthusiastically by the other five "original" franchises, is that Montreal always had the pick of the litter in Quebec, stocking its roster with superstar after homebrew superstar. Nothing could be further from the truth.

The original Canadiens of 1909-10, designed to represent Montreal's French community, were led by two francophones (a word unknown then) stars: Edouard Newsy Lalonde and Didier Pitre. Both were Ontario boys: Lalonde, a star lacrosse player from nearby Cornwall, and Pitre from halfway across the continent in Sault Ste Marie. When Howie Morenz (German-Canadian) ruled the roost in the 1920s and '30s, alongside line-mates Aurel Joliat and Billy Boucher, the trio also was born and bred in Ontario.

The Canadiens who won two Cups in the mid-1940s had Maurice Richard and Emile (Butch) Bouchard on the marquee, but only five players with French surnames wore the fabled CH, and several of their stars like Elmer Lach, Hector (Toe) Blake and Ken Reardon were non-Quebeckers.

The Habs swarm Glenn Hall's goal.

The real powerhouses began with the arrival of Frank Selke in 1946, and continued on through the stewardship of Sam Pollock, from 1964-78. In that period of time, the Habs won sixteen Stanley Cups.

The Flying Frenchmen truly took off in the 1950s with five consecutive Stanley Cup victories, and Canadiens wrote a new definition for hockey dynasties, a record that has been challenged, but never matched. In the late 1960s and early 1970s, a new generation of Flying Frenchmen brandished the torch, winning six Cups in nine years while holding off powerhouses like the Bruins and Hawks, but the best was yet to come.

The Canadiens scaled Himalayan heights in 1976 and '77. Having won the Stanley Cup in 1975-76, the team was given a simple task by coach Scotty Bowman – defend the championship at all costs.

The Canadiens swept aside all opposition, losing only eight of eighty regular-season games, and only one game at the Forum. The team also set a new NHL standard by winning sixty games. (Nineteen seasons later, Detroit Red Wings would win sixty-two games, but in a longer season and against much weaker opposition.)

Montreal scored three hundred and eighty-seven goals (4.83 goals per game) during the season, while allowing opponents only one hundred and seventy-one (2.14 goals against per game). They swept through the regular season with a 60-8-12 record, and lost only two of fourteen games in the playoffs to win their second consecutive Stanley Cup.

In three seasons between 1975 and 1978, the Canadiens would lose only twenty-nine of two hundred and forty games, a testament to the great balance, leadership and consistency that would also carry them to four consecutive post-season championships. No team has come remotely close to that record in the Modern Era, not the five straight Canadiens of the 1950s, nor the six-of-nine team of the late 1960s and early '70s, the four straight Islanders, or the five-of-seven Oilers.

And while a combination of rampant expansion and free agency has ended the era of NHL dynasties, the Canadiens still managed to finish out the century with Cup wins in 1986 and 1993 to keep their record going.

Two years, same result. Maurice Richard won the 1952 semi-final (above). A year later, Elmer Lach's overtime goal led to an ecstatic celebration and the Stanley Cup.

Maurice Richard had set the tone for the series in the first game when he scored a pair of goals en route to a 5-1 Montreal win. The Habs followed with a 4-0 whitewash in the second contest at the Forum, thanks to a hat trick by Boom Boom Geoffrion. Late in that contest, Montreal's all-purpose winger and checking center Ken Mosdell broke his leg and his absence was noted when the Bruins stormed back to even the series with 4-1 and 3-2 wins at the Garden. When Sugar Jim Henry stood the Habs on their ears in a 1-0 win at the Forum, the Bruins headed home with the series lead, and Lynn let loose with an unPatrick-like "the Habs are dead."

The boast appeared to be endorsed by his players, who took a 2-0 lead in the first period of game six in Boston, but the Canadiens tied the game. Paul Masnick kept Montreal alive with the winner in double overtime and the teams headed north for the deciding game.

Detroit Red Wings name Sid Abel as their new coach, replacing Jimmy Skinner. Abel goes on to coach the Red Wings for the next ten years.

Montreal's Dickie Moore sets an NHL record for most points in a season, scoring a goal and an assist for his ninety-sixth point of the year, in a 4-2 Canadiens win at New York. Moore breaks Gordie Howe's record of ninety-five points, set in 1952-53.

March 22, 1959

Another Montreal injury appeared to boost the Bruins. Early in the second period, Richard crashed into the Boston zone and circled defenseman Bill Quackenbush, only to be crushed on a vicious, but fair, bodycheck by Leo Labine. Obviously concussed, with a six-stitch gash on his forehead, Richard remained in the Forum clinic for most of the next two periods. Late in the game, Canadiens coach Toe Blake was surprised to see his superstar sitting on the bench.

"*Can you go in?*" Blake asked, ignoring teammates who were indicating in sign language that the Rocket was in mental orbit.

"*I can play,*" came the gruff reply, and Richard jumped over the boards on the next shift. Late in the game, the puck went deep into the Canadiens' zone and Butch Bouchard picked it up and nimbly fed it to Richard as Bruins' forecheckers closed in. Richard eluded two Boston players and another in the neutral zone, and had the No. 9 locomotive at full steam when he came up against Quackenbush a second time. Richard edged by the tall defender and avoided a backchecking Milt Schmidt, hooking the puck past Henry and into the net for the winning score. Billy Reay's insurance goal was an afterthought.

Lynn Patrick added: "*A truck wouldn't have stopped Richard on that play.*"

Lynn would remain with the Bruins for the next fifteen years. He and Art Ross got along well, unlike the latter's relationship two decades earlier with Frank Patrick. When Ross retired in 1955, Lynn Patrick became general manager, in charge of Boston's hockey operations.

Craig Patrick of the Jr. Canadiens shares a moment with his father Lynn.

April 14, 1960

Jean Béliveau scores twice as the Canadiens become the first team to win five consecutive Stanley Cups, with a 4-0 win over Toronto. Montreal wins the Cup in eight straight games.

Hull and Mahovlich

Bobby Hull and Frank Mahovlich both entered the NHL in the 1957-58 season, quickly climbed to the front ranks and dominated the left wing position for the next fifteen seasons. The flamboyant,

Frank Mahovlich

gregarious, and blond Hull, nicknamed The Golden Jet, vied for attention with the introverted, dark-haired Mahovlich, called The Big M.

With his golden hair, rippling muscles and overpowering slap shot, Hull was a crowd favorite from the day he joined the Chicago Blackhawks, the key man in the revitalization of a sad-sack franchise. The sight of Hull with the puck breaking down the wing to unload a slapper on a quivering netminder was a highlight of the game in the 1960s. He was renowned as a player who never refused a request for an autograph and, for a six-team regional league that was striving for national attention, he was the star who earned heavy media exposure and set down much groundwork for the NHL's expansion.

Hull's fifty goals in the 1961-62 season tied Rocket Richard's record, which Hull then broke with fifty-four in 1965-66. But despite Hull's presence, a 1961 Stanley Cup victory was the lone one for a talented Hawks team.

Hull frequently had battles with the team's ownership and management over what he considered was a small salary for the feats he had accomplished, notably an always-packed Chicago Stadium. He was locked in a major struggle over a new contract in 1972 when the rival World Hockey Association came calling. Hull's signing of a ten-year, two million, seven hundred thousand-dollar contract with the Winnipeg Jets, plus a one-million-dollar signing bonus shared by the WHA teams, gave the new league the credibility it needed to get started.

Mahovlich was a tall, elegant player whose smooth style allowed him to make the game look easy. That earned him derision from the Toronto fans who never felt he delivered on his true potential, even though he played a large role in the four Stanley Cup titles won by the Leafs in the 1960s.

The Big M was a sensitive sort and once was forced to the sidelines by psychological problems arising from his strained relationship with Leafs boss Punch Imlach.

Mahovlich was traded to Detroit in 1968, where he excelled on a line with Gordie Howe and Alex Delvecchio. Dealt to the Montreal Canadiens in 1971, the Big M played perhaps the finest all-round hockey of his career and immediately contributed to Cup victories in 1971 and 1973. After three years with the Canadiens, where he played alongside his younger brother Peter, he saw the youth movement coming at the Forum and returned to Toronto and the Toros, finishing his career in the WHA.

Bobby Hull and Frank Mahovlich have been retired more than two decades, and still the debate rages over which of the two was the game's best-ever left wing. It will go on well into the new millennium.

Bobby Hull celebrates his 28th birthday.

Muzz Patrick (left) and his Tacoma Rockets

After retiring as a player, the happy-go-lucky Muzz Patrick also plunged into minor league coaching, heading to the family's old western haunting ground to hone his skills. He began in the American Association with St. Paul, and moved to Tacoma of the Pacific Coast League in 1950, and then on to Seattle. In 1954, John Kilpatrick threw out an SOS and Muzz answered the call, becoming the third Patrick to coach the Blueshirts. What helped was that Muzz's Seattle team was returning from a disastrous road trip to Saskatoon and other cold spots in the PCL when the phone rang.

Muzz felt uncomfortable as the second Patrick to replace Frank Boucher behind the New York bench, the same Frank Boucher who had replaced his father, Lester, as Rangers coach.

The Big M forces Gump Worsley to extend himself, to no avail.

(top) **Frank Selke and Jean Béliveau**

take turns signing on the dotted line,

while Dick Irvin looks on.

(below) **Sam Pollock, flanked by**

David Molson and Jean Béliveau.

"Although he didn't seem too upset about it, I felt badly replacing Frank as coach, even though it was just an interim situation and he was, of course, still the general manager," Muzz said. "With me being a Patrick, the move may have looked like the thin edge of the wedge." That's exactly what it was, and at the end of that season Frank Boucher was fired after almost three decades in the organization as a player, coach and manager, and Muzz took over.

Brothers Lester and Frank had faced each other in the mid-1930s from behind the benches of the Rangers and Bruins, now Lynn and Muzz Patrick were in the same position, twenty years later. Unfortunately, the brothers fought it out in the league's basement while Montreal, Toronto and Detroit exchanged the keys to the NHL penthouse.

Lester Patrick and Art Ross had built strong franchises in the 1930s and 1940s that began to lose ground in the 1950s. Montreal, especially, benefitted from three decades of sound, visionary management from Frank Selke (1947-64) and Sam Pollock (1964-78), while Conn Smythe in Toronto and Jack Adams in Detroit built strong, renewable organizations that were passed along to such strong coach/managers as George (Punch) Imlach and Sid Abel.

> [*Montreal, especially,*
> *benefitted from three decades*
> *of sound, visionary management*
> *from Frank Selke and Sam Pollock*]

April 26, 1962

Jack Adams announces his retirement from hockey, after serving thirty-five years as the Detroit Red Wings' general manager. Coach Sid Abel is given the double title of GM and coach.

Jean Béliveau is named Captain of the Montreal Canadiens, succeeding Doug Harvey, who had been traded to the New York Rangers.

October 11, 1961

ALL-STAR TEAMS

1951

1ˢᵗ TEAM ★ ★ ★ ★ ★ ★ ★ ★ ★ ★ ★ ★ ★ ★ ★ ★

Coach   *Hector (Toe) Blake*
Executive   *Frank Selke*

Doug Harvey
Defense

Bobby Orr
Defense

Terry Sawchuk
Goalie

Gordie Howe
Right Wing

Jean Béliveau
Center

Bobby Hull
Left Wing

1975

ALL-STAR TEAMS

★ ★ ★ ★ ★ ★ ★ ★ ★ ★ ★ ★ ★ ★ ★ ★ ★ **2ᴺᴰ TEAM**

Coach   **George (Punch) Imlach**
Executive **Sam Pollock**

Frank Mahovlich
Left Wing

Pierre Pilote
Defense

Bernard Geoffrion
Right Wing

Jacques Plante
Goalie

Phil Esposito
Center

Tim Horton
Defense

A Real Major League

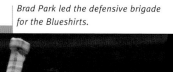

Brad Park led the defensive brigade for the Blueshirts.

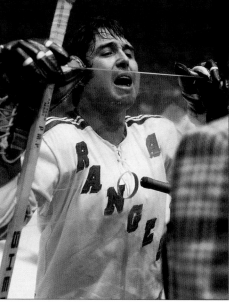

Gump Worsley defending against Bobby Hull.

Lynn Patrick's Boston Bruins were in three Stanley Cup finals in the 1950s, losing to the Canadiens each time, and that would be it for a decade.

It was even worse for Muzz Patrick's Rangers. The team missed the post-season tournament between 1950-51 and 1954-55, lost to Montreal in the 1955-56 and 1956-57 playoffs, and to Boston in 1957-58, before missing the playoffs in seven of the next eight years.

By 1990s standards, those teams were powerhouses: New York had Andy Bathgate, Bill Gadsby, Dean Prentice, Earl Ingarfield, Lou Fontinato, Gump Worsley, Red Sullivan, Larry Cahan, Harry Howell, Jack Evans, Andy Hebenton, and Camille Henry, with Jean Ratelle, Rod Gilbert, Vic Hadfield and Brad Park en route in the 1960s.

Boston's line-up included Fern Flaman, Fleming Mackell, Leo Boivin, the Uke Line of Bronco Horvath, John Bucyk and Vic Stasiuk, as well as Doug Mohns, Leo Labine, Jerry Toppazzini, and Don McKenney.

April 18, 1963

Toronto's Dave Keon sets a playoff record for most shorthanded goals in one game – he scores twice during a 3-1 win over Detroit in game five of the final. The victory gives the Maple Leafs the 1963 Stanley Cup Championship.

Punch Imlach's Retirement Home

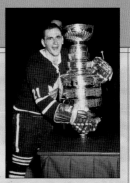

The great comedian, the late Johnny Wayne, said it best about the Toronto Maple Leafs team that won the Stanley Cup in 1967.

"It won't be knee operations that chop down this team," Wayne said. *"It will be prostate surgery."*

The Centenary Leafs were the oldest team in NHL history to win the Cup in one of the biggest upsets in playoff history, expanding to four the number of crowns the team won in the decade. Ten of the nineteen men on the playoff roster were over thirty-five years of age, led by the amazing geriatric goalies, Johnny Bower, forty-three, and Terry Sawchuk, thirty-eight.

These Leafs had several survivors from the teams that had won three straight in 1962-64, notably Frank Mahovlich, Dave Keon, Bob Pulford, Tim Horton, Allan Stanley, George Armstrong and Red Kelly.

What is significant is that this Golden Age movement was all part of George (Punch) Imlach's plan. When the new general manager and coach took control of the Leafs in 1958, the club had a strong core of players from its junior development teams, Marlboros and St. Michael's Majors which included players like Mahovlich, Dick Duff, Billy Harris, Ron Ellis and Pulford, with Keon on the way. All of this young talent needed on-ice direction, and Imlach set about acquiring it.

Imlach was a master at the low-cost acquisition of veterans with much left to contribute. Goalie Bower, for instance, was thirty-three when he was pried out of the minors to be the Leafs

mainstay, and successful veterans like Kelly and Stanley were important cogs in all four Leafs wins. Other old-timers such as Bert Olmstead, Andy Bathgate, Don McKenney, Marcel Pronovost, Pierre Pilote and Ed Litzenberger made briefer, but just as important, contributions after being acquired by Imlach.

Bobby Baun enjoyed the 1967 Stanley Cup.

"Punch built teams with a good combination of young legs and old heads," said Armstrong, the Leafs captain and leader in their last period of success. *"A big part of our success was having veterans to use in important situations, and their example of what it took to win rubbed off on the young guys."*

Imlach's bridal philosophy of "something old, something new, something borrowed, something blue" carried the Leafs to a five-game victory over defending champion Chicago in the 1962 Cup final, and then to six and seven-game wins over Detroit in 1963 and '64. The 1964 victory was the stuff of legend, with Bobby Baun pulling Toronto even in the series with an overtime goal in game six, while playing on a broken ankle, and the Leafs returning home to close out the set 4-0 in game seven.

The Centennial Year victory over Montreal was a case of two goalies who refused to lose. Bower and Sawchuk were magnificent in the series, won in six by Toronto in what turned out to be Imlach's last hurrah.

Punch Imlach delivered results.

David Keon played at both ends of the ice.

January 18, 1964

Detroit's Terry Sawchuk leads the Red Wings to a 2-0 win over Montreal, to become the NHL's all-time shutout leader, with ninety-five. George Hainsworth had retired with ninety-four.

Chicago's Pierre Pilote picks up two assists to give him fifty-eight points for the year, an NHL record for points by a defenseman, in a 3-2 loss at Montreal. Pilote broke the twenty-one-year-old record of fifty-seven points set by Babe Pratt.

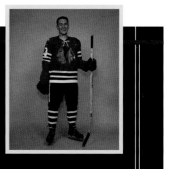

March 20, 1965

But they trailed the juggernauts in Montreal, Toronto and Detroit. The Canadiens had, by far, the most bountiful player harvest each year and the 1948-55 period saw the arrival of Doug Harvey, Tom Johnson, Dollard St. Laurent and Jean-Guy Talbot on defense, Jacques Plante in goal, Bernard Geoffrion, Dickie Moore, Jean Béliveau, Floyd Curry, Ken Mosdell, Henri Richard, Don Marshall and Bert Olmstead up front.

They joined a team that already featured the incomparable Rocket Richard, captain Butch Bouchard and veterans like Billy Reay and Bud MacPherson. In the wings were Claude Provost, André Pronovost, Phil Goyette, Charlie Hodge, Bobby Rousseau, Claude Larose, Bill Hicke, Yvan Cournoyer, Terry Harper, Jacques Laperrière, Ted Harris and Jacques Lemaire.

Montreal's Jean Béliveau

(opposite and below right)

was an offensive threat

game-in, game-out, alongside

such gifted teammates

as the Roadrunner, Yvan Cournoyer.

JEAN BÉLIVEAU

Four on four

WHEN DID YOU FIRST MEET BOBBY ORR?

At a hockey banquet in Oshawa in the spring of 1964. Jojo Graboski, who was a legend in Quebec senior hockey because of his incredible skating prowess and who played with the Quebec Aces before my time, introduced me to a 16-year-old Bobby Orr that night.

WHEN DID YOU FIRST SEE HIM PLAY HOCKEY?

I had seen a few newsreels on the sports news, but I didn't see him play until his first season, in 1966.

WHAT WAS YOUR IMPRESSION OF HIM?

He was only 18 years old, but I can honestly say that I have never seen a player of that age with his maturity and hockey sense. He scored his first-ever National Hockey League goal against us, in our first game against him, and his second in the league.

WAS HE THE DOMINATING PLAYER WHO HAS BEEN ELEVATED TO HEROIC STATUS BY FOLKLORE?

Like any player, Bobby had his ups and downs. He was the finest player of his era, but he would suffer mistakes and bad games for the simple reason that the people he made his mistakes against were the best, and were capable of capitalizing quickly. All he did was prove he was human.

HE WAS HUMAN, FOR SURE, BUT HAS THE MYTH OUTGROWN THE MAN?

Not at all. In his early days, too many opponents both on the ice and in the stands were looking for feet of clay. He took too many chances, they said. He got caught up ice. He was weak inside his own zone. Everyone was a critic.

SO THE HYPE BEGAN BEFORE HE JOINED THE LEAGUE?

Watching him play, and playing against him, I knew right away that he was something special. Also, having experienced the same big build-up, big-criticism roller coaster in my early years in the league, I knew what he was going through and I sympathized.

WHAT IS YOUR DESCRIPTION OF BOBBY ORR'S IMPACT, IN A NUTSHELL?

It was anything but hype. Simply put, he had the greatest impact of any player to come along in my lifetime. He earned his place in hockey by single-handedly changing the game from the style played in my day to the one played today.

HOW DID BOBBY ORR CHANGE HOCKEY?

He redefined the defenseman's role, bringing him into a new, more aggressive offensive strategy, and opening the door for all-out attacks off quick transitions. His rushing exploits made it difficult, if not impossible for defensive teams to zero in on Boston forwards. Bobby could race ahead of the play, immediately putting pressure on our defensemen while catching forwards off guard.

Or he could come from behind a screen of teammates, cut left or right at speed, thereby drawing two or three defenders to him, before laying off a pass to someone in the clear. Although some of the earliest defenders had rushed the puck in the days of seven-man hockey (with the rover), this was an innovation.

WHAT WAS HIS GREATEST WEAPON?

It is probably a tie between his ice vision and hockey sense, and his skating ability. Bobby was very rare in that he was a strong, two-legged skater; he could cut to the left or right at speed with equal effect. Most skaters, even today, favor one side or the other. That a defenseman could do this, especially against other, slower-footed defenders, was a very special talent.

WAS HIS "GAME" THAT RADICALLY DIFFERENT?

Prior to his arrival in the league, defensemen rarely jumped up into the play. They were supposed to "head-man" the puck (throw it up quickly to the point forward, or he who was furthest ahead on the attack) and then follow the play up ice.

HOW ELSE DID THIS CHANGE THINGS?

It changed the make-up of the prototypical defender. Before Orr, defensemen were generally big, blocky guys – heavy hitters who tended to move slowly and awkwardly. If a defenseman was a slow or lumbering skater, he would rarely be able to jump up into the offensive flow. He'd be constantly backing up or standing still because he was unable to come up to and challenge an attacking forward. Slow skaters are always at a disadvantage, no matter what their position.

If you slow down at the opponent's blue line, your pass, your shot and your move will all be slow. But, if you're skating like Orr did, all your moves are running at the same speed – carrying the puck, stickhandling and releasing the shot. Thus Orr dictated the pace not only of a given game, but all future games, by cranking up the speed limits to previously unknown levels.

SO TEAMS WENT LOOKING FOR GOOD OFFENSIVE DEFENSEMEN?

They went looking for good offensive and defensive defensemen. The mobile defenseman not only helped your attack, he had the speed to counter the attack of the other team's mobile defenseman. Needless to say, he could handle the fast-skating forwards, too.

BUT HE WAS JUST ONE PLAYER; ISN'T THIS A BIT DRAMATIC?

One player, the right player, can literally change the allure and tempo of a game, as Bobby Orr did most every night. Orr presented problems the opposing team never had to face before. For example, when the puck was in your end, the wingers would go directly to the point. With Orr on the ice, wingers would have to be in motion sooner. This disrupted team strategy and brought pressure on teams that the fans could not appreciate at first. When the Bruins faced off in our zone, it did not matter who they had up

front – Esposito, Hodge, Cashman, Bucyk or McKenzie. How we lined up was dictated by one factor, the position of Bobby Orr. When the puck was dropped, everyone's attention was divided, with nervous glances in Orr's direction predominating.

WERE THERE OTHER ADJUSTMENTS TO ORR?

Of course. The man-to-man, lane game would change with the speedy defense-man able to come from the back, or attack at any time, thus creating out-numbered situations. He had the ability to move the game laterally from boards to boards, Also as important, powerplay and penalty-killing strategies would change when he was on the ice in a defensive or offensive role.

WHAT IS HIS LEGACY?

Serge Savard, Guy Lapointe and Brad Park in his "graduating class" all tried to pick up things from his game and incorporate them into theirs. After that, you might call his legacy Chris Chelios, Paul Coffey, Brian Leetch, Phil Housley, Denis Potvin, Larry Robinson, Ray Bourque, Doug Wilson and Borje Salming... all mobile defensemen who were the linchpins of their teams' offenses and defenses. The defenseman, as team quarterback, was Bobby's creation.

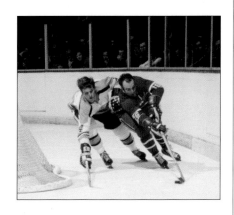

*Ted Lindsay
and his father Bert, (left)*

There also were two significant editions of the Toronto Maple Leafs. The first was Conn Smythe's post-war blue-and-white, with such stalwarts as Syl Apps, Teeder Kennedy, Gus Mortson, Jim Thomson, Vic Lynn, Bill Barilko, Howie Meeker, Wild Bill Ezinicki, Harry Watson, the Metz brothers, Sid Smith, Tod Sloan, Cal Gardner and Max Bentley. It was the first NHL team to win three Stanley Cups in a row (1947-49) and five in seven years if one includes 1945 and 1951.

The second edition emerged after a Toronto dry spell in the early 1950s. Punch Imlach took over the team in 1958, and took the trade route to acquire a veteran roster that won four Stanley Cups

Terry Sawchuk

in six years (1962-64 and 1967). That team included a defensive corps of goalies Johnny Bower and (later) Terry Sawchuk, blue-liners Carl Brewer, Allan Stanley, Tim Horton, Kent Douglas, Bob Baun, Larry Hillman, Al Arbour and a primarily homegrown front line of Bob Pulford, Frank Mahovlich, Dave Keon, George (Chief) Armstrong, Dick Duff, Billy Harris, Jim Pappin, Ron Ellis, Bob Nevin and Ron Stewart. Imlach was a master of the timely transaction, adding veteran performers as circumstances warranted to fill a position on a forward line or defense.

Alex Delvecchio

Detroit had Sawchuk or Glenn Hall in goal, Bob Goldham, Black Jack Stewart, Marcel Pronovost and Red Kelly on defense, and Ted Lindsay, Gordie Howe, Sid Abel, Alex Delvecchio, Norm Ullman, John and Larry Wilson, Earl Reibel, Marty Pavelich, Tony Leswick and Glen Skov up front.

And, after years in the wilderness, Chicago Blackhawks were being rejuvenated by an airlift from their junior team in St. Catharines. Future stars who would restore respectability to the Windy City included Bobby and Dennis Hull, Pierre Pilote, Stan Mikita, Chico Maki, Ken Hodge, Phil Esposito, Kenny Wharram, and Elmer (Moose) Vasko.

It was a six-team National Hockey League in all of its glory, with rabid hockey fans in each city ferociously proud of their team and familiar with all of the players on the five other clubs.

Stan Mikita

The 1961 Cup champion Blackhawks

Although the Rangers and Bruins were competitive, they somehow could not escape the league's nether regions in that era. Still, the Patricks went after each other tooth-and-nail throughout that period.

Famous referee and raconteur Red Storey remembers a European exhibition tour by the Bruins and Rangers after the 1959 season. The five-week, twenty-three game tour had moments of entertaining hockey, and other moments, too. As Red recounts: "*One night in Geneva, the teams were playing a beautiful game, great skating and passing and stickhandling, and the fans weren't making any noise at all. The Patricks came into the officials' room after the second period, and Muzz asked: 'What's wrong? This is the best game we've had over here and they're sitting on their hands.' I told him that all I knew is that it was a helluva hockey game.*

"*Then Lynn said: 'I think I know what's wrong. They've read all the time about how violent the NHL is and they're not interested in seeing nice hockey. They want to see a little rough stuff. I'm going back to my room and I'm going to tell my team to belt every Rangers' sweater they see.' Muzz said: 'Oh yeah? Well, I'm going back to my room and tell them to kick the crap out of every Bruin they see!' They were really getting mad at each other and as they were leaving the room, I stopped them. 'Hold it just a minute. Are you going to tell them that I know this?'*

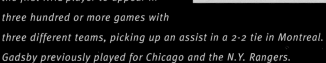

February 5, 1966

Detroit's Bill Gadsby (4) becomes ▶ the first NHL player to appear in three hundred or more games with three different teams, picking up an assist in a 2-2 tie in Montreal. Gadsby previously played for Chicago and the N.Y. Rangers.

Scotty Bowman is named head coach of the St. Louis Blues, replacing Lynn Patrick, who resigns to concentrate on his duties as general manager. It is Bowman's first head coaching job in the NHL.

November 20, 1967

Muzz Patrick moved behind

the Rangers bench

for a season-and-a half in 1954,

and then moved upstairs

to the general manager's job.

Puckstoppers Extraordinaire

Glenn Hall's five hundredth straight game is feted.

Terry Sawchuk, Glenn Hall and Jacques Plante were men of very different personalities and goalies with disparate styles. In fact, the only thing they had in common was that they stopped the puck better for longer than any others at their position.

They entered the NHL at the start of the 1950s and endured at perhaps the most demanding job, both physically and mentally, in sport until the early 1970s. The style employed by goalies now is based on an amalgam of the approaches used by Plante, Sawchuk and Hall.

Hall pioneered the "butterfly" style of the 1990s used by top goalies such as Patrick Roy. He dug the toes of his skates into the ice and bent his knees, his pads covering as much of the net's low portion as possible.

"I didn't have strong arms so I had trouble keeping my stick down on the ice," Hall said. *"To compensate, I used my pads to cover the bottom of the net."*

Jacques Plante, masked man.

Sick to his stomach before every game and often between periods, Hall established a record that never will be broken when he played in five hundred and two consecutive games with Detroit and Chicago. He revived his career with the expansion St. Louis Blues, was play-off MVP in 1968, and shared the 1968-69 Vézina Trophy with teammate Plante.

A sullen, often surly man who had a long list of injuries, espe-

cially to his back and arms, Sawchuk was the definitive reflex goalie, reacting after the shooter had made his move. He was also known for his uncommon, radar-like ability to focus on the puck carrier and move with him in his crease, "squaring off" as it is known. In his career, mostly with Detroit, Boston and Toronto he had a record one hundred and three shutouts. At thirty-eight, he shared the net with Johnny Bower, forty-three, when the Toronto Maple Leafs won the Stanley Cup in 1967.

Plante was the great "angles" player among goalies, reducing the net available for shooters by his positioning and then using cat-like quickness to nullify any mistakes.

"The saves I liked best were the ones where I never touched the puck," Plante said. *"When I played the angle correctly, if the shooter missed me with the puck, it missed the net."*

A loner with a large palette of idiosyncrasies, Plante was the major innovator in how goalies played. He was the first goalie to leave the crease to handle loose pucks, especially blocking shoot-ins along the boards and leaving the puck for his defensemen, and the first to wear a face mask on a regular basis after he was cut badly in the face by a shot in New York in 1959.

In the eighteen seasons when all three manned the goals for various teams in the NHL, they earned thirteen first, and twelve second All-Star team nominations. While Sawchuk and Plante have passed away, Hall still sees duty as a goalie consultant in the National Hockey League.

Terry Sawchuk and Johnny Bower share the Vézina Trophy.

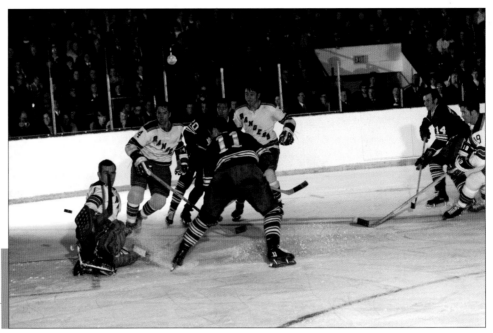

Arnie Brown (4), Brad Park (2) and Jean Ratelle (19) move in to help goalie Ed Giacomin against the Leafs.

"They said no; I was on my own. As soon as we got back to the ice, I called over the captains, Red Sullivan of the Rangers and Fernie Flaman of the Bruins, and told them: 'Look, I know the rules. I know your instructions. I just want you to take a good look at me and George and Bill (linesmen George Hayes and Bill Morrison). These are white-and-black sweaters. Don't hit them. Apart from that, you're on your own for the third period.'

"They ran from here to Regina to hit each other. George and Bill and I just stood around and marvelled at it. All we did was stay out of the road. We could have called some boarding and some hooking, but mostly they were just great body-checks. At one point, there were only five guys standing up on the ice, the two goalies and the three of us. The game finished and, amazingly, nobody died and we didn't have to call an ambulance. The crowd gave them a ten-minute standing ovation, and some fans said it was the best show they'd ever seen in that building. That was what Lynn and Muzz wanted, so we let them play that way the rest of the tour."

January 15, 1968

Minnesota's Bill Masterton dies two days after suffering a head injury in a game against Oakland. It is the first death as a result of a game injury in the history of the National Hockey League.

The Philadelphia Spectrum's roof blows off, forcing the expansion Flyers to play their final month of the season on the road, with their home games moved to Quebec City.

March 1, 1968

The NHL Doubles Up; the Expansion of 1967

When the Brooklyn Americans folded in 1942, the NHL became a six-team league and stayed that way for twenty-five years. Teams in Toronto, Montreal, Boston, Detroit, New York and Chicago filled more than ninety per cent of their available seats into the 1960s. Even such long-term weak teams as the Blackhawks, Rangers and Bruins did not lose money, which fostered no inclination for change among the owners.

The growth of television revenues available to the other major pro team sports provided the motivation for the NHL to enlarge its population. A six-team league primarily restricted to the northeast portion of the continent garnered little attention in the national media. To attract TV money, the NHL needed to be in more markets and spread across the continent.

Rumors of rival leagues being formed, notably talk in the mid-1960s of a major league on the West Coast, helped focus the NHL governors.

Applications for expansion franchises at two million dollars each were invited and, in 1965, the NHL approved six new teams, Los Angeles, Oakland, Minnesota, Pittsburgh, Philadelphia and St. Louis, to begin play in the 1967-68 season. Buffalo, Vancouver, Cleveland and Baltimore were turned down in the original expansion.

The teams were stocked in an expansion draft and, with established clubs protecting twelve players, few front-line players were available. But the top five clubs in the new division finished in a space of six points, and the expansion teams had a highly respectable 40-86-18 won-lost-tied mark against the six established teams.

Montreal's Sam Pollock presided over the NHL's Expansion Committee and suggested that to help speed along the process of parity, the new teams should not be allowed to trade their top choices from the amateur entry draft, for a period of five years or so. They refused,

The Rangers line up

against the Expansion Seals

*Bill Jennings, Bruce Norris
and NHL President Clarence Campbell,
oversee the latest league realignment.*

saying the Old Guard had no control over their businesses, and then paid for it dearly. Trading many of the Canadiens' excess bodies to stockpile draft choices, Pollock made some of the new teams respectable right away, but guaranteed that the Canadiens would always be drafting some of the best new talent that came along, Guy Lafleur included.

The St. Louis Blues, with a roster of NHL veterans, had early success, winning the new division playoffs in the first three seasons before losing the Stanley Cup final to the Canadiens, twice, and Boston. Philadelphia would be the first of the Class of '67 to win the Stanley Cup, in 1974 and again in 1975.

Expansion continued with the addition of Buffalo and Vancouver in 1970, New York Islanders and Atlanta Flames in 1972, Washington Capitals and Kansas City Scouts (later Colorado Rockies, then New Jersey) in 1974. By the 1976 season, ten years after the major expansion, the league had tripled to eighteen from six teams.

Lynn Patrick and Sid Salomon III celebrate their new team.

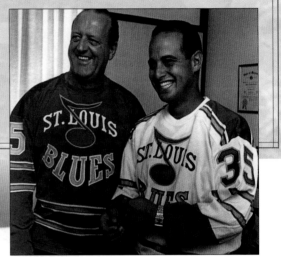

NATIONAL HOCKE
DIVISION REALIGNMEN
DIVISION III
CHICAGO
KANSAS CITY
MINNESOTA
ST. LOUIS
VANCOUVER

DIVIS
BOST
BUFF
CALIF
TORO
1970

April 6, 1968

L.A. Kings become the first club in NHL history to win its first two playoff games, when they beat Minnesota 2-0 in game two of the Stanley Cup quarter-finals.

Boston's Phil Esposito scores twice to become the first player in NHL history to score one hundred points in a season. His two goals come in a 4-0 win over Pittsburgh.

March 2, 1969

J.C. Tremblay (bottom right), Yvan Cournoyer and Jean Béliveau (4) harass the Toronto net.

Red Kelly

The Muzz Patrick stewardship of the Rangers ended in the 1960s, as much for a trade he wanted to make but couldn't, as for a trade that he did make that infuriated the Madison Square Garden faithful, although it worked out to New York's advantage in the long term. In 1960, after a feud with All-Star defenseman Red Kelly over reports that he had made his star play with a broken ankle the previous year, general manager Jack Adams of the Red Wings was determined to trade the recalcitrant player. A veteran of Frank Patrick's Vancouver Millionaires, Adams was fond of telling reporters that his stint in the British Columbia metropolis was the best possible school of hockey management that anyone could attend.

Adams and Frank were close friends, and once traded NHL stars in seconds. Both men were at the Forum to take in the Maroons-Leafs Stanley Cup final in 1935, when Patrick turned to Adams: "*If I had Cooney Weiland,*" he said of Detroit's shifty center, "*my club would be here.*"

Adams retorted: "*And if I had Marty Barry,*" he said of Boston's smooth big pivot, "*we'd win the Cup.*" They looked at each other, laughed, and shook hands on the deal. Both players were stars with their new teams.

When Adams sought to move Kelly, he looked toward a Patrick, in this case Frank's nephew. They quickly agreed on Kelly and winger Billy McNeill for veteran defenseman Bill Gadsby and winger Eddie Shack. Kelly refused to report, however, threatening retirement, and even league president Clarence Campbell couldn't convince him.

June 11, 1969

In the annual NHL summer draft, the Chicago Blackhawks claim rookie goalie Tony Esposito from the Montreal Canadiens, for twenty-five thousand dollars.

Eventually, Kelly went to Toronto for journeyman Marc Rheaume, who would play forty-seven games with the Red Wings. Red Kelly was converted to center and played eight seasons with Toronto, a major contributor to four Stanley Cups for the Leafs.

May 22, 1970

The Buffalo Sabres and Vancouver Canucks are officially granted NHL franchises, for expansion fees of six million dollars each.

Gil Perreault scores his thirty-fifth goal of the season to set a new NHL record for rookies, as the Sabres win 5-3 over the Blues. Oakland's Norm Ferguson, Minnesota's Danny Grant and Maroon's Nels Stewart shared the previous record.

March 18, 1971

Muzz also made a trade that helped Toronto. On February 22, 1964, he moved popular team leader and star Andy Bathgate to Toronto along with Don McKenney, for five players, including Dick Duff, Bob Nevin, Arnie Brown, Bill Collins and the rights to junior defensemen Rod Seiling. All of the players Muzz received would help the Blueshirts for a long time, or bring even more talent to Madison Square Garden, but Bathgate and McKenney ensured a Cup for the Leafs that spring, and "trade the manager" signs abounded on Broadway.

The final straw came at the end of the season when goalie Jacques Plante, acquired from the Canadiens a year earlier, went public with criticism of Rangers management, and Muzz confronted him publicly in a shouting match after a press conference. Team president Bill Jennings witnessed the outburst and several weeks later, Muzz was moved upstairs to a Garden's vice-presidency, and Emile Francis replaced him as GM, holding the job for eleven years.

Bobby Orr,
Oshawa Generals

In 1960, Lynn Patrick made his greatest contribution to the Bruins, although he would be gone by the time the benefits accrued. Patrick and Wren Blair attended the Ontario Minor Hockey Association bantam provincials that spring. Blair was the coach and GM of the Kingston Frontenacs of the Eastern Canada Professional League and was scouting two local defensemen. Within ten minutes of play starting, neither Patrick nor Blair could have told you the names of those two players because they were mesmerized by a tiny defenseman who played for Parry Sound. Still of peewee age, Robert Gordon Orr had been moved up a competitive category because he had made a shambles of his own age group and here he was, in the provincial playdowns, playing keepaway with the puck. The Boston executive machine went into high gear and within two years, Orr was part of the Bruins organization. For the first time in years, the team could see the light at the end of the tunnel.

*Muzz was moved upstairs
to a Garden's vice-presidency,
and Emile Francis replaced him as GM*

The Eagle Lands on the NHLPA

An attempt to form a National Hockey League players' union or association in the late 1950s, led by Ted Lindsay of the Detroit Red Wings, was snuffed out mercilessly by the NHL owners. To make sure that the message got across, most of the organizers (Lindsay, Jimmy Thomson and Tod Sloan of Toronto) were traded to the NHL's version of purgatory at the time, the Chicago Blackhawks.

Ten years later, led by young Toronto attorney Alan Eagleson, the players tried again, and this time they were successful in achieving league acceptance of their association.

Eagleson first appeared on the NHL scene as a friend and adviser to Bob Pulford and several other Leaf players. He was hired by the family of young defenseman Bobby Orr to represent the brilliant young player in 1966 contract negotiations with the Boston Bruins, obtaining a record contract for his client. That same year, Eagleson was instrumental in settling a strike by players against Eddie Shore, tyrannical owner of the American Hockey League's Springfield Indians.

Bruins goalie Ed Johnston and Orr asked Eagleson to meet with the team's players to discuss forming a players' association. Eagleson and Orr met with all of the players in the league, team-by-team, and within a few months, the majority of NHL players had signified their support.

Pulford was the first president of the NHL Players' Association and at the league's annual meeting in 1967, the governors refused to allow Eagleson to address them, but heard the Leaf veteran. Realizing that the vast majority of players backed the idea, the team owners readily agreed to negotiate with the association and Eagleson.

The association soon had the NHL minimum salary increased to ten thousand dollars from seven thousand, five hundred dollars per season, with improvements in the medical plan and players' pension.

Through his player agency and leadership of Canada and the NHL's international hockey involvement, Eagleson became the game's biggest powerbroker, most famous perhaps for his role in arranging international confrontations like the Canada-Russia Summit in 1972, the 1979 Challenge Cup and a series of Canada Cup tournaments.

He was executive director of the NHLPA until 1991, when he resigned, replaced by Bob Goodenow. Eagleson later was charged and convicted of theft and fraud, received a jail sentence and a one million dollar fine. Whatever his indiscretions, they pale in comparison with his accomplishments over a quarter of a century.

Bobby Orr Career Highlights

March 20, 1948

Robert Gordon Orr is born in Parry Sound, Ont.

September 3, 1966

Bobby Orr signs his first NHL contract with the Boston Bruins – a two- year deal paying seventy-thousand dollars plus a signing bonus – the top salary in the game.

April 26, 1967

Boston's Bobby Orr is winner of the Calder Memorial Trophy as the NHL's most outstanding rookie.

May 10, 1968

Bobby Orr is winner of the Norris Memorial Trophy for the first of eight straight seasons, what will be an NHL record for defensemen.

March 15, 1969

Orr records the sixtieth point of the season (with an assist), surpassing the NHL record (set by Chicago's Pierre Pilote in 1964-65) for most points by a defenseman.

March 20, 1969

He scores his twenty-first goal of the season, a record for defensemen, breaking the mark set by Detroit's Flash Hollett in 1944-45. It comes at 19:59 of the final period, on Orr's twenty-first birthday, in a 5-5 tie against Chicago, in Boston.

March 15, 1970

Bobby Orr has two goals and two assists to become the first defenseman in NHL history to reach one hundred points in a season; in a 5-5 tie with Detroit.

March 22, 1970

Boston's Bobby Orr scores two goals and two assists in a 5-0 Bruins win over Minnesota. His assist total of seventy-eight breaks the NHL record set by Phil Esposito in 1968-69.

April 5, 1970

Bobby Orr has an assist in the final game of the season (a 3-1 Boston win over Toronto) to become first NHL defenseman to win the Art Ross Trophy, as the league's top scorer. Orr finishes the year with thirty-three goals and eighty-seven assists for one hundred and twenty points in seventy-six games.

April 16, 1970

He is the first defenseman in NHL history to score goals in four straight playoff games, tallying twice as Boston beats the Rangers 4-1 in New York, in game six of the Stanley Cup quarter-finals.

May 5, 1970

Bruins' Bobby Orr has two assists to raise his playoff point total to eighteen, an NHL record for defensemen in a playoff year. Boston beats the Blues 6-2 in

game two of the Stanley Cup final, at St. Louis.

May 8, 1970

Boston's Bobby Orr is winner of the Hart Memorial Trophy as the NHL MVP, becoming the first defenseman to win the award in twenty-six seasons; it goes along with his Art Ross (first) and Norris Memorial Trophy (third).

May 10, 1970

Bobby Orr's overtime goal at 0:40 gives Boston a 4-3 win over St. Louis, and the 1970 Stanley Cup championship, in four straight games. Orr receives the Conn Smythe Trophy as playoff MVP.

May 4, 1972

Bobby Orr sets a career record for play-off scoring by defensemen with his seventeenth goal in forty-seven playoff games. The previous mark of sixteen had been set by Detroit's Red Kelly in ninety-four playoff games. Boston loses to the Rangers, 5-2 at New York.

May 5, 1972
Bobby Orr becomes the first player in NHL history to win the Hart Trophy (MVP) for three straight seasons, and the Norris Trophy for five straight years.

May 11, 1972
Boston beat NY Rangers 3-0 In game six of the final to win the 1972 Stanley Cup. Bobby Orr became only the fourth player to score two Cup-winning goals in his career.

December 21, 1972
An assist by Bobby Orr sets an NHL record for career points (five hundred and forty-one) by a defenseman. It comes in Orr's four hundred and twenty-third career NHL game, an 8-1 win over Detroit. Doug Harvey held the previous record, with five hundred and forty points in one thousand, one hundred and thirteen games.

January 1, 1973
Bobby Orr ties an NHL record for defensemen with six assists in an 8-2 Bruins win at Vancouver. The feat was previously accomplished by Babe Pratt in 1944, and Pat Stapleton in 1969.

November 15, 1973
He scores three power play goals and adds four assists to become the first NHL defenseman to record seven points in one game, as Boston beat the New York Rangers, 10-2.

November 17, 1973
Orr contributes four assists in an 8-0 Boston win against Detroit, giving him four hundred and fifty-six career assists, the most by an NHL defenseman. Doug Harvey held the previous mark of four hundred and fifty-two assists. It came in Orr's four hundred and fifty-eighth NHL game.

March 12, 1974
An assist enables Bobby Orr to reach the one hundred-point mark for the season, in a 4-0 win over the Sabres. Orr becomes the first NHL player to score one hundred points for five straight seasons.

June 16, 1975
Boston defenseman Bobby Orr is named to the NHL's first All-Star team for the eighth straight year.

September 24, 1976
Team Canada wins the first Canada Cup with Darryl Sittler's overtime goal providing the margin of victory. The 5-4 win over Czechoslovakia gives Canada a two-game sweep of their best-of-three final. Bobby Orr is selected MVP of the Canadian team.

October 7, 1976
Bobby Orr plays his first game with the Chicago Blackhawks, scoring a goal and an assist in the Hawks 6-4 win at St. Louis.

March 8, 1977
After an examination of his damaged knee, Bobby Orr announces he will be on the shelf for the remainder of the 1976-77 season, but says he is not contemplating retirement.

October 28, 1978
Orr scores the final goal of his NHL career, his two hundred and seventieth. It comes against Rogie Vachon as the Blackhawks lose at Detroit, 7-2.

November 8, 1978
Bobby Orr announces his retirement from the NHL. His final career totals were two hundred and seventy goals and six hundred and forty-five assists, for nine hundred and fifteen points in six hundred and fifty-seven games.

June 12, 1979
At age thirty-one, Bobby Orr is the youngest player to be inducted into the Hockey Hall of Fame.

22,24,26,28
СЕНТЯБРЯ

ХОККЕЙ

СССР·КАНАДА

The Russians are coming!

The early 1970s saw big happenings in hockey, notably the birth of the World Hockey Association and the continued expansion of the NHL. But the big word in hockey circles at the time was "Russia."

Starting with a 1954 upset win in the world championships, the caliber of hockey in the then-Soviet Union grew steadily until the country's national team dominated global amateur hockey. Canada was able to win titles in 1958, '59 and '61 with senior teams of minor pro caliber, but through the 1960s, the Russians reigned in the world and Olympic tournaments.

Vladislav Tretiak

Canadians always had a somewhat smug attitude towards the Soviet success, claiming that NHL players and teams would have little trouble handling the men who wore CCCP proudly on their chests. When the first eight-game Summit Series was announced for 1972, pitting the best Canadian-born NHL players against the Soviet National Club, forecasts were for a Team Canada romp.

In what is very likely the most gripping, strongest hockey competition ever staged, Team Canada triumphed by a scant margin of four wins to three, with one game tied. For those who had predicted a walkover, it must be noted that it took Paul Henderson's famous goal thirty-four

The Russians are coming!

seconds from the end of the final game, to ensure victory in a match watched on television by the vast majority of Canadians.

In the first four games of the series played in Canada, the Soviets had two wins, Canada one, with one tied. The opening game of the series at the Forum in Montreal, on September 2, was a gigantic shock to the Canadian hockey psyche, a 7-3 romp for the Russians.

When the Russians won the first game of four in Moscow, Team Canada appeared certain to lose the series. But in a superb display of pluck and effort, the Canadians won three one-goal games, Henderson scoring the winner in each, against the Soviets' brilliant young goalie Vladislav Tretiak.

Phil Esposito

The best player in the series was center Phil Esposito, who became the Team Canada leader, and many have called his performance in the Summit the finest individual effort in hockey history. He had lots of help, from stalwarts like Bobby Clarke, Yvan Cournoyer, Pete Mahovlich, Gary Bergman, Pat Stapleton and Bill White. Canadian fans could not help but notice the performance of several Soviet players and, after the series, Tretiak, Alexandr Yakushev, Valeri Kharlamov, Boris Mikhailov and Vladimir Petrov were household names in Canada.

Vladimir Petrov

The WHA All-Stars were beaten by the Soviets in a 1974 series, as the '72 Summit had created a big demand for more Soviet-NHL play. In late December, 1975, and early January, 1976, two Soviet club teams, Central Red Army, the perennial champions whose roster had most of the national team players, and Soviet Wings, each played four games against NHL clubs.

Memorable in that exchange was the game in Montreal on New Year's Eve, when the Army team and the Montreal Canadiens, who were on their way to four consecutive Stanley Cup titles, played a 3-3 tie in an extraordinary game, despite the Soviets being outshot 38-13 by the home team. The next day, the Wings were soundly thrashed 12-6 by Buffalo's French Connection.

Valeri Kharlamov

A week later, the defending Cup champs, the Philadelphia Flyers, beat the Army team, 4-1, in Philly, in a game that saw the Broad Street Bullies at their best, or worst, depending on your point of view.

For Canadian hockey fans, the game between two legendary teams, the Canadiens and Central Red Army, was an evening to long remember. It signified the obvious: international hockey was here to stay, and North American fans wanted more of it.

June 10, 1971

In the NHL amateur draft ▶
held in Montreal, the
Montreal Canadiens use
the first pick overall to
select Guy Lafleur.

Detroit's Marcel Dionne scores two goals and two assists ▶
to reach seventy-five points, an NHL record for rookies, as
the Red Wings win 6-3 at Los Angeles. Dionne breaks the
old mark of seventy-two points, set by Buffalo's Gilbert
Perreault the previous season.

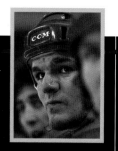

March 22, 1972

The Broad Street Bullies

Melees were a way of life.

The teams that joined the NHL in the 1967 expansion had varying degrees of success. While the St. Louis Blues attained quick prosperity with a roster of useful veterans, the climb to the league's upper echelons was slow and difficult for most of the new clubs.

The first expansion team to reach the pinnacle of the Stanley Cup was the Philadelphia Flyers, establishing NHL penalty records en route to earning the nickname the Broad Street Bullies. While brawling and aggressive play made them the terrors of the league, the Flyers also were a well-disciplined team that executed the systems of veteran coach, Fred Shero.

The Flyers had enjoyed modest success in their early years, but in the playoffs, larger opponents shoved around the team's contingent of small, skilled players. To end that, general manager Keith Allen drafted and traded for big, belligerent players.

An important acquisition was center Bobby Clarke in the 1969 amateur draft. He became their top scorer and team leader. Another key man was goalie Bernie Parent, who had jumped to the WHA after an undistinguished NHL career in Boston and Toronto, but returned to the Flyers a year later.

Tough guys Dave (Hammer) Schultz, Bob (Hound Dog) Kelly and Don Saleski fought all comers but the team also had excellent talent in Clarke, Rick MacLeish, Bill Barber, Bill Flett, Ross Lonsberry, Orest Kindrachuk, and Reggie Leach and a physical defense led by brothers Joe and Jim Watson, Moose Dupont and veteran Ed Van Impe.

A day at the office for the Bullies

In 1974, the Flyers beat the Boston juggernaut of Esposito and Orr in a six-game final, topped off by Parent's 1-0 shutout in the final game. A year later, the Buffalo Sabres of the famed French Connection were also dismissed in six games, with Parent once again clinching the cup with a whitewash, this time 2-0. His remarkable performances between the pipes made the Flyer goalie the first-ever back-to-back winner of the Conn Smythe Trophy as playoff MVP.

Bernie Parent shut out the world.

In 1965, a year before Orr's arrival in the NHL and after a fifth straight season of last-place finishes for Boston, Weston Adams brought in Hap Emms as his general manager. Lynn Patrick was offered a vice-presidency, as well, but he saw expansion coming. He moved west to coach for Dan Reeves, the owner of the Los Angeles Blades of the Pacific Coast League who was thought to have the inside track on the new Los Angeles NHL franchise. As it turned out, Reeves was outbid by Jack Kent Cooke and Lynn was out in the cold. Two months later, he received a call from the Rangers' Bill Jennings and was told that his name had been recommended to the new St. Louis franchise.

Within three weeks, he was general manager of the Blues, a team that would appear in the Stanley Cup final in the first three years of its existence. Lynn would remain with the Blues as GM, and later, as senior vice-president, until 1977.

Ironically, Lynn Patrick would relive his own 1934 Rangers rookie season with the St. Louis Blues in 1974. His son Craig, twenty-eight, had played three relatively modest seasons with the California Golden Seals when coach Al Arbour and the owners recommended that he be acquired by the team. Lynn balked, remembering his debut with his father's team in New York. He was outvoted and Craig played a year with the Blues before he was traded to Kansas City, then drifted down into the minors.

His dad was succinct. *"Craig was too defense-minded for a winger."*

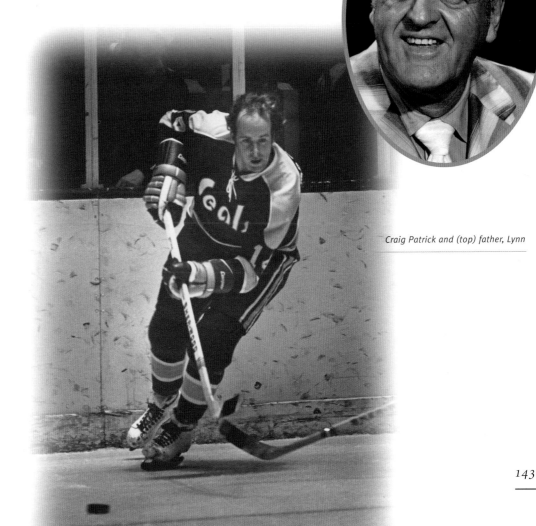

Craig Patrick and (top) father, Lynn

April 23, 1972

Hockey Canada announces that an eight-game series between the best NHL players and the Soviet national team is to be played in September.

Bobby Hull signs with the Winnipeg Jets of the WHA for two hundred and fifty thousand dollars a year for ten years and a million dollar signing bonus, launching the NHL-WHA salary war.

June 27, 1972

Unlike Lester, Lynn and Muzz Patrick were too busy with their teams to contribute professionally to the development of hockey in the United States. Lynn did make a contribution, in the persons of two of his four sons, Craig and Glenn (thirty-eight NHL games with California, St. Louis and Cleveland). Craig was the better hockey player, but by his own admission a "journeyman." In 1969, he was one of the leaders of the University of Denver Pioneers when they won the NCAA Division I championship in the U.S.

At that time, USA hockey could only produce journeymen. The six-team National Hockey League was an exclusive preserve for Canadians, as the number of Americans had dropped off during the 1940s. By the early 1960s, the only American in the league would be Minnesota native Tommy Williams, who played with Boston. He was the only permanent NHLer to contribute to the Olympic gold medal at Squaw Valley in 1960, putting in six hundred and sixty-three big league games with Boston and three expansion teams.

The 1960 U.S. team, primarily staffed by Minnesotans like goalie Jack McCartan, Roger and Billy Christian, Williams, Bill Cleary, Jack Kirrane and John Mayasich, surprised a Canadian team looking ahead to the Soviets, 2-1, and then outscored the Russians, 3-2, and the Czechs, 9-4, for the gold behind McCartan's spectacular goaltending. A last-minute addition to the team, the University of Minnesota Golden Gophers goalie was the star of the Olympic tournament and described by Coach Jack Riley as the "*most outstanding goalie I've ever seen. Without him, we wouldn't have been successful at Squaw Valley.*"

Boston's Tommy Williams was the lone American in the NHL in the 1960s.

European Inroads

The runaway proliferation of big league hockey to twenty-eight teams from six in five years from 1967 to '72, with expansion of the NHL and the birth of the WHA, enormously intensified the demand for talent.

The Canadian minor hockey system, long the main supplier of talent, could not produce enough quality players to meet the need, and while U.S. hockey was growing rapidly as a source, it was not yet a major factor.

Up to that point, European players were not rated as having high potential by the pros. Of course, the talent in two top hockey countries, the Soviet Union and Czechoslovakia, was out of reach because of the Iron Curtain. In most pro discussions of players from Sweden and Finland, the two democracies where hockey was big, the term "chicken" was employed often. NHL clubs felt that the Scandinavian players lacked the toughness to compete on smaller North American ice surfaces.

NHL teams had taken modest looks at European players before. In the late 1950s, the Boston Bruins invited Tumba Johansson, the great Swedish center, to their training camp, but he failed to impress. Swedish winger Ulf Sterner played four games for the New York Rangers in 1964-65 and finished the season in minor pro hockey before returning home.

But the population explosion in pro teams inspired a closer look at the Europeans, and scouting of the Swedes and Finns was increased.

In 1972, the Detroit Red Wings signed Swedish defenseman Thommie Bergman, and he had a solid rookie campaign, the first of nine major league seasons with the Wings and Winnipeg Jets of the WHA.

Stripped bare by WHA raids on their roster, the Toronto Maple Leafs sent scout Gerry McNamara to check out much touted Swedish winger Inge Hammarstrom. McNamara insisted the Leafs not only sign Hammarstrom, but also his teammate, defenseman Borje Salming, who would be the first European to become a major NHL star, a six-time All-Star in a seventeen-season NHL career.

At the time, defection was the only way a Czechoslovakian player could reach the pros, and that country's top player, big center Vaclav Nedomansky took that route to the WHA Toronto Toros. Big Ned had a ten-year stint in the WHA and NHL.

The first pro team to build a winner around European players was the WHA Winnipeg Jets. Swedish forwards Anders Hedberg and Ulf Nilsson teamed with Bobby Hull to form a brilliant line while defensemen Bergman and Lars-Erik Sjoberg, forwards Mats Lind, Willy Lindstrom and goalie Curt Larsson plus Finns Heikki Riihiranta and Veli Pekka Ketola, gave the 1976 WHA championship team a distinctly Scandinavian flavor. Many of these players would move into the NHL when the WHA was absorbed three years later.

Borje Salming

Lester Patrick *(center)*

and sons Lynn and Muzz

after the Silver Fox's induction

in the Hockey Hall of Fame

in Toronto.

McCartan managed a mere dozen NHL games with the Rangers, four in 1960 and eight in 1961, in what would be a fifteen-year professional career, finishing up with the Minnesota Fighting Saints of the World Hockey Association in 1972-74. McCartan's time on the New York roster saw him listed behind future Hall of Famers Lorne Worsley and Jacques Plante on the team's depth chart – poor luck or poor timing, or both.

McCartan's quandary and the lot of the American professional hockey player would change dramatically over the next two decades. When Team USA stunned the hockey world with a 1980 Olympic championship at Lake Placid, more than half of the team would be absorbed into the NHL within months of the historic feat. One Team USA star, defenseman Ken Morrow, would turn in a rare hockey double, skating with "NHL silver," the Stanley Cup, on Long Island, three months after winning gold upstate at Lake Placid.

Expansion to six U.S. cities in 1967 was the key. With the addition of Philadelphia, St. Louis, Pittsburgh, California, Minnesota and Los Angeles, came movement in hockey throughout the United States, and one hundred and twenty more National Hockey League jobs.

Expansion would drive professional hockey for the rest of the twentieth century. The Patricks, Muzz and Lynn, and later Craig, would have front row seats as the modern game emerged.

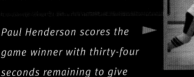

Paul Henderson scores the game winner with thirty-four seconds remaining to give Team Canada a 6-5 win over the Soviets in Moscow, in game eight of the historic 1972 series.

September 28, 1972

May 10, 1973

Yvan Cournoyer scores the winning goal, and adds two assists, as Montreal beats Chicago 6-4 in game six of the finals, to become the 1973 Stanley Cup champions.

World Hockey Association

Bobby Hull and Gordie Howe

The owners and executives of NHL teams cracked jokes galore at the 1971 league meeting in the Bahamas when they heard rumors that a rival league had moved beyond the planning stage. The laughter died quickly when the World Hockey Association became a reality in the 1972-73 season, to change the face of big league hockey forever.

Founded by California promoters Gary Davidson and Dennis Murphy, the WHA, with twelve teams in its first season, acquired authenticity when winger Bobby Hull, one of the NHL's marquee stars with the Chicago Blackhawks, jumped to the new league, joining the Winnipeg

Bobby Hull

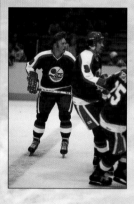

Jets on a ten-year, big money contract. Other NHL stars, including Gerry Cheevers, Bernie Parent, Derek Sanderson, J.C. Tremblay and Ted Green joined him in the new league.

In its seven-season existence, the WHA's eighteen teams played in twenty-seven cities, but the on-ice product was not its greatest legacy.

The league inspired a bidding war for players that pushed salaries upward rapidly, forcing the NHL to abandon its amateur draft rules and claim players less than twenty years of age. As well, the new league recruited heavily in Europe for players, notably Sweden and Finland, opening the doors to a rich source of talent.

An assortment of legal hassles and court actions were expensive for both leagues, and several WHA teams vanished in a sea of debt. Talks were initiated in 1977 between the WHA and NHL on a merger that was accomplished at the end of the 1978-79 season when four WHA clubs (Edmonton, Quebec, Hartford and Winnipeg) joined the NHL.

Noteworthy in the WHA's hectic history was NHL great Gordie Howe, his sons Mark and Marty as teammates in Houston and Hartford, and Wayne Gretzky, at seventeen, making his pro debut with the Indianapolis Racers before being traded to the Edmonton Oilers. As well, youngsters Mark Napier, Rod Langway, Gaston Gingras, Buddy Cloutier, Rob Ramage, Mark Messier and Mike Gartner all played their first professional games in the WHA before moving on to star in the NHL over the next two decades.

Ted Green

Bernie Parent set off a feeding

frenzy among NHL players when

he accepted a lucrative offer from

the WHA's Miami Screaming Eagles.

The team never saw the light of day

but Parent became a Philadelphia

Blazer in 1973.

STANLEY CUP

1950-51	TORONTO MAPLE LEAFS
1951-52	DETROIT RED WINGS
1952-53	MONTREAL CANADIENS
1953-54	DETROIT RED WINGS
1954-55	DETROIT RED WINGS
1955-56	MONTREAL CANADIENS
1956-57	MONTREAL CANADIENS
1957-58	MONTREAL CANADIENS
1958-59	MONTREAL CANADIENS
1959-60	MONTREAL CANADIENS
1960-61	CHICAGO BLACKHAWKS
1961-62	TORONTO MAPLE LEAFS
1962-63	TORONTO MAPLE LEAFS
1963-64	TORONTO MAPLE LEAFS
1964-65	MONTREAL CANADIENS
1965-66	MONTREAL CANADIENS
1966-67	TORONTO MAPLE LEAFS
1967-68	MONTREAL CANADIENS
1968-69	MONTREAL CANADIENS
1969-70	BOSTON BRUINS
1970-71	MONTREAL CANADIENS
1971-72	BOSTON BRUINS
1972-73	MONTREAL CANADIENS
1973-74	PHILADELPHIA FLYERS
1974-75	PHILADELPHIA FLYERS

1952
DETROIT RED WINGS

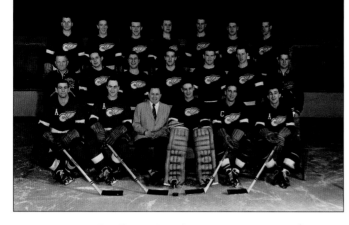

1954
DETROIT RED WINGS

1956
MONTREAL CANADIENS

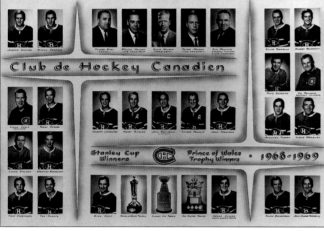

1969
MONTREAL CANADIENS

1967
TORONTO MAPLE LEAFS

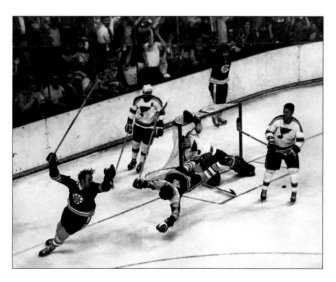

1970

BOSTON BRUINS

IV Fourth Quarter

1976
20

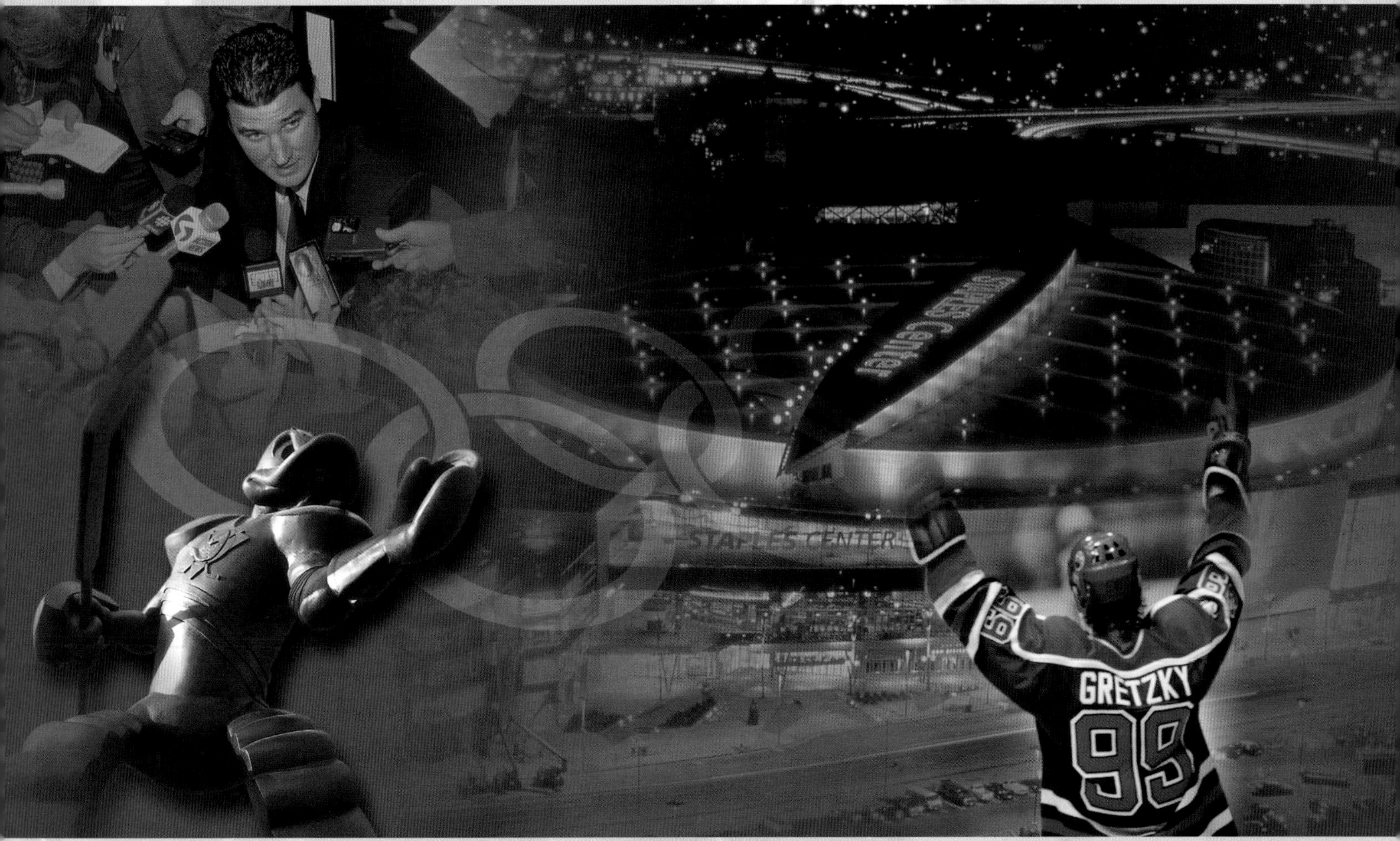

SPANNING THE CONTINENTS

The Patricks and the Americanization of the NHL

The Staples Center gleamed and glistened in its anchorage right beside the downtown Convention Center in Los Angeles on this October weekend in 1999. And while one wag in the press described it as a gigantic Swiss Army knife, few *Angelinos* cared. They had their new toy and the excitement was palpable. The new home for the Kings of the National Hockey League, as well as the National Basketball Association twins of the Lakers and Clippers, would be center stage to many future Made-in-Los Angeles memories.

os Angeles was the latest city to treat itself to an entertainment multiplex of and for the New Millennium. After 1995 or so, marketers and public relationists disdained the 1990s in their hyperbole: All "state-of-the-art" or "leading-edge" developments were teleported automatically from the 1990s into the next millennium.

As with similar structures across North America, the new building had a plethora of private loges with more features than an expensive hotel suite, a glass atrium, "smart" seats, the standard Jumbotron© with its endless database of computer-generated special effects, and a mind-blowing decibel-hawg of a sound system. Local touches, lest the building be confused with (horrors!) new multiplexes in Buffalo or Nashville, included a palm-treed promenade and terrazzo floors.

As one might expect with such an event of local and regional import, the *Los Angeles Times* Sunday edition, big enough already on most weekends, was swollen further on October 17, 1999, with a special supplement of stories about the opening of the Staples Center.

One caught the attention much more than the others, for its headline: *When will it become obsolete?*

In other words, this spaceship has landed; another will be along in a few years when the ever-dwindling attention span of the denizens of the New Millennium demands something bigger, brighter and faster, heavy on the bells and whistles. Nothing is permanent.

The reality of the world of professional hockey at the end of its first century, and all pro sports for that matter, was that change was now measured in nanoseconds. Players, executives, teams and buildings were as expendable, even as disposable, as last year's PC.

This *tsunami* of change was a creature of the century's fourth quarter; actually the decade of the 1990s. How had pro hockey changed so radically?

October 8, 1975

▶ Doug Jarvis plays the
first of his NHL record
nine hundred and sixty-four
consecutive games.

Darryl Sittler sets an NHL record with ten points in one
game – on six goals and four assists in an 11-4 Toronto
romp over Boston, at Maple Leaf Gardens. He also sets
another record for hat tricks scored in consecutive periods.

February 7, 1976

The 1990s – the decade

when hockey fans got

the best of both worlds,

bringing their TV sets

to live events.

Team executives in 1976 still read the same management manuals as their predecessors. Some, actually, could be described as "predecessors": Sam Pollock still ran things in Montreal, and other graduates of Frank Selke U. included Bill Torrey on Long Island and Cliff Fletcher in Atlanta.

Punch Imlach was the boss in Buffalo, Harry Sinden was only the fifth GM Boston ever had – and still is – while Tommy Ivan would soon turn over the Blackhawks to Bob Pulford after twenty-two years at the helm. Other veteran hockey executives included Keith Allen in Philadelphia and Emile Francis in St. Louis.

Experienced, aware hockey people staffed the front offices of most of the eighteen NHL franchises that year, throwing occasional nervous glances at the World Hockey Association, the upstart league formed four years before in 1972 that had forever tilted the balance in the money game towards the players.

The situation was well under control in the executive suite, and the National Hockey League had the geographical dispersal it had sought when it doubled in size in 1967. Team managers were proud of the moves they had made, individually and collectively, to modernize the game – completely renovating the Forum in Montreal and Madison Square Garden in New York, expanding into U.S. markets, instituting the universal draft, and actively seeking out communications opportunities with network television.

Lanny McDonald,
Colorado Rockies

There were mid-course adjustments. The California Seals experiment with owner Charles Finley was deemed a failure, and the team became the Cleveland Barons for a single season, 1976-77, before merging with the Minnesota North Stars. Kansas City Scouts survived two seasons (1974-76), and became the Colorado Rockies for six (1976-82) before settling in some New Jersey swampland as the Devils for the 1982-83 season. Atlanta Flames flickered for eight seasons, and then hotfooted it north to Calgary for the 1980-81 season.

Still, the game had changed little on or off the ice. Pro hockey followed traditions developed throughout the century. The haves and have-nots were evident, and the gap between both groups showed no signs of shrinking. The league's elite was essentially unchanged, as were the bottom feeders. The system in place guaranteed that expansion teams could count on a half-decade of futility before they could achieve even modest competitive fire. Expansion fees were swelling the coffers of the senior teams, without a perceptible threat to the hegemony of the Old Boys Club.

The status quo was bolstered by three consecutive dynasties, Montreal Canadiens, New York Islanders and Edmonton Oilers, teams that would match up well with any of the century's powerhouses. The trio owned the first fifteen years of the fourth quarter. Montreal had the best balance, the Isles the most grit, and the Oilers the most flash, and all three won with style. The Canadiens and Islanders won four straight Cups in turn, and then the Oilers took five in seven seasons, with Montreal and Calgary winning the others.

Several things happened within the time frame (1976-1990) of the three dynasties. The Canadiens were the last NHL juggernaut to win consistently with a team composed primarily of Canadian players, with a few Americans (Bill Nyrop, Rod Langway, Rick Chartraw) thrown in for good measure.

The Islanders were helped by the Scandinavian Connection of Anders Kallur, Stefan Persson, Tomas Jonsson and Mats Hallin; solid, skilled players drafted in the mid-to-late 1970s who contributed on both sides of the puck.

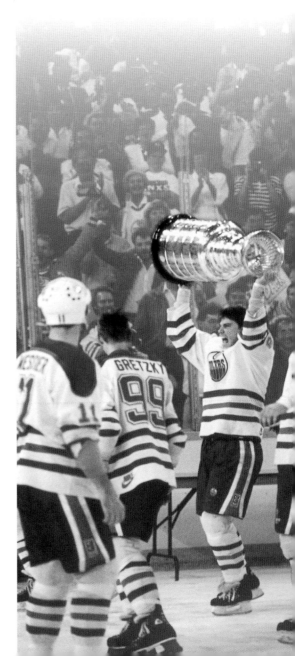

The Dynasties

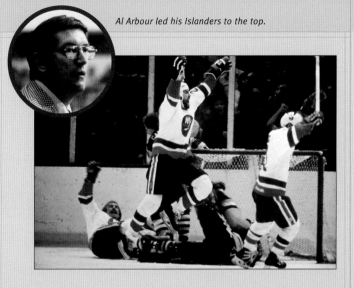

Al Arbour led his Islanders to the top.

In the view of many hockey experts, the days of NHL dynasty teams – domination of the Stanley Cup throne for an extended stretch of seasons – are gone, mainly for economic reasons. To win a series of titles requires star players, who push a team's payroll to a level too high to maintain.

Thus, the three teams who dominated the Cup from 1976 to 1990, the Montreal Canadiens, the New York Islanders and Edmonton Oilers, are probably the last of the mighty teams.

Owning rosters with great stars and excellent depth in "foot soldiers", the three clubs collected the title fourteen times in fifteen years and, while the Pittsburgh Penguins and Detroit Red Wings won two consecutive crowns each in the 1990s, they were unable to extend their streaks.

Montreal and New York were creatures of the first major expansion in 1967, both essentially built from within via the draft by crafty manager-architects, Sam Pollock in Montreal, and New York's Bill Torrey. When the GMs of the six new expansion teams rejected Pollock's advice to institute a rule that forbade the trade of top draft picks for five years, it was Pollock who made the best use of the opportunity, trading the players from the championship teams of the 1960s to secure those who would drive the Stanley Cup winners of the 1970s.

The Canadiens collected four consecutive victories from 1976-79 under the coaching of Scotty Bowman. Keys were the goaltending of Ken Dryden, three superb defensemen in Larry Robinson, Serge Savard and Guy Lapointe, the exceptional forward line of Guy Lafleur, Steve Shutt and Jacques Lemaire plus defensive specialists Bob Gainey and Doug Jarvis.

When Montreal faltered in a second attempt for five straight Cups in May 1980, a carbon copy of the *bleu-blanc-rouge* took over. The Islanders from top to bottom resembled the Canadiens, with Torrey building the team throughout the decade with Pollock-like patience and focus. Al Arbour took them under his wing and coached them to the top, just as his mentor, Scotty Bowman, had done before him.

The Islanders played a simple game based on sound positional play and discipline. Goalie Billy Smith, defensemen Denis Potvin and Stefan Persson, and forwards Bryan Trottier, Mike Bossy, Clark Gillies, Butch Goring, Bob Nystrom and John Tonelli gave the team exceptional depth.

"Our strength was the ability to match whatever style an opponent tossed at us," Arbour said. *"We could skate, score, check or play tough as the situation demanded."*

While the Isles were dominating, the Oilers were building to challenge them. After being swept by the Islanders in the 1983 final, the Oilers were ready to win a year later. The flamboyant team won five Cups in seven seasons (1984-'85-'87-'88-'90).

The highest scoring team in NHL history, the Oilers, assembled by general manager-coach Glen Sather were led by center Wayne Gretzky, who now owns a large section of the NHL record book. The forward duos of Gretzky and Jari Kurri, Mark Messier and Glenn Anderson, defensemen Paul Coffey, Kevin Lowe, Charlie Huddy and Randy Gregg, and goalie Grant Fuhr, were the mainstays.

Apply the salaries of the late 1990s to the roster of those three exceptional teams, and the excessive cost of such teams is very evident.

The Oilers took it a step further. While Europeans such as Kent Nilsson (late in his career), Willy Lindstrom, Jaroslav Pouzar and Reijo Ruotsalainen were effective players, Finns Jari Kurri and Esa Tikkanen took starring roles on a talent-rich team, and highlighted the mass migration of European players into the league in the 1980s.

Esa Tikkanen

The Iron Curtain was rusting, the Berlin Wall tumbling, and the only real Cold War remaining was on ice rinks. Americans, Russians, Czechs, Swedes and Finns were all part of ice hockey's new Détente, and the line formed on the right at Immigration for players seeking North American dollars.

In the middle of this was another Patrick, Craig, grandson of Lester and son of Lynn. Like his father and uncle Muzz before him, Craig moved to Montreal during his high school days, playing hockey with the Lachine Maroons and the Junior Canadiens and attending school at Verdun Catholic High School.

Serge Savard (right) and teammate Rogatien Vachon (below)

The 1964-65 Baby Habs were a special edition; five of their players – Patrick, Serge Savard, Jacques Lemaire, Rogatien Vachon and Carol Vadnais – would enjoy significant NHL playing careers before moving on to serve in NHL front offices. A sixth, their coach, Scotty Bowman, would forge a Hall-of-Fame career off the ice, as well. The Patrick bloodlines showed. Craig was a solid performer with Montreal (thirteen goals and eighteen assists for thirty-one points in fifty-six games), but no threat to jump quickly into the NHL.

April 1, 1976

Philadelphia Flyers' Reggie Leach becomes the second player in NHL history to score sixty goals in a season, scoring in an 11-2 Flyers win over Washington.

*Hockey was in my blood,
and I was fortunate enough
to get to live my dream*

The Patrick parents had directed Craig and brothers Dean and Glenn to other careers, just as Lester and Grace Patrick had done to Lynn and Muzz.

"My parents did everything they could to not encourage me to get into hockey, but I knew what I wanted to do," Craig recalled. *"In fact, they wouldn't drive me to practices and games, I had to get rides. They wouldn't encourage us at all. I remember one of my elementary school teachers calling our home and sending notes that said: 'Can you get this kid to do anything but draw pictures of hockey games?' Hockey was in my blood, and I was fortunate enough to get to live my dream."*

After his time in Montreal, Craig attended the University of Denver and captained the Pioneers to the NCAA Division I championship in 1969, almost a decade after the U.S. Olympic team had triumphed at the 1960 Winter Olympic Games at Squaw Valley.

That watershed event in U.S. hockey history had little fall-out. In the early sixties, the number of Americans in the NHL dropped to one, Boston winger Tommy Williams, who had played on the gold medal team. It remained that way through the 1960s – with no groundswell of young recruits across the U.S. Nine years later, the NCAA-champion Pioneers were all Canadians, with the notable exception of Patrick, their captain, whose grandparents and parents were Canadian.

"Squaw Valley may have done some good," Patrick recalled. *"I remember watching it. I was already involved in hockey, so it didn't affect me in any way, but it was a thrill to watch them win. I remember kids in that era talking about it. I don't think they started playing hockey because of it, but people paid attention."*

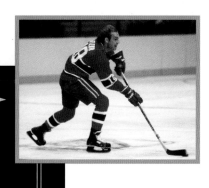

Guy Lafleur scores the winning goal ▶ as Montreal beats Philadelphia 5-3 in game four, sweeping the final for their nineteenth Stanley Cup Championship.

May 16, 1976

Glenn Patrick and

brother Craig toiled

for Cleveland and

Washington respectively.

"Kids in the U.S. up to a certain age have always been able to compete with Canadians, but once you get to a certain age level, the caliber of the play goes up in Canada because of the better competition," he said. *"Nowadays, there are enough kids playing down here so that the level of competition has improved. Back then, Americans on Junior A teams in Canada were rare."*

After college, Craig set out on a hockey career that included stints with the U.S. national team in 1969-70 and 1970-71, and a five-game amateur tryout with the Montreal Voyageurs, the Canadiens' legendary American Hockey League farm team that was strong enough to regularly defeat some NHL expansion teams. In 1971-72, he made the NHL with California Golden Seals. Over the next eight years, he would play four hundred and one regular-season games with a quartet of expansion teams, the Seals, St. Louis Blues, Kansas City Scouts and Washington Capitals, scoring seventy-two goals and ninety-one assists. He also turned in thirty games with the WHA's Minnesota Fighting Saints in 1976-77, scoring six goals and eleven assists.

Younger brother Glenn would play thirty-eight NHL games with the Blues, Seals and Cleveland Barons between 1973-74 and 1976-77, and another twenty-three with the Edmonton Oilers of the World Hockey Association. Just as it was in the first quarter of the century, two members of the Patrick family played in the top pro league of the day. Two members of the Patrick family also would play significant roles in NHL front offices in the fourth quarter.

In 1966, team President Bill Jennings and the New York Rangers sought to honor the memory and contributions of their first executive to hockey with the presentation of the Lester Patrick Trophy, an annual award "for outstanding service to hockey in the United States." The first (posthumous) winner was Jack Adams, and a year later, his favorite hockey player, Gordie Howe, was honored.

New York's Phil Esposito scores his six hundredth
NHL goal in a 5-1 Rangers' win over Vancouver; the
third player in NHL history to reach this plateau.

*The Lester Patrick trophy underscored
the permanence of the Patrick family
in the National Hockey League*

Gordie Howe receives the trophy in
1967 as Muzz and Lynn Patrick look on.

"It is pretty special for players like Glenn and myself to play in a league which annually bestows an award named after our grandfather. It makes me especially proud that my grandfather was recognized in the U.S. for what he did for hockey," said Craig.

The trophy also served to underscore the permanence of the Patrick family in the National Hockey League.

"There haven't been many years where there hasn't been a Patrick in the NHL," said Craig. *"When my Dad died in 1979, he was still with the St. Louis Blues. The last time I can remember where there wasn't anyone would be 1947-48 when my Dad and Muzz had retired as players to coach in the minors, and my grandfather had just retired as an executive. And Dad was back the next season to coach the Rangers."*

The Other Leagues

From Beauce to Bakersfield, Amarillo to Anchorage, Portland (Oregon) to Portland (Maine), the other leagues have existed under constantly changing names and configurations through much of the century.

The true minor professional circuits in which all players were paid to play actually started in the mid-1920s when the National Hockey League expanded to the United States. The folding of the Pacific Coast league (then called the Western Hockey League) in 1926, placed more players on the open market than were needed to staff the new NHL clubs, and three minor loops were created.

Previously, several strong "amateur" circuits had existed in which the players were paid, but not openly.

What serious hockey fans might find the most unusual about minor professional hockey is the fact that the 1990s are by far and away the most prosperous time for hockey at the sub-NHL level.

When the decade started, only thirty-one minor pro teams existed, the lowest number since the 1920s.

Colorful American Hockey League action in the 1990s

In the 1999-2000 season, however, a total of one hundred and eleven minor pro clubs were dispersed in seven leagues – the American, International, East Coast, United, Western Professional, West Coast, and Central leagues. Fifty of those teams are in the southern U.S. where, for most of the century, hockey pucks were about as familiar as backyard igloos.

The top development leagues for NHL teams are the American Hockey League and the International Hockey League, while some teams in the ECHL have affiliations with NHL clubs or teams in the AHL or IHL. The vast majority of current and past NHL players logged preparation time in the minors, including many Europeans.

The AHL was born in 1936 as the IAHL, when the International Amateur and Can-Am leagues merged, while the second IHL began play in 1945. The "I" was dropped on the IAHL when its Canadian cities vanished because of Depression era woes.

Albany River Rats

Two original AHL clubs still going strong are the Springfield Indians, who became the Falcons in 1993, and the Providence Reds, who took a short hiatus in the mid-1980s to return in 1992 as the Bruins.

Islander Mike Bossy sets an NHL record for goals by a rookie, with his forty-fifth of the year in a 7-1 win over Chicago, breaking the mark of forty-four set by Buffalo's Rick Martin in 1971-72.

The North Stars beat Philadelphia 7-1 to end the Flyers' NHL record thirty-five-game unbeaten streak (25-0-10); before fifteen thousand, nine hundred and sixty-two fans at Minnesota, the largest crowd in team history.

The minor pro leagues have had their own "superstars"; players who excelled long-term at the various levels but could never make a breakthrough in the NHL. High scorers Willie Marshall, Mike Nykoluk, Guyle Fielder, Bruce Boudreau, Eddie Dorohoy, Harry Pidhirny, Fred Glover, Willie O'Ree, Chick Chalmers, Andy Hebenton (after a solid NHL career with Boston and New York), and Ray Powell, proliferated in minor pro hockey. Among the star netminders were Marcel Paille, Marcel Pelletier, Bob Perreault, Gilles Mayer, Ross Brooks and Jack McCartan.

Worcester IceCats

Jean Béliveau, Quebec Aces

There was the occasional "minor leaguer-makes-good" success story. Goalie Johnny Bower – who spent a dozen seasons in minor pro with teams like the Cleveland Barons, Vancouver Canucks and Providence Reds between 1945 and 1958 – played a full season with the New York Rangers who wanted to teach Lorne Worsley a lesson in 1953-54. He was picked up by Punch Imlach and won four Stanley Cups with Toronto in a career that wrapped up in 1969.

Hartford Wolfpack vs Springfield Falcons

Bower was thirty-four when the Leafs came calling.

And then there was the very special success story. In 1951-52 and 1952-53, Canadiens fans held their collective breath as Jean Béliveau decided to remain with the "amateur" Quebec Aces, coached by Punch Imlach, rather than sign with Montreal, which held the big center's pro rights. He was in no hurry; he was making more money in the Quebec Senior Hockey League than Gordie Howe and Maurice Richard were paid as the NHL's best players. When he finally moved to the NHL, he immediately took over the title as the league's best-paid athlete.

No other minor pro stars would ever be able to make that claim.

AN AMERICAN HOCKEY REVOLUTION

....

Craig Patrick vs Team Canada

Craig Patrick assessed his playing career with the same fine eye he turns on potential recruits at the draft table.

"I was not very good, that's why I got traded so many times," he said. *"I had decent skills, but I turned pro at twenty-five which didn't leave me a lot of time to have a good pro career. I managed to play in the Canada Cup in 1976, which I was pretty proud of, but I never was a top quality player. If I was on the third line, I had a chance to contribute."*

His career breakthrough came in 1979, when he played on the U.S. team at the World Championships in Helsinki, Finland.

"Herb Brooks was the coach and we had a good relationship," Craig reminisced. *"I had played with him before, but I got to know him a lot better during that championship. He took me aside one day in Helsinki: 'I've offered the job of my assistant (of the U.S. Olympic team) to someone else, but if it's turned down, would you be interested?' I said, 'absolutely.' We went back home, and he called back less than a month later.*

"We moved out to Minneapolis. While we were out there, I discovered that the general manager had a full-time job and couldn't handle all the GM duties, and I picked up several of those, too."

When Team USA arrived at Lake Placid for the 1980 Winter Games, Craig Patrick was Herb Brooks' right-hand man. In the year prior to the Games, the team entered several tournaments with fair to middling results, and played the Canadian team even in a lengthy North American-wide exhibition series. A week before the Games, the collegians, who averaged twenty-two years of age, played an exhibition game with the powerhouse Soviet Union. The veteran Russians had several players who had taken part in the Soviet-Canada series of 1972, captain Boris Mikhailov and goalie Vladislav Tretiak prominent among them. The previous year, they had defeated an NHL All-Star team two games to one in the Challenge Cup. Therefore, it was no surprise when they rolled over the Olympic "kids" 10-3.

The Miracle on Ice

The next time the teams met was the medal round of the Games. Gathering momentum as they went and spurred on by a fiercely partisan crowd, the Americans took a record of four wins and a tie into the Russian game, and had shocked the world by playing the Soviets to a 3-3 deadlock midway through the third period. The late afternoon contest was broadcast live across the U.S. by ABC, and announcer Al Michaels and his color man Ken Dryden sensed a moment of history was upon them.

Team captain Mike Eruzione broke through the Russian defense and scored to give his team the lead, and a team of "nobodies" with names like Verchota, Schneider, Janaszak, Harrington, Strobel and Johnson threw up an impenetrable wall in front of their Boston-raised goalie Jim Craig. An entire country held its breath, living and dying with every Red wave as the Soviets mounted attack after attack, bombarding Craig with thirty-nine shots.

"We weren't aware what was going on outside the arena," Patrick said. *"We moved basically from dorm to meeting room to rink, that was our life. The only chance we had to see the excitement in the country was in the arena at the games, but we weren't aware of all this hype that was going on. Then as the Olympics went on, we started to receive more and more telegrams and tons of messages."*

Team USA staved off the Soviets to forge the Miracle on Ice, clinched the Olympic gold medal with a 4-2 defeat of Finland, and U.S. hockey took a giant leap forward, especially in the pro ranks.

May 21, 1980

The Atlanta Flames are sold to a group of Canadian businessmen, who announce that they will move the team to Calgary.

Phil Esposito and Craig Patrick

Rangers' center Phil Esposito plays in his final NHL game, ▶ a 3-3 tie with Buffalo, at Madison Square Garden. Esposito retires as the second highest scorer in NHL history — trailing only Gordie Howe — with seven hundred and seventeen career goals and one thousand, five hundred and ninety points.

January 9, 1981

Jaromir Jagr (Czech Republic)

> *The 1998 Olympic Games in Nagano, Japan saw NHL stars in gold medal action for the very first time*

Dominik Hasek (Czech Republic)

Sergei Fedorov (Russia)

Saku Koivu and Adam Foote, of Finland and Canada, respectively

The World's Game

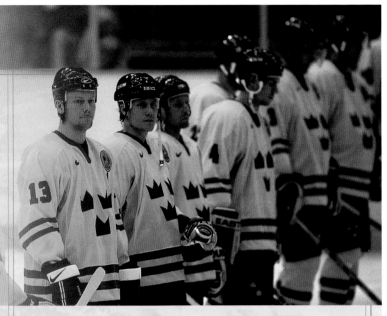

The early meetings between NHL players from Canada and Soviet Union clubs had a "them vs. us," communism vs. democracy, quality that created great interest.

Hockey was split into two distinct camps, separated by the Iron Curtain, by the mid-1970s after Swedish and Finnish players had moved to the NHL and WHA in increasing numbers. The 1972 Summit Series started the east-west exchanges that produced great hockey moments.

Team Sweden has always been a threat.

Guy Lafleur and Marcel Dionne with Bobby Orr, Team Canada 1976 MVP

But even though players from all countries now are in the NHL, when the best in the world play for their home countries' national teams, the competition is special. The World Cup of hockey in 1996 and the participation of NHL players in the 1998 Olympic Games proved that. The six top world hockey powers, Canada, the U.S., Russia, the Czech Republic, Sweden and Finland are being pushed now by Slovakia, Germany, Switzerland, Belarus and Austria.

Five Canada Cup tournaments involving the top six were staged from 1976 to '91 with Canada winning four of them. Memorable in that competition was the 1987 tournament in which the Soviets and Canada played three one-goal games in the final, and the play of Wayne Gretzky and Mario Lemieux was a highlight. The first four tournaments produced a Canada-Russia final, but in 1991 it was Canada over the U.S. for the title.

The Canadian domination ended in the 1996 World Cup when the U.S. team won the title over Canada. At the 1998 Olympics, when the NHL closed down for two weeks to allow players to participate, long-time foes, the Czech Republic and Russia met in the final. Goalie Dominik Hasek backed the Czech wins over Canada and the Soviets to earn the gold medal.

A Soviet-NHL match-up twice replaced the NHL All-Star game: In the 1979 Challenge Cup in New York when the Soviets won two of three games, and *Rendez-vous 1987* in Quebec City when the teams split two games.

In the final of the five tournaments, Canada and the Russians traded victories while Canada defeated Czechoslovakia, Sweden and the U.S. in the others.

May 27, 1982

Colorado Rockies are sold and moved to New Jersey, where they become the Devils.

The Miracle on Ice team visits the White House.

Like Craig Patrick, Herb Brooks could make a poignant comparison with the 1960 Cup win. He had been the last player cut from the Squaw Valley team, and one of his stars in 1980 was forward Dave Christian, son of Billy Christian and nephew of Roger Christian, leaders on the '60 squad.

"I've been asked if the Lake Placid victory encouraged young Americans to take up hockey, or apply themselves more seriously to it," said the Minnesota native. *"I think it jump-started a lot of kids in the direction of the game, no question."*

More importantly, Brooks added, it opened up the National Hockey League to great athletes from many countries. *"It brought hockey from all over the world together in the NHL."*

With the Minnesota North Stars joining the league in 1967, the drafting of American talent had begun, especially those players in the team's backyard. U.S. trained players began trickling into the league in the 1970s, Patrick among them. Most, however, were mid-round or late-round draft selections and journeymen when they reached the league. Few were drafted early. Defenseman Reed Larson had been selected twenty-second (second round) in 1976, and Tom Gorence and Rod Langway were picked at the thirty-fifth and thirty-sixth spots (second round) the following year.

Three members of the 1980 Olympic team were selected in the higher rounds just before the Games: Steve Christoff, twenty-fourth in the second round in 1978; Mike Ramsey, eleventh, in the first round, and Neal Broten, forty-second, in the second round in 1979. All were college players.

October 23, 1983

Philadelphia's Rich Sutter scores a goal in his first NHL game, the sixth Sutter brother to score a goal in the league.

In the NHL Entry Draft held in Montreal, the Pittsburgh Penguins select Mario Lemieux first overall.

June 9, 1984

Boss and The Flower

Guy Lafleur and Mike Bossy

Guy Lafleur and Mike Bossy had extraordinary records in Quebec junior hockey, and then were viewed very differently in assessments for the NHL draft.

Lafleur was a unanimous choice as first pick in the 1971 Entry Draft, a sure-fire NHL star claimed with a pick acquired by the Montreal Canadiens in a trade with the California Seals.

Although he had scored three hundred and eight goals in four junior seasons, Bossy was not regarded as a good NHL prospect in the 1977 draft. He was rated as weak defensively and not physical enough in a "goon" era of an NHL talent pool diluted by big league hockey's proliferation. Thus, the New York Islanders could make him their fifteenth pick, mainly at the strong insistence of their Quebec scout, the late Henry Saraceno.

But in the NHL, the careers of the two right wingers ran parallel, although they were different kinds of players. In eleven of twelve seasons from 1975 to 1986, Lafleur (six times) and Bossy (five times) were the selections at right wing on the league's first All-Star team. The Flower, as Lafleur was nicknamed, played on five Stanley Cup winners, while Bossy was the scoring engine in the Islanders' four straight Cup crowns (1980-83).

Because he had produced one hundred and thirty goals and two hundred and nine points in his final junior season for Quebec Remparts, and eighty-six points in twenty-nine playoff games in two years, Lafleur's solid rookie season (twenty-nine goals, sixty-four points) was viewed as ordinary. Alternating at center and wing for much of three seasons, he did not break out until his fourth season when he scored fifty-three goals and totalled one hundred and nineteen points.

Lafleur was the NHL's golden star for the next six years, which were packed with numbers and achievements as any player ever. In that stretch, he had a total of seven hundred and sixty-six points, based on three hundred and twenty-seven goals and four hundred and thirty-nine assists.

Le Démon Blond as he was known in his home province, won three scoring titles, two Most Valuable Player (Hart Trophy) awards and the Conn Smythe Trophy as playoff MVP. During his most successful run, he was partnered by either Pete Mahovlich or Jacques Lemaire at center, and Steve Shutt on the left wing.

Lafleur's well-documented off-ice activities may have taken a toll as his performance declined steadily and led to his retirement in 1985. But, after three years out of the game, he returned in 1988 with the New York Rangers, then capped off his playing career with two seasons in Quebec, showing only occasional flashes of the top Flower.

Prior to Bossy's arrival with the Islanders, that very talented team was seen as a "scorer short" of a legitimate challenge for the Stanley Cup. The Isles welcomed the Montreal native with open arms, slotting him in on a line with Bryan Trottier and Clark Gillies.

Among the most gifted natural goal scorers ever to play, Bossy scored fifty or more goals in a record nine straight seasons, and enjoyed five seasons of sixty or more, a mark he shares with Wayne Gretzky. Only Mario Lemieux (.823 goals per game) had a higher average than Bossy's .762. He also scored eighty-five goals in one hundred and twenty-nine playoff games, almost identical to the post-season production of his home city's most famous right winger, Maurice Richard, who had eighty-two goals in one hundred and thirty-three games.

"No player ever worked harder to be a complete player than Bossy," said Islanders coach Al Arbour. *"He was burned by people saying he wasn't good defensively and took that part of his game to a very high level. He was the best I ever saw at taking the chance that was available and turning it into a goal."*

Chronic back problems cut his career short at the age of thirty-one after ten seasons. There is no telling how many goals he may have scored given another five or six seasons of full health.

The breakthrough to the top of the Entry Draft came in 1981. Bobby Carpenter of St. John's Prep School in Massachusetts was selected in the first round, third overall, and found himself on the cover of *Sports Illustrated*. Another high school star, Dave Preuss of St. Thomas High School in Minnesota, was picked in the second round at the thirty-fourth spot. Carpenter would enjoy an up-and-down career in the NHL, scoring three hundred and eighteen goals and four hundred assists in one thousand, one hundred and twenty-two games. He also was the first American to have a fifty-goal season, scoring fifty-three with forty-two assists for Washington Capitals in the 1984-85 season. And he wasn't even the prize of his draft year.

Selected late in the second round by Montreal, at the fortieth spot, was a defenseman from Chicago named Chris Chelios. A year later, the Canadiens picked three American players in the first two rounds, collegiate defenseman Kent Carlson, and high schoolers David Maley and Scott Sandelin, while the Sabres featured a first-round selection named Phil Housley, a carrot-topped high school senior who, like Carpenter, would move directly into NHL competition.

Ultimate draft status for U.S. hockey came in 1983. Forward Brian Lawton of Mount St. Charles High School in Providence, R.I., was claimed first overall, while Detroit's Pat LaFontaine was selected third, and goalie Tom Barrasso of Acton-Boxboro High in Massachusetts was fifth. All three were in the NHL the following season.

"No matter where these players came from, high school for Housley, Lawton and Barrasso, or the Quebec junior league for LaFontaine, Americans began to play starring or leadership roles on their NHL teams, opening the way for even more players at all levels," Craig Patrick said.

Esa Tikkanen, Randy Gregg and Grant Fuhr

May 22, 1986

Montreal Canadiens become the first team to win one hundred games in the Stanley Cup finals, with a 1-0 win over the Calgary Flames, in game four.

December 11, 1985

Edmonton Oilers beat the Blackhawks 12-9, in Chicago, in the highest scoring game in modern NHL history. The team set another record with twelve goals scored in the second period.

Jari Kurri scores the winner in the seventh and deciding game of the Stanley Cup final as the Oilers beat the Flyers 3-1 to win their third Cup in four years.

May 31, 1987

Joey Mullen

The Made-in-America roll call was impressive: Joey Mullen, the first U.S.-born player to score five hundred NHL goals, and his brother Brian; the three Broten brothers, Neal, Paul and Aaron; Chelios and his University of Wisconsin defense mate Gary Suter; Mike Modano, the Hatcher brothers, Kevin and Derian; Housley, Brian Leetch, John LeClair, Mike Richter, Tom Barrasso, Guy Hebert, one-thousand-point man LaFontaine, Jimmy Carson, Jeremy Roenick, Tony Amonte, Keith Tkachuk, and Bryan Berard.

European-trained players also were swelling NHL rosters in the 1980s. While few took the dramatic route of the Stastnys, Peter and Anton, spirited out of Czechoslovakia and Austria in the dead of night by officials of the Quebec Nordiques, players like Kent (Magic) Nilsson, Pelle Lindbergh, Borje Salming, Thommie Bergman, Mats Naslund, Petr Svoboda, Hakan Loob and Ulf Samuelsson were major contributors to their teams.

The next generation with names like Sundin, Forsberg, Selanne, Bondra, Bure, Fedorov, Mogilny, Ozolinsh and Tverdosky would be even more exciting. While it appeared that Canada now was relegated to producing spear carriers, stars still were emerging from The True North.

Peter Stastny

January 4, 1988

Toronto defenseman Borje Salming becomes the first European-trained player to appear in one thousand career NHL games, in a 7-7 Maple Leafs tie with Vancouver.

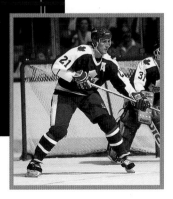

NORTHERN LIGHTS

....

Two such stars were right out of a George Lucas movie, representing the forces of Darkness and Light, both in their ascension to the National Hockey League and in their performances once they had arrived.

Eric Lindros and Paul Kariya's careers ran parallel in many ways, from their delayed entries into the NHL and their successes in international play at the junior and senior levels, to the concussions and lengthy stays on the injury lists that have plagued them.

Lindros, The Next One, is a Darth Vader-like Dark Menace on the ice, his six-feet, five-inch, two hundred and forty-pound body pounding opponents into submission as he leads the aptly named Legion of Doom into the NHL wars. That image thrusts his prodigious skills into the background.

Like Béliveau and Gretzky before him, his arrival in the NHL had been long-awaited when he was drafted in 1991 by the Quebec Nordiques. Unlike his predecessors, he resolutely refused to join Quebec and played a year of international hockey with Canada's 1992 Olympic team, silver medalists at Albertville, France. More agonizing for the staunch Quebec fans, the eighteen-year-old played for Team Canada in the 1991 Canada Cup, playing games in Montreal and Quebec where fans implored him to change his mind to no avail. If he was frustrated by the contract impasse that fall, he took it out on the opposition, knocking Martin Rucinsky of Czechoslovakia and Sweden's Ulf Samuelsson out of the tournament with thunderous hits.

Lindros's recalcitrance forced the Nordiques to deal him the following summer and that also turned out to be high drama as two teams, the Flyers and the Rangers, each claimed that he had been dealt to them. It took a special mediator to move him to Philadelphia, in exchange for a raft of players, draft choices and cash.

Kariya also delayed his entry into the NHL, playing a season with the Canadian national team in preparation for the Lillehammer Olympic Games before joining the Anaheim Mighty Ducks. A speedster with a devastating shot and superior play-making abilities, the Japanese Canadian was the first freshman to win the NCAA's Hobey Baker Award as outstanding U.S. college player after he led the University of Maine to the championship in 1993.

Whatever doubts about his diminutive size (five-feet, nine inches, one hundred and seventy pounds) were dispelled when he joined the Mighty Ducks. In his second season, he scored fifty goals and fifty-eight assists and was selected to the NHL's first All-Star team at left wing, while winning the Lady Byng Trophy as the league's most gentlemanly player.

While Lindros' arrival in the NHL was the culmination of a program to nurture huge players, Kariya's success balanced things out, turning NHL scouts and teams on to the merits of smaller, skilled players. Both are proof that Canada can still produce superstars, even though that ratio has fallen.

GM Craig Patrick with

coach Herb Brooks *(right)*

and coach Craig Patrick

with his Rangers in

1980-81 *(below)*

Craig Patrick and the Lake Placid team paved the way for the increased numbers of U.S. players. He played an even larger role in the introduction of U.S.-trained coaches. In 1980, he was hired as director of operations for the New York Rangers, under GM Fred Shero, and coached the team for sixty games that season. Speculation that summer was that the Rangers' job was Herb Brooks' for the asking, but when no offer was forthcoming, the Minnesotan headed overseas for a season in Switzerland.

When Craig took over as Rangers' general manager in June, 1981, the youngest man (thirty-five) to fill the post, and the third Patrick, he immediately tabbed Brooks as his man, even though there were reservations in some quarters.

"I felt he was the best coach available and the fact that Herb came from college ranks didn't change my decision," Patrick recalled. *"Herb was aware of the 'college coach' thing, and might have felt uneasy about it a little bit. I think there were times when he over-reacted a bit because he felt that people only saw him as a college coach, but he did a good job for us."*

In three full seasons, and part of a fourth, Brooks took the Rangers to the division final twice, and semi-final once. When it appeared that the team wasn't responding any more, he was let go in the middle of the 1984-85 season. He would return to school hockey with St. Cloud State, and then eventually the NHL with the New Jersey Devils and the Minnesota North Stars. Herb Brooks and Craig Patrick would reunite within the Pittsburgh organization in the late 1990s.

Patrick served as Rangers general manager through the 1985-86 season, until he was replaced by Phil Esposito, and returned to his *alma mater* as Athletics Director at the University of Denver for two years. There was still a Patrick presence in the league. Muzz Patrick's son Dick was in the Washington Capitals organization (he would serve as team president and governor in the late 1990s), and it would not be long before Craig returned.

In December, 1989, Craig Patrick's biggest NHL adventure began when he took over as general manager and coach of the Pittsburgh Penguins, replacing Tony Esposito and Gene Ubriaco in those posts.

"When I first got to Pittsburgh, everyone wanted to know who I had in mind to coach," Patrick said. *"Truth be told, I had nobody in mind at that point, so I coached the team until the end of the season until we decided what we wanted. I knew in February what kind of coach we needed, and who I wanted."*

The right man for the job was another U.S.-trained college coach, Bob Johnson. "Badger Bob", as he was known, came out of high school and college ranks in Minnesota to take over the University of Wisconsin team for fifteen years, winning three NCAA titles along the way and coaching such rising NHL stars as Chris Chelios and Gary Suter.

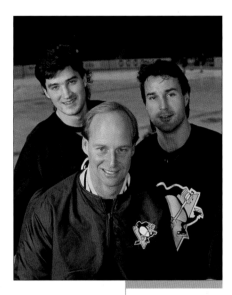

Mario Lemieux, Craig
Patrick and Paul Coffey

In 1982, he was appointed head coach of the Calgary Flames and it was generally acknowledged that he had done a stellar job, taking his team to the 1986 Stanley Cup final, eliminating the powerful Edmonton Oilers along the way. A season after his Flames had lost to the Canadiens in five games, Bob Johnson returned to amateur hockey, accepting a job as executive director of USA Hockey.

"I called Bob at USA Hockey and said, 'You're the guy I want.' He was reluctant at first because it was an important job, and his programs were starting to show results," said Patrick. *"He was what we needed. His demeanor and teaching ability were important, especially with a young Pittsburgh team that included players from all over, and a strong nucleus built around Mario Lemieux, Larry Murphy, Paul Coffey and Tom Barrasso. I needed a coach with Bob's communication skills and knowledge of the game. There might have been other people like that somewhere, but at the time he was at a premium."*

Badger Bob came aboard, and in one of those bittersweet stories, led the Penguins to a Stanley Cup in the spring of 1991. It was bittersweet because Bob Johnson, whose son Mark had been on the Miracle on Ice team in 1980, died of brain disease the following November. Craig Patrick had ensured the Cup victory with the first of many astute trades as Pittsburgh GM, sending John Cullen, Zarley Zalapski and Jeff Parker to Hartford for Ron Francis, Ulf Samuelsson and Grant Jennings, at the trading deadline on March 4.

The following season, veteran coach Scotty Bowman took over the reins. He had served as director of player personnel for the Pens during the previous year, and slid into the coaching job with nary a hitch. The team, still devastated by the death of their former coach, struggled during the season, playing only seven games above .500. Another late-season deal acquired forward Rick Tocchet, goalie Ken Wregget and defenseman Kjell Samuelsson from Philadelphia in return for Mark Recchi, Brian Benning and a flip of draft choices. Three months later, the Penguins had a second Stanley Cup.

March 30, 1988

Edmonton's Grant Fuhr sets an NHL record for games played by a goalie in a season, appearing in his seventy-fourth game and eclipsing Philadelphia goalie Bernie Parent's mark of seventy-three, set in 1973-74. Oilers defeat Minnesota 6-3.

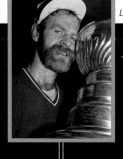

Lanny McDonald

◄ Calgary Flames beat the Canadiens 4-2 to win the 1989 Stanley Cup Championship; the first time ever that the Canadiens lose a final series on home ice.

May 25, 1989

The Sutters

Brother acts have been a common phenomenon through NHL history. There is a lengthy list of two siblings who made it, a few trios (Bob, Bill and Barclay Plager; the Hunters, Mark, Dave and Dale; Charlie, Lionel and Roy Conacher and a foursome (Frank, George, Bob and Bill Boucher).

But Grace and Louis Sutter of Viking, Alberta, were the top producers of hockey players. Six of their sons, Brian, Duane, Darryl, Brent and the twins, Rich and Ron, had good NHL careers. The eldest in the family of seven sons, Gary, did not try for a hockey career but, as Brent said: *"Gary would have made it because, when we were young, he was the best of us all."*

Rich and Ron

Brian was the first Sutter to make the NHL with the St. Louis Blues, then progressed to coaching with the Blues, Boston Bruins and Calgary Flames. Darryl played with the Chicago Blackhawks and later coached that team and the San Jose Sharks.

Duane was a member of the New York Islanders' four Stanley Cup winners in the 1980s and Brent his mate for two wins with the Isles. Both finished their careers with the Blackhawks. Rich and Ron were with several teams in the NHL.

Not blessed with large amounts of natural talent, the Sutter brothers had determination, hard work and aggressiveness as their strong points. They were not big men, but that did not discourage them from taking on all comers. Their approach saw them all suffer injuries.

"The Sutter boys' flaw, if you can call it that, is that they all play the game as if they were forty pounds heavier than they are," said Jacques Demers, a long-time NHL coach who had Brian with the Blues. *"They all weighed in the one hundred and seventy to one hundred and eighty-pound range but went into the corners like they were two hundred and twenty-five. That leads to injuries."*

Their mother had a slightly different look at the careers of her half dozen offspring.

"They did well in hockey, but to me, as a mother, the best part was that they had good manners and never have been in any trouble," Grace Sutter once said.

Brent vs Brian

Coach Darryl Sutter and brother Duane catch the action

June 17, 1989

Mats Sundin of Sweden is the first player selected (by Quebec Nordiques) in the NHL Amateur Entry Draft held at the Metropolitan Sports Center in Bloomington, MN. This marks the first time that a European player is the top pick in the draft.

Mario Lemieux was a gifted, tremendous athlete who played the game a lot different than anyone else

Did it mean anything to Craig Patrick that he had won a Cup at the management level, as his grandfather had, but a feat that had eluded his father and uncle?

"Muzz and Lynn did great jobs, but unfortunately didn't win the Cup," he replied. *"One thing I've learned in NHL management is that you've got to be fortunate to win."*

The twin championships ushered in the 1990s, and it appeared that the Penguins were set for several more, like the Oilers before them, when misfortune struck. By this time, the huge talent of Mario Lemieux had even eclipsed that of Wayne Gretzky, and the Penguins were expected to add one or two more Stanley Cups to their trophy case. In the spring of 1993, those hopes came crashing down when the Islanders upset them in the playoffs, only to lose to the eventual champion Montreal Canadiens. The New York upset was a minor tremor compared to a previous shock that rocked the team.

"I always felt that anyone who's been around the Penguins has to feel blessed to have been able to watch Mario Lemieux, day-in, day-out, all those years," said Patrick. *"He was a gifted, tremendous athlete who played the game a lot different than anyone else. I didn't get a chance to be near Jean Béliveau and all the other greats... but I can't imagine anyone ever having been better."* As it turned out, the six-foot, four-inch superstar was fragile.

In the first Cup season, Patrick had secured the services of Ron Francis in the late-season trade because he wasn't certain if Super Mario would be available. That season, surgery to repair a herniated disk had limited Lemieux's season to only twenty-six games. He would play almost that many in the playoffs, scoring sixteen goals and forty-four points in twenty-three post-season contests. Sixty and sixty-four game seasons followed before disaster struck.

In January of 1993, bothered by a lump in his neck, Mario underwent tests and the results were devastating. He had Hodgkin's disease, a specialized form of lymphatic cancer. The good news was that the average survival rate was eighty-one per cent, and if the condition were caught early, as in his case, those odds increased into the high nineties. Treatment was a combination of radiation and chemotherapy and days after the announcement, Super Mario was officially a cancer patient.

He underwent radiation on February 2, and doctors refused to allow him to return to play when he made the request. On March 1, he underwent a second radiation treatment at two o'clock in Pittsburgh, got on a plane to Philadelphia, and was in the opening line-up when the game started shortly after seven-thirty. He received a ninety-second standing ovation from the fiercely partisan Flyers fans, and scored a goal and an assist in Pittsburgh's 5-4 loss. Lemieux still managed an astonishing one hundred and sixty points in only sixty games that season, taking the scoring championship, but his physical woes would catch up with him.

We all lived and died with Mario
through the hard times, and that made it all
the more special to see what he accomplished
when he could make it out onto the ice

In 1993-94, more back problems including a herniated muscle sidelined him for all but twenty-two games, and in August 1994, the message that everyone had dreaded, came. With doctors flanking him at a special news conference, Mario Lemieux announced he was taking a year's medical leave, and sat out the entire 1994-95 campaign.

He returned for two more seasons, playing seventy and seventy-six games and scoring one hundred and sixty-one and one hundred and twenty-two points respectively, leading the league both times. His health a prime concern despite his young age, thirty-two, he retired at the end of the 1996-97 season, with six hundred and thirteen goals and one thousand, four hundred and ninety-four points, in a mere seven hundred and forty-five games over thirteen seasons.

"We all lived and died with Mario through the hard times, and that made it all the more special to see what he accomplished when he could make it out onto the ice," said Craig Patrick.

"I think we can all honestly say that we've never seen such a talent in this league, and we probably won't ever again."

The man who had saved the franchise in Pittsburgh was gone, and he'd be called upon to do it again two years later.

January 12, 1992

NHL history is made when the New Jersey Devils use four Russian-born players (Vyacheslav Fetisov, Alexei Kasatonov, Valeri Zelepukin, and rookie Alexander Semak) in a 5-2 win over the Kings, in New Jersey.

Pittsburgh Penguins beat Chicago 6-5 in game four of the final to repeat as Stanley Cup champions. It was their eleventh straight playoff victory.

June 1, 1992

Montreal Canadiens beat the Los Angeles Kings 4-1 at the Forum in Montreal, to win the 1993 Stanley Cup Championship in five games. Patrick Roy wins the Conn Smythe Trophy as playoffs MVP.

Toronto's Mike Gartner scores twice to become the first player in NHL history to score thirty or more goals in fifteen straight seasons; in the Leafs' 6-3 win over visiting Quebec.

June 9, 1993

Meanwhile, change ravaged the NHL, on the ice and off. As mentioned earlier in this chapter, the league had gone multi-national, on the ice at least. A generation after Canadians had basked in the glory of "Us versus Them" confrontations with the Soviets, the Soviet Union was no more. Russian hockey stars were fan favorites throughout the league, as popular and recognizable as the top Canadian and American players.

Scotty Bowman, who had coached the Canadiens against the Central Red Army team on the memorable New Year's Eve in Montreal, and later the NHL All-Stars against the Soviet Union at the Challenge Cup in 1979, made that point dramatically on the night of October 27, 1995. Five of his Red Wings hopped over the boards for a powerplay that night: Vladimir Konstantinov and Vyacheslav Fetisov were on defense, while Igor Larionov, Slava Kozlov and Sergei Fedorov were up front. All five had once played for Central Red Army. On this night, it was a curiosity.

By 1999, hockey fans north of the world's longest undefended border regularly bemoaned a shortage of Canadians in the league. In October, the National Hockey League released its latest country-of-origin figures that showed that Canadians now comprised fifty-six per cent of NHL players, down from ninety-seven per cent when the league doubled in size to twelve teams in 1967. It was the first time that the proportion of Canadian pros in the league had dipped below sixty per cent.

The numbers served to recall the changing face of the game, even though they weren't new; the proportion of Canadian players in the league had been stable for about five years. Also stable was the percentage of American-born players, at sixteen per cent of the total.

The rising power was the Czech Republic with fifty players, with another ten from Slovakia. At the start of the 1999-2000 season, there were forty-seven Russians, thirty-seven Swedes and twenty Finns in the league, and an assortment of players from other countries, including Germany, Kazakhstan and Belarus.

The New Europeans

Alexei Yashin

The necessity of stocking European players to produce a successful team was a fact of NHL life at the end of the 1990s, their integration into the game's thinking complete.

Not only were the Europeans needed to lift team skill levels, they were among the league's top scorers (seven of the top twelve in points in the 1998-99 season, leading point-getter on eleven teams), major box office draws and team leaders. Europeans were named captains of five teams – Swedes Mats Sundin (Toronto) and Kenny Jonsson (Islanders), the Czech Republic's Jaromir Jagr (Pittsburgh), Russian Alexei Yashin (Ottawa) and Finn Saku Koivu (Montreal).

In the twenty NHL seasons from 1979-80 to 1998-99, only one Stanley Cup championship team, the 1992-93 Canadiens, did not have a European player on the roster. Every other Cup winner over the two decades had Europeans in key roles, including the 1985-86 Canadiens with Swedes Mats Naslund and Kjell Dahlin, and Czech Petr Svoboda.

Saku Koivu

"European players are no longer an 'issue' in NHL thinking, but an integral part of team building, the same as players from Canada and the U.S.," said Bill Torrey, president of the Florida Panthers, and architect of the Islanders' four-straight dynasty in the early 1980s that integrated five players from Sweden into its line-up.

"The integration is total now. Back in the late 1970s, a few teams added a Swede or a Finn to fill in a hole in the roster and lift their level of skill. Now our team lists contain only the names of hockey players, with no reference to nationality. The league has expanded considerably (seven new teams in the 1990s) and maintained a high level of play because the Russian, Czech, Slovakian and other Iron Curtain players became available early in the decade."

The World Hockey Association, competing with an established league for players, opened the door wide to players from Sweden and Finland during the 1970s, and both dominant teams in the 1980s, the Islanders and Oilers, had Europeans in prominent roles.

That the NHL has become a "world" league heading into the new century is demonstrated by six Europeans on the league's first and second All-Star teams in 1998-99, sixteen Europeans in the twenty-eight first-round selections in the 1999 Entry Draft, and a "World versus North America" format in the annual All-Star game. Three of the four contenders for the 1998-99 Hart Trophy as the league's Most Valuable Player were Europeans – MVP Jagr, Yashin, Dominik Hasek of the Buffalo Sabres (MVP the two previous seasons), and Teemu Selanne of the Anaheim Mighty Ducks.

Hasek also led the ascension of European goalies into Number One positions on NHL teams. Nikolai Khabibulin (Phoenix), Roman Turek (St. Louis), Arturs Irbe (Carolina) and Tommy Salo (Edmonton) followed as the main men in the nets for their teams.

On the blue line, such men as Niklas Lidstrom (Detroit), Sergei Zubov (Dallas), Alexei Zhitnik (Buffalo), Sandis Ozolinsh (Colorado) and Vladimir Malakhov (Montreal), were in the front ranks. Any list of the league's most exciting forwards would include Jagr, Selanne, Sundin, Yashin, Peter Forsberg (Colorado), Pavel Bure (Florida), Sergei Fedorov and Slava Kozlov of Detroit.

Teemu Selanne

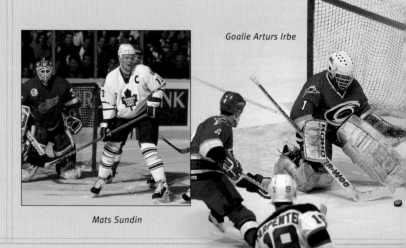
Goalie Arturs Irbe

Mats Sundin

The Dominator

Explore the textbook on the proper way to play goal in the NHL, and there's simply no slot in it for Dominik Hasek, who has perhaps the most unorthodox style in NHL history. But that has not prevented him from becoming "The Dominator."

"The only thing Hasek does right by the goaltenders' book is stop the puck," said John Muckler, former GM of the Buffalo Sabres.

Stand-up approach? Forget it. The butterfly style? What's that? But armed with an extraordinary set of reflexes and a large amount of athletic ability, Hasek has achieved great heights in the goaltending profession.

Hasek falls down a great deal, doesn't handle the puck especially well on his daring safaris out of the net to field it and loses his stick more times than any goalie. He often drops his stick and uses his blocker hand to smother the puck, eschewing the catching hand approach of other goalies.

"I don't think much about how I might look playing goal," Hasek said. *"My job is to keep the puck out of the net, and I'll do it any way I can."*

In his NHL career of four hundred and fourteen games through the 1998-99 season, mainly with the Buffalo Sabres, Hasek had a 2.26 goals against average, lowering that mark to 2.05 in fifty-six playoff games. He was the first goalie to win the Hart Trophy as most valuable NHL player since Jacques Plante in 1962 when he collected it in both 1996-97 and 1997-98.

Another Hasek career highlight came in the 1998 Olympics in Japan when he backed his homeland's gold medal victory in the NHL's first participation in the Games. Hasek had an average of 0.97 in six games and stopped all five Canadian shootout tries.

Born in Pardubice, Czechoslovakia, Hasek was playing for his hometown in that country's major league at sixteen and on the national team a year later.

THE GREAT ONE COMETH

Whatever the nationality of the players, and the prejudices, or not, of the fans, some of the best hockey ever was played in the fourth quarter of the century. Gordie Howe and Bobby Hull both retired from the Whalers after a curtain call in 1979-80, a year after the injury-plagued career of Bobby Orr came to a premature end. The succession was assured, however, as a raft of superb talents were igniting hockey passions throughout the league.

The incomparable Guy Lafleur, Bob Gainey and Larry Robinson held sway in Montreal, while the talented trio of Denis Potvin, Bryan Trottier and Mike Bossy filled the Nassau Coliseum for a decade. Darryl Sittler, Lanny McDonald and Borje Salming galvanized Maple Leaf Gardens in the late 1970s as the Espositos, Ratelles, Gilberts, Parks, Middletons, and Dionnes held sway elsewhere into the 1980s.

And then came The Great One and Mario the Magnificent. Wayne Gretzky and Mario Lemieux took a back seat to no one from the previous eras of the game. Both were magnificently skilled players who teamed up with gifted teammates from both sides of the Atlantic throughout the 1980s and '90s.

Wayne Gretzky was the story of professional ice hockey in the fourth quarter of the twentieth century. Canada was first introduced to him as a tow-headed, four-foot, four-inch novice (ten years old) in 1971-72 who scored an incredible three hundred and seventy-eight goals, to go along with one hundred and thirty-nine assists, as a member of the Brantford Nadrofsky Steelers in the Ontario Minor Hockey Association. That earned him television interviews and a meeting with his idol, Gordie Howe.

The hockey world followed his progression after that, the skinny Brantford kid routinely playing with players five and six years his senior. His breakout year was 1976 when, as a member of the Sault Ste. Marie Greyhounds, he also played for the Canadian junior team in the world championship in Montreal and Quebec City, and was top scorer, although Canada finished fourth.

September 30, 1994

The Mighty Ducks of Anaheim set NHL records for most victories (thirty-three) and most road wins (nineteen) by a first-year team as they win 3-1 in Vancouver.

NHL Commissioner Gary Bettman announces the postponement of the start of the 1994-95 NHL season, due to a labor dispute between the NHL's owners and players.

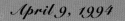
April 9, 1994

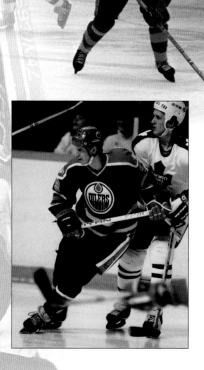

Wayne Gretzky was the story
of professional ice hockey
in the fourth quarter
of the twentieth century

A year later, at seventeen, Wayne Gretzky was a professional, scoring one hundred and ten points in only sixty games in the World Hockey Association, a season shared between stints with the Indianapolis Racers and the Edmonton Oilers. Spindly legged, barely one hundred and fifty pounds soaking wet, and younger looking even than his teenage years, Gretzky moved to the National Hockey League with what remained of the WHA in the fall of 1979. Here the hyperbole would end; here The Kid would be playing with (the real) Big Boys, on a not-so-strong team, and reality would prove to be a stern mistress.

Someone forgot to tell The Kid. He took his herky-jerky style and weird wind-up for his slap shot to hockey's fastest and strongest league, tied established star Marcel Dionne for the league scoring title (finishing ahead of Guy Lafleur, *et al* in the process) and was awarded the Hart Trophy as the NHL's MVP.

Wayne Gretzky would go on to have the National Hockey League's most successful career in terms of pure offense, win four Stanley Cups with the Oilers, and put more fans in seats in North American arenas than the fabulous Gordie Howe (his idol) and Maurice Richard combined. There would be two hundred-point seasons, there would be a season of ninety-two goals, there would be a career of three thousand points (!!! – one exclamation point per thousand, The Kid earned it), but nothing would surpass that first year when the skinny blond guy who barely qualified for his driver's license, won the Hart Trophy.

How quickly would he take over the NHL? Ask Richard Sévigny, the Canadiens back-up goalie who, showing loyalty to his guy, stated that Guy Lafleur would put Gretzky "into his back pocket" in their best-of-five playoff series in 1981. Wayne (as he would be known from then on) merely set a playoff record for assists (five) in the first game of the series at the Forum and engineered a sweep of the mighty Habs.

Later that year, there was a contretemps, as Gretzky and his mates were humiliated 8-1 by the Soviets in the final of the Canada Cup. The Great One bounced back with a vengeance, obliterating the Rocket's fifty goals in fifty games mark by reaching the half-century mark in game thirty-nine, on his fifth goal of the night, and then almost doubling that total with ninety-two on the season (and two hundred and twelve total points).

March 25, 1995

Detroit's Scotty Bowman becomes the first coach in the NHL to record nine hundred career victories, when the Red Wings beat the Canucks 2-1 in Vancouver, improving Bowman's lifetime record to 900-417-236.

The Quebec Nordiques franchise is given approval by the NHL Board of Governors to move to Denver. The team will later be re-named the Colorado Avalanche.

June 21, 1995

Igor Larionov and Slava Fetisov

Red Wings make history by playing five former Soviet Union players (Vyacheslav Fetisov, Vladimir Konstantinov, Igor Larionov, Sergei Fedorov and Vyacheslav Kozlov) as a unit during a 3-0 win at Calgary. All five had played for Central Red Army.

In August, 1988, Peter Pocklington guaranteed that he would graduate from the most-hated man in Alberta to the most-hated man in Canada when he traded/sold The Great One to the Los Angeles Kings. In the long run, it was a beneficial move for the league as Gretzky revived a moribund franchise in the second largest media market in the U.S. He would take the Kings to a Stanley Cup final in 1993, losing to the Canadiens, and then move on to St. Louis and the Rangers before retiring. Pocklington would get his back, as his Gretzky-less Oilers would win the Stanley Cup in 1990.

The spindly legs never went away, nor did the shirt-tucked-in-on-the-right-side-of-his-pants, a style copied by thousands of minor hockey stars around the world. The Gretzkys became Canadian royalty, all known by their first name; paterfamilias Walter, wife Janet, kids Ty, Paulina and Trevor, brothers Brent and Keith.

On April 18, 1999, with all of North American looking on and agonizing over every shift, The Great One played his last game in the National Hockey League, a 2-1 overtime loss to the Penguins at Madison Square Garden. Late in the game, trailing 1-0, Gretzky set up the Rangers' lone goal of the contest and millions of hockey fans expelled a continent-wide sigh of relief. It was point number two thousand, eight hundred and fifty-seven in regular season play, but it outweighed all of its predecessors. It meant that The Great One could go out in a manner to which he was accustomed.

Just prior to the game, NHL Commissioner Gary Bettman announced that from the end of the New York game onwards, no player in the league would ever again wear number 99.

It seemed fair.

Gretzky and Lemieux were the centerpieces of the National Hockey League, but there was much more for sports fans in the 1980s and '90s.

Wayne Gretzky Career Highlights

January 26, 1961
Wayne Gretzky is born in Brantford, Ont.

November 2, 1978
After eight games with the Indianapolis Racers of the WHA, Gretzky is sold to the Edmonton Oilers (along with Eddie Mio and Peter Driscoll). Gretzky goes on to score one hundred and four points in seventy-two games and is named WHA Rookie of the Year.

October 10, 1979
Edmonton Oilers rookie Wayne Gretzky plays in his first NHL game, and picks up an assist in a 4-2 loss to Chicago.

February 24, 1980
He becomes the first player in NHL history to score one hundred points in a season before his twentieth birthday, as well as reach the century mark in his first NHL season. His one hundredth career point is an assist in his sixty-first career game, a 4-2 Oilers loss to Boston.

April 2, 1980
Gretzky becomes the first teenager to score fifty goals in a season, when the nineteen-year-old tallies for the Oilers in their 1-1 tie against Minnesota, at Northlands Coliseum.

February 14, 1981
Wayne Gretzky overtakes L.A.'s Marcel Dionne in the 1980-81 scoring race, and goes on to win the Art Ross Trophy as the NHL's top scorer this season – and for each of the next six years.

March 29, 1981
Edmonton's Wayne Gretzky breaks Phil Esposito's NHL record for most points in a season (one hundred and fifty-two) with three assists in a 4-2 Oilers win at Detroit.

April 1, 1981
He breaks Bobby Orr's single season record for assists, with his one hundred and fourth of the season, in a 4-4 Oilers tie with the Colorado Rockies. Gretzky would finish the season with a record one hundred and nine assists.

December 27, 1981
In his thirty-eighth game of the season, Wayne Gretzky scores a hat trick to record the fastest one hundred points in NHL history, in a 10-3 Oilers win over the Kings, in Edmonton.

December 30, 1981
Wayne Gretzky scores five goals in the Oilers 7-5 win over the Flyers, to reach fifty goals in thirty-nine games, shattering Maurice Richard's record of fifty goals in fifty games, which had been tied by Mike Bossy.

February 24, 1982
Gretzky beats Don Edwards for his seventy-seventh goal of the season, surpassing Phil Esposito's previous mark. Gretzky has a hat trick on this night, and goes on to score ninety-two goals for the season. Oilers win 6-3 at Buffalo.

March 25, 1982
Wayne Gretzky has two goals and two assists to become the first player in NHL history to score two hundred points in a season. The four points in a 7-2 win over Calgary give Gretzky two hundred and three points for the campaign.

October 5, 1983
Gretzky scores a goal and an assist during a 5-4 win over Toronto in the 1983-84 season opener. It is the beginning of an NHL-record, fifty-one-game scoring streak.

May 19, 1984
He scores two goals and an assist as the Edmonton Oilers beat the Islanders 5-2 in game five of the final, becoming the 1984 Stanley Cup champions – and the first former WHA team to win the Stanley Cup.

December 19, 1984
While playing in his four hundred and twenty-fourth career game, Gretzky has two goals and four assists to become the fastest player to reach one thousand career points, breaking Guy Lafleur's record of seven hundred and twenty games. The Oilers beat the visiting Kings, 7-3.

April 9, 1987
Edmonton sets a Stanley Cup playoff record for most goals in a game, defeating L.A. 13-3, in game two of the Smythe Division semi-finals. Wayne Gretzky has six assists in the game, including his one hundred and seventy-seventh career playoff point, to pass Jean Béliveau and move into first place on the all-time playoff scoring list.

March 1, 1988
Gretzky picks up a first-period assist to extend his career total to one thousand and fifty, overtaking Gordie Howe as the NHL's all-time leader in career assists. Howe had one thousand and forty-nine in twenty-six years, while Gretzky passed him in nine years. Oilers beat the Kings 5-3.

May 26, 1988
He plays his final game as an Edmonton Oiler in a 6-3 win over Boston, as the Oilers win the Stanley Cup for the fourth time in five years. Gretzky wins the Conn Smythe Trophy with forty-three points in nineteen playoff games.

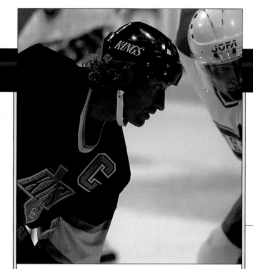

August 9, 1988

In a blockbuster, Wayne Gretzky, Mike Krushelnyski and Marty McSorley are traded to the Kings from Edmonton in exchange for Jimmy Carson, Martin Gélinas, three first-round draft choices (1989, 1991, 1993) and cash.

April 24, 1989

Wayne Gretzky scores his eighty-sixth career playoff goal, passing Mike Bossy who held the previous record. The Kings lose 5-3 to Calgary in game four of the Smythe Division final.

June 6, 1989

The Great One becomes the first player in NHL history to win the same award nine times when he is named the recipient of the Hart Trophy after his first season with the Los Angeles Kings.

October 26, 1990

He is the first player in NHL history to reach the two thousand-point milestone, with an assist in the Kings' 6-2 loss at Winnipeg. Gretzky's career stats at this juncture total six hundred and eighty-four goals and one thousand, three hundred and sixteen assists, in eight hundred and fifty-seven NHL games.

March 14, 1991

Wayne Gretzky sets an NHL record with an assist in his eighteenth consecutive game – breaking the mark he shared with Paul Coffey.

April 20, 1992

Gretzky picks up four assists to become the first player in NHL history to record three hundred career playoff points, in an 8-5 Kings win over the Oilers, in game two of the Smythe Division semi-final, in Los Angeles.

May 7, 1993

He scores twice to become the first player in NHL history to score one hundred play-off goals. Gretzky also adds an assist to lead the Kings to a 7-4 win over the Canucks, in game three of the Smythe Division final.

May 29, 1993

Gretzky sets a Stanley Cup record with his eighth career playoff hat trick, and adds an assist to lead the Kings to a 5-4 win over the Leafs in game seven of the Campbell Conference final.

March 23, 1994

Gretzky scores career goal number eight hundred and two, surpassing Gordie Howe as the league's all-time leading goal scorer. It comes in his 15th NHL season, as the Kings lose 6-3 to Vancouver at the Forum.

March 18, 1996

St. Louis' Wayne Gretzky scores his one thousandth pro hockey goal (including NHL, WHA, regular season and playoffs), in a 3-1 Blues win at Los Angeles, to join Gordie Howe and Bobby Hull in a very exclusive club.

July 21, 1996

New York Rangers announce the signing of free agent Wayne Gretzky.

December 1, 1996

Gretzky is the first player in NHL history to reach the three thousand-point plateau (including playoffs), with an assist in the Rangers' 6-2 win over the Canadiens, at MSG.

October 26, 1997

Wayne Gretzky picks up two assists in the Rangers 3-3 tie with Anaheim, at MSG, surpassing Gordie Howe's previous record of one thousand, eight hundred and fifty helpers.

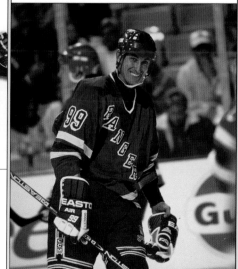

March 29, 1999

The Great One scores his one thousand and seventy-second all-time goal, surpassing Gordie Howe as the leading scorer in pro hockey history (twenty NHL seasons and one season in WHA) as the Rangers defeat the visiting Islanders, 6-2.

April 29, 1999

The Hockey Hall of Fame selection committee votes unanimously to waive the traditional three-year waiting period for induction for Wayne Gretzky, who had retired eleven days earlier.

The Rivalries

Called *La Guerre* and the Uncivil War, these rivalries kept Quebeckers and Albertans keenly interested on cold winter nights.

Both similarities and differences existed in the Quebec Nordiques vs Montreal Canadiens, and Calgary Flames vs Edmonton Oilers squabbles that peaked in the 1980s.

The Oilers and Nordiques had toiled in the relative anonymity of the World Hockey Association and resented coming to the National Hockey League hat-in-hand for the 1979 merger of the leagues. Other similarities are that both rivalries took some time to stoke, then became fires almost impossible to extinguish; and each had a David-and-Goliath context, Calgary and Quebec's David to Edmonton (Wayne Gretzky) and Montreal's Goliath (Guy Lafleur) and the long shadow of the Forum).

Hot Quebec Nights

La Guerre had everything; teams owned by rival breweries, the established vs. the new, "English" vs "French", and a new outlet for three centuries of animosity between the old capital and the metropolis. Quebec City could never forgive the Canadiens for taking two favored sons, Jean Béliveau and Guy Lafleur in earlier decades, and resented the taunts of Montrealers that in the WHA, the Nords toiled in an inferior league as had previous Quebec teams in the minors.

When the Nordiques won the WHA's Avco Cup in 1977, it created only a small ripple because the Canadiens had just won their second of what would be four consecutive Stanley Cups. Quebec fans clamored for a Canadiens-Nordiques series, but Montreal fans ridiculed the idea.

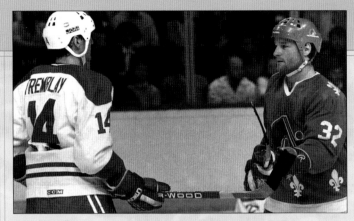

Mario Tremblay vs Dale Hunter

When the Nordiques did enter the NHL, it took two seasons before the rivalry heated up, and that happened when the teams moved to the same division in 1981-82. The Nords had drafted well with young stars Dale Hunter, Buddy Cloutier, and Michel Goulet, surrounded them with quality veterans like Marc Tardif, Andre Savard, and Tony McKegney, and then acquired the catalysts for a decade of success when they spirited Anton and Peter Stastny out of Czechoslovakia.

The Nordiques first win of note over Montreal came in overtime in the final game of their 1982 playoff, the first between the teams. Hunter circled the net and somehow snuck the puck under the pad of the Canadiens' goalie Rick Walmsley, a goal that still is a rumor.

In the teams' most emotional game – the 1984 Good Friday Massacre – the Canadiens eliminated the Nordiques. Quebec had a 2-0 lead late in the second period of the sixth game at the Forum, a return to Le Colisée likely, when a riot broke out. The main instigator was Quebec's Louis Sleigher, a former Canadiens draft choice who sucker-punched Montreal defenseman Jean Hamel, an original Nordique. An all-out brawl ensued, the period ended early, but the game misconducts assessed to several players on both teams were not announced until the teams came out for the third period. That led to a second brawl, fuelled by players who had been ejected from the game.

Montreal came back with four unanswered goals, two by Steve Shutt, to win the series. A year later, Quebec won a dandy confrontation on Peter Stastny's game-seven overtime goal at the Forum.

The Canadiens won the last two playoff rounds against their provincial rivals, including a 1993 six-game series en route to the Stanley Cup, after the Nordiques had won the first two games. The Nordiques missed the playoffs a year later, and then lost to the Rangers in 1995 before moving to Colorado.

Montreal scores!

Wayne and Jari

Oil on Troubled Waters

Images from The Uncivil War are just as vivid. Gretzky, Kurri, Coffey and Messier celebrated win after win by the Oilers in the 1980s, interrupted by a few shining moments for the Flames.

An enduring scene is the anguished expression on Edmonton rookie defenseman Steve Smith seconds after his errant clearing attempt went into his own net off the back of Grant Fuhr's leg, eliminating the Oilers in a seventh game in 1986.

The Oilers flattened the Flames the next spring, but the Calgarians earned bragging rights with a 1989 Stanley Cup win, a last hurrah for the Flames' popular Lanny McDonald. The only way the triumph could have been more satisfying was if the Flames had ousted the Oilers to reach the peak.

Lanny McDonald

The teams met in their most recent playoff series in 1991, a bitter, grinding match-up won in seventh-game overtime by the Oilers. Especially galling for Flames fans was the fact that Calgary won game six in overtime in Edmonton, only to have the Oilers repay the favor in the seventh game in Calgary.

The teams have met five times in post-season play, the Oilers winning four series, with three of those series decided in a seventh game. During the years from 1983 to 1991, Alberta teams won the Stanley Cup six times.

It has been a decade since the last Calgary-Edmonton post-season acrimony. However, unlike the mothballed Montreal-Quebec hostilities, hope "springs" eternal for a Battle of Alberta each year.

Islanders-Rangers, Canadiens-Nordiques and Flames-Oilers face-offs punctuated the special rivalries that kept fans warm in the depths of winter. At century's end, NHL hockey was in good shape on the ice: Teemu Selanne, Mike Modano, Jaromir Jagr, Dominik Hasek and Patrick Roy, Joe Sakic, Peter Forsberg, Mats Sundin, Chris Chelios, Raymond Bourque, Mark Messier, Jeremy Roenick, Keith Tkachuk, Paul Kariya, Eric Lindros and John LeClair all performed with distinction every night.

The game underwent its most significant change off the ice, however.

Trevor Linden vs Mark Messier, 1994 Stanley Cup final

THE NHL GOES CORPORATE

When the National Hockey League's last decade of the twentieth century swung into action, only one rink from the Original Six era had been mothballed, Detroit's Olympia. Chicago Stadium, Boston Garden, the Forum, Maple Leaf Gardens and Madison Square Garden still were the centerpieces of their storied franchises. At the end of the same decade, however, only Madison Square remained and plans were under way for a spectacular mid-Manhattan entertainment center to meet the needs of the NBA Knicks, the Rangers and the myriad other events that keep MSG hopping year-round.

The names of the new facilities also spoke volumes about where professional sports had gone, and how it would be in the New Millennium: the United (airline) Center in Chicago, Boston's Fleet (bank) Center, Montreal's Molson (brewery) Centre and the Air Canada (airline) Centre in Toronto. Joining them around the circuit were the Marine Midland (bank) Arena in Buffalo, the Pepsi (soft drinks) Center in Denver, the National Car Rental Center in Miami, the Corel (computer software) Centre in Ottawa, the First Union (bank) Center in Philadelphia, the Kiel Center in St. Louis, San Jose Arena, Tampa Bay's Ice Palace, General Motors (automobiles) Place in Vancouver, and Washington's MCI (telecommunications) Center.

The entertainment palaces of the 1990s

As well, several existing arenas had been rechristened with corporate identities, including the Canadian Airlines Saddledome in Calgary, Edmonton's Skyreach (formerly Northlands Coliseum) Center, and New Jersey's Continental Airlines (Brendan Byrne) Arena.

NHL Commissioner
Gary Bettman

The era of the revenue stream had arrived, where to survive professional franchises had to "sell" their arenas to corporations, negotiate one-sided deals with revenue partners in three levels of government, and take over every cent of the entertainment dollar directed toward their events. It was the era of the corporate box, where the business community entertained lavishly in hotel suites that had somehow been "teleported" into the choicest locations of the modern arenas. The subsequent expense account feeding frenzy drove ticket prices for all seats around the "loges" sky high, and made it exceedingly difficult for middle-class hockey fans to buy single-game passes, let alone afford season's tickets.

Still, the NHL needed the full support of the business community to make ends meet, and managers would shake the money tree until every needle fell out.

Where the players had seen the pendulum swing back their way in the 1970s with the arrival of the World Hockey Association, what transpired in the early 1990s rocked the NHL to its core. A pair of labor disruptions in 1992 and 1994 contributed to a spiral of escalating salaries, which saw the league average climb to one million, three hundred thousand dollars in 1999, from the two hundred and fifty thousand dollars mean of 1990.

"I trace this process back to when the NHL Players' Association decided to make all salaries public," Patrick said. "From that point on, our finances have really been in trouble. We're trying to find more revenue to pay the salaries we're paying."

"I can understand why some players might get upset when somebody they think they're better than, and usually they are, was getting X amount of dollars, and they were getting less. That affected what we do in management. We kept giving the big money to them until there was nothing more to give."

NHLPA executive director
Bob Goodenow

Every franchise needed a new, multifunctional building to survive, to provide the revenues that were needed to keep pace with escalating salaries and costs.

Spanning the Continents

193

June 25, 1997

Detroit's Scotty Bowman records
his one thousandth NHL coaching
victory as the Red Wings win 6-5
in overtime, at Pittsburgh.

The National Hockey League officially approves
expansion to a thirty-team league by the year 2000,
with the announcement of new clubs in Nashville,
Atlanta, Columbus, and Minneapolis.

February 8, 1997

In Canada, that didn't always guarantee success. Early in the 1990s, there were eight Canadian franchises – Vancouver, Quebec, Montreal, Ottawa, Toronto, Winnipeg, Calgary and Edmonton. The Quebec and Winnipeg franchises were refused public help by several levels of government when they sought to build new facilities, and the teams moved to Colorado (Quebec) and Phoenix (Winnipeg) in mid-decade. Most poignant for diehard Nordiques' fans was the fact that the Colorado Avalanche won the Stanley Cup ten months after leaving Le Colisée.

Two teams, Edmonton and Calgary, invested millions of dollars in renovations to their buildings, while Ottawa, Montreal, Toronto and Vancouver all built new arenas. These moves didn't guarantee survival, as those franchises discovered by the end of the decade.

The Ottawa Senators, a revived franchise and one of the game's most exciting young teams, were poised to move to the United States at century's end, and there were fears that a similar fate could await other Canadian teams in Edmonton, Calgary and Vancouver. Unbelievable but true, some voices were even raised in Montreal about the long-term viability of the venerable Canadiens in the era of the sixty-eight cent Canadian dollar, especially considering what the team called an eleven-million-dollar annual municipal tax burden for the recently built Molson Centre.

Alexei Yashin, jumping in Ottawa

Saving Canada's Game

When the National Hockey League added the four surviving teams from the World Hockey Association in 1979, it was a major boost for the big league game in Canada. Quebec, Edmonton and Winnipeg joined Toronto, Montreal and Vancouver. The number expanded to eight when Atlanta moved to Calgary in 1980 and Ottawa joined in a 1992 expansion.

The situation for Canadian NHL teams was radically changed in the 1990s, however. Two teams (Quebec to Colorado in 1995, Winnipeg to Phoenix in '96) left Canada for financial reasons, nine teams were added in the U.S. "Sunbelt," and the only team remaining from the WHA merger was the Oilers.

The future was cloudy for Canadian teams at the end of the century, especially those in the "small" markets: Ottawa, Edmonton and Calgary. Two factors played a big role in the Canadian clubs' problems – the almost forty-per-cent gap between the Canadian dollar and its U.S. counterpart – and the tax situation faced by Canadian teams, as compared with that of their U.S. rivals.

Two expansion teams of the 1990s, Ottawa and Nashville, presented a stark contrast in the approaches taken by American and Canadian governments to new sports franchises. The Senators began play in the tiny Civic Centre when they joined the league, and built the two hundred million-dollar Palladium (later renamed the Corel Centre) in suburban Kanata in 1996. Because there was no access road to the property, the team also had to pay for one.

By 1999, the Senators had paid one hundred and sixty million dollars in taxes to all levels of government. In one season, 1998, the team and the building paid almost thirty-seven million dollars in taxes, while ticket revenues were only thirty-four million. Entertainment and property taxes in Ontario and Quebec were at fault. The Senators lost seven million dollars a year on average in the late 1990s, and the anticipated loss in 1999 was ten million.

The bluegrass was very much greener in Nashville in the same period. The city built an eighteen thousand, five hundred-seat arena in 1996, two years before the arrival of the Predators. At the hockey team's request, the city spent fourteen million dollars to remodel the facility, adding new corporate boxes, and then built a practice rink for the team, as well.

Home in Nashville

When the Predators joined the league, the city paid twenty-five per cent of the eighty million dollar expansion fee. The Predators keep all revenues from ticket sales, luxury boxes, rink board and scoreboard advertising, parking, and team merchandise, and forty per cent of concessions. None of the four new U.S.-based teams, Nashville, Atlanta, Minnesota and Columbus, pays property taxes.

The cost of Nashville's "annual rent" commitment was fifty thousand dollars.

Moreover, the cost of hockey players was lower in the United States. Most NHL players and their agents accepted lower salaries in the U.S. because the cost of living and income taxes were much lower, especially in Texas and Florida where there was no state income tax.

This imbalance led to the unbelievable in 1999; some hockey observers even labelling Montreal a "small market" team, and outgoing team president Ronald Corey, who was suing local government to recoup the annual levy of eleven millions dollars against the Molson Centre and the Canadiens, agreeing with that assessment.

"That one tax alone costs us three top-flight hockey players a year, and puts us at a significant disadvantage," he said.

Teams sought relief from three levels of government (national, provincial, municipal), a movement spearheaded by Ottawa owner Rod Bryden.

Rod Bryden

"If, say, the Florida Panthers bring in twenty-five million dollars, they'll have twenty million to spend on players." Bryden said. *"If we bring in twenty-five million, we might have three million dollars for talent after we pay for our building and the real estate taxes. It would be a tremendous help if governments recognized hockey as an industry and gave us the tax concessions other industries receive."*

At century's end, ownership groups in Houston, Portland and Oklahoma City were participants in an invisible tug-of-war over the Senators.

Rats & Bats & Cephalopods

Not all octopi were wet and cold...

Over the many years of pro hockey's first century, many items flew around arenas during games: Sticks, pucks, bodychecks and Frenchmen.

Not all flights, however, began on the ice.

April 15, 1952, game four of the Stanley Cup final. The hometown Red Wings were up 3-0 in games, heading for a second series sweep, after dismissing the Leafs in the semi-final. They won that night, an eighth straight victory and a Stanley Cup first.

Eight wins... a championship... a record – what symbolic gesture or metaphor could bring this momentous occasion to the next level for the Motor City fans?

The answer came flying out of the stands, hit the Olympia ice with a SPLAT, and lay there quivering for minutes while hockey players and officials froze. Sticks and fingers were pointed and Stadium personnel were summoned. A shovel and a bucket eventually were produced and the unique detritus was removed from the playing surface.

Hours earlier, brothers Jerry and Pete Cusimano, fishmongers at the nearby Eastern Market realized they had a product that signified the magic number: The eight-tentacled octopus would become a playoff regular in Detroit for almost half a century. The only thing that saved cephalopods from extinction in Michigan would be Detroit's spotty playoff performance in those five decades.

May 20, 1975. The venerable Aud in Buffalo was a sweatbox as game three of the final against Philadelphia got under way. It was so warm that the referee stopped the game several times so that the players could skate around to dissipate the fog that rose from the ice.

Midway through the game, a bat flew out of the rafters and buzzed Bernie Parent in the Flyers net. It was the only flying object the Philadelphia netminder couldn't stop during that playoff, and the game ground to a halt until Sabres winger Jim Lorenz demonstrated remarkable hand-to-eye co-ordination. The bat cadaver was trundled away and the Flyers went on to win their second straight Stanley Cup.

Fast forward to the mid-1990s and the 1996 playoffs... in Miami. The three-year-old Florida Panthers had little to distinguish themselves from other recent expansion teams in Ottawa and Anaheim as the 1995-96 season began. The team was equal parts untested rookies and castaways, one that had watched the previous two playoffs on television.

Early in the season, forward Scott Mellanby was taping sticks in the bowels of the rickety Miami Arena when a rat darted into the room and right toward him. Mellanby, a veteran who had deflected pucks that moved much faster, reacted like any hockey player with a stick in his hands would; when the rat bounced off the opposite wall, it was an ex-rodent.

That night, Mellanby scored twice in a 4-3 win over the visiting Flames, and the "rat trick" was born. By the following spring, and with prominent Florida residents as owner Wayne Huizenga and Jack Nicklaus looking on, every Panthers' playoff goal at the Miami Arena was greeted by a rain of rodents, rubber, plastic and otherwise.

It worked for all of May and much of June as Boston, Philadelphia and Pittsburgh were dispatched by the Panthers. The world was spared a Stanley Cup Rat Parade, however, when the Colorado Avalanche swept Florida in the final.

That summer, the NHL played Pied Piper and instituted new regulations banning fan-generated flights of rats and octopi.

Misguided bats of the mammalian sort may still proceed with caution, however.

Bernie Parent swings (at a) bat (background), while Colorado celebrates a Stanley Cup amid a rink full of rats.

The sixty-eight cent Canadian dollar costs us some hockey players, and the municipal tax burden is money we could invest in our hockey operations

"*In today's marketplace, you might be able to compete with one hand behind your back, but not two,*" said Canadiens' outgoing president Ronald Corey, who left the team in mid-1999 after seventeen years at the helm. "*The sixty-eight cent dollar costs us some hockey players, and the eleven million-dollar municipal tax burden, which none of the U.S.-based teams has to pay, is money we could invest in our hockey operations, to shore up our farm teams, scouting or acquire talented hockey players, or even keep our own once they reach free agency.*"

The NHL's small market teams were not confined to Canada. In 1997, claiming a restrictive fan base and no help impending from local governments, owner Peter Karmanos moved the Hartford Whalers to Raleigh, North Carolina, a part of the United States known for its fervid following of a winter sport invented by a Canadian. Unfortunately for the renamed Carolina Hurricanes, that sport was James Naismith's basketball, and the Research Triangle was addicted to the college version. Three seasons later, as the hockey team finally moved into its new arena almost unnoticed by the local community, the jury was out on the franchise's chances in the region.

Formerly the Hartford Whalers

December 1, 1997

The Canadiens become the first team in history to play five thousand NHL games, in a 1-0 loss to the Penguins, in Montreal. The team's record since 1917 is 2,625 wins, 1,603 losses and 772 ties.

ALL-STAR TEAMS 1976

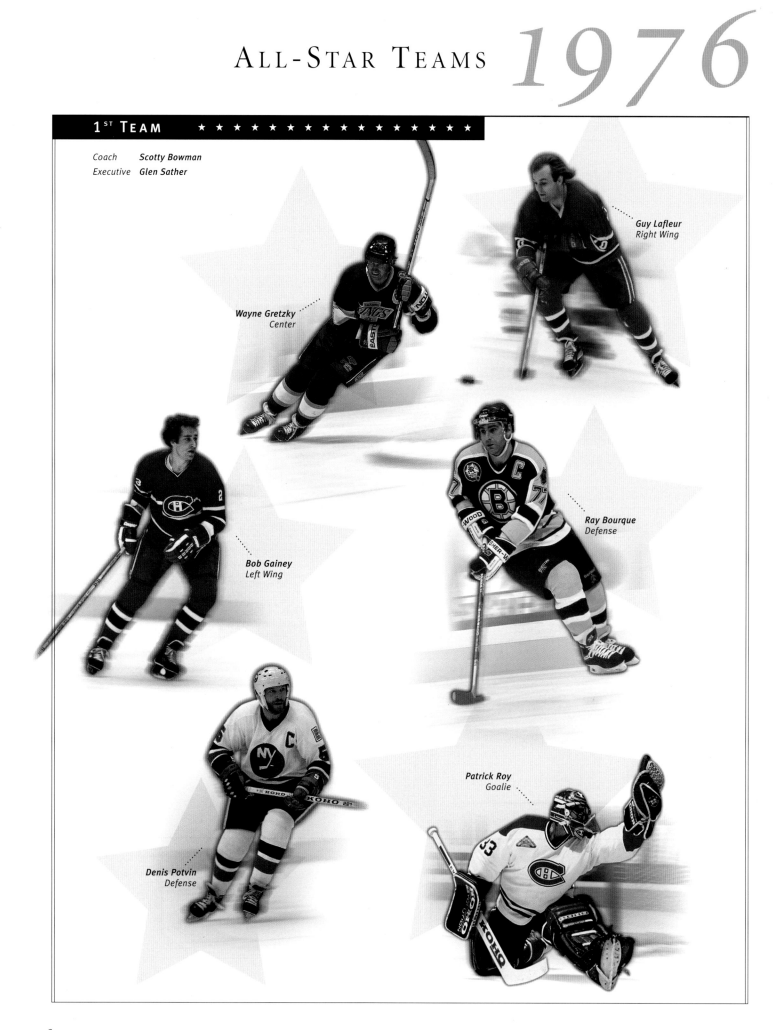

1ˢᵀ TEAM ★ ★ ★ ★ ★ ★ ★ ★ ★ ★ ★ ★ ★ ★ ★ ★ ★ ★

Coach   **Scotty Bowman**
Executive   **Glen Sather**

Guy Lafleur
Right Wing

Wayne Gretzky
Center

Bob Gainey
Left Wing

Ray Bourque
Defense

Denis Potvin
Defense

Patrick Roy
Goalie

2000 ALL-STAR TEAMS

★ ★ ★ ★ ★ ★ ★ ★ ★ ★ ★ ★ ★ ★ ★ ★ ★ **2ND TEAM**

Coach **Al Arbour**
Executive **Bill Torrey**

Mario Lemieux
Center

Jaromir Jagr
Right Wing

Steve Shutt
Left Wing

Paul Coffey
Defense

Dominik Hasek
Goalie

Larry Robinson
Defense

Spanning the Continents

199

Accepted into the league in the 1967 expansion, Pittsburgh celebrated its thirtieth anniversary with its second bankruptcy, and by the late summer of 1999, less than eight weeks from the new season, the team teetered on the edge of extinction.

For a second time in his still-young life (going on thirty-four), Mario Lemieux would save the hockey franchise in his adopted city. When he first signed with the Penguins in 1984, the team had averaged six thousand fans a game over the previous two seasons. By the late 1980s and with Lemieux's Pens poised to win the Stanley Cup, a hockey ticket at the Igloo was the hardest thing to find in the city.

Pittsburgh won its Cups, Mario Lemieux suffered the setbacks to his health that forced his retirement, but the Czech version of the superstar "wide body", Jaromir Jagr, took over and kept Pittsburgh competitive on the ice, at least. Players' salaries were sky-high, and soon some of Jagr's more prominent teammates were heading to other teams, through free agency.

Jaromir Jagr

"*In the last three or four years, we let some people go – Ron Francis, for example – because we were out of money,*" said Craig Patrick. "*And what had become obvious to us, was that the situation was going to get worse before it got better.*" Lemieux and Francis gone, some fans boycotted the Penguins because they felt management wasn't doing all it could to remain competitive.

When Lemieux left, the club still owed him an estimated thirty million dollars in deferred payments and guaranteed salary from a forty-two million-dollar contract signed in 1992. Boston businessman Roger Marino had taken over the fiscal side of the team from co-owner Howard Baldwin in 1997 and, in 1998, the unthinkable happened: Pittsburgh's Mr. Hockey sued the team to recoup some thirty-three million dollars owed to him.

February 22, 1998

The Czech Republic, led by goalie Dominik Hasek, captures the men's ice hockey gold medal at the Olympic Winter Games in Nagano with a 1-0 win over Russia. It marks the first time that NHL players are allowed to compete.

April 7, 1999

Colorado's Patrick Roy sets an NHL record for goaltenders, with his ninth career thirty-win season, in a 4-1 win over the visiting Nashville Predators. Roy previously shared the record of eight thirty-win seasons with Tony Esposito.

The NHL announces new rule changes for regular season overtime starting in 1999-2000; from now on, teams will play four-on-four (skaters) and each team would receive one point for the tie, with an additional point going to the overtime winner.

June 21, 1999

Marino responded that the expense of paying Lemieux when he was no longer playing was a financial burden on the Penguins, especially considering the significantly lower attendance at the Igloo since his retirement. The owner added that the team would lose ten million dollars for the current fiscal year.

When the team filed for bankruptcy protection in October, 1998, Marino said the Penguins had lost thirty-seven million dollars over the previous two seasons. The future was bleak; no one in Pittsburgh with money appeared ready to step up.

Mario Lemieux used money owed to him as a stake and put together a management group that eventually etched out an agreement that everyone could live with – banks, insurance companies, the NHLPA, SMG (the arena landlord), Fox Sports Net Pittsburgh, and other creditors in the local business community. U.S. Bankruptcy Judge M. Bruce McCullough worked with Lemieux throughout the summer.

When it appeared everyone was on board, another snag occurred and Judge McCullough got the league to agree to a final deadline of eleven o'clock on Tuesday, August 24. If all agreements were not finalized by that time, he would push to have the team liquidated. *"From my experience, people have to have a real deadline to get serious. Painful as it was going to be... if it didn't get done, I was going to blow it up,"* the judge said.

Lemieux's attorney Doug Campbell mobilized some heavy hitters in the private and public sectors, and the final agreement was forged at one o'clock Wednesday morning. On Friday, August 27, at two o'clock in the afternoon, an amount of more than fifty million dollars was released from Lemieux's escrow account to pay the team's bills and the deal was done. If Lemieux were the center on this line, his wingers were Judge McCullough and his lawyer Campbell, and all three were accomplished stickhandlers.

Spanning the Continents

For a second time in his still-young life, Mario Lemieux would save the hockey franchise in his adopted city

"*Mario is the whole reason why Pittsburgh hockey has been successful,*" Patrick remarked. "*He seems to have the same approach. He's very similar in the office to the way he was on the ice; totally in control and fully aware of everything that's happening all the time. He's always been a tremendous asset to this hockey club. No one else could have saved this club from bankruptcy and dispersal.*"

On September 1, 1999, the NHL Board of Governors confirmed Mario Lemieux as the new owner and chairman of the Pittsburgh Penguins hockey team. Craig Patrick sits at his right hand as president and CEO of the team.

The second question at Super Mario's post-confirmation press conference should have been the first: *"What can you do to control player salaries?"*

Lemieux showed he had lost none of his skating ability: *"We have a lot of work to do. I'm new in this process, but I'll learn the business."*

[*I've said many times that we have one of the best general managers in the league in Craig Patrick*]

When asked if he would be involved more with the business side, or the hockey side of the operation, he lauded the man already in place. *"I'll be more involved in the business side. I've said many times that we have one of the best general managers in the league in Craig Patrick. He's done an excellent job throughout his career in Pittsburgh and I have a lot of confidence in him. He's the one who's going to run the hockey side."*

Both men expressed optimism about the future, for Pittsburgh and the league.

"Small market teams can compete; all teams can compete," said Patrick. *"I don't think that the big spenders are necessarily going to win all the time. If you run your business properly, you can bring in the right people at the right place and time, and try to stay profitable. Then you can stay competitive.*

"I'm encouraged this year the way the teams have addressed their payrolls. It seems that most of them have been losing money and we certainly can't afford to lose money on payroll. Other teams are looking at it that way, too. I think that's a good sign for the future of the game."

Mario Lemieux sees *"a lot of upside to the game, and the future is very bright for the NHL."*

"It's more about ideas, than money," he added, echoing words spoken eighty-eight years before, by Frank and Lester Patrick.

"The game is better than it was a few years ago. The players are better and the game is in better shape. Anything I can do to improve the game, or come up with ideas to improve the game, I would be willing to do that. I think I have some ideas to make the game better for the players and fans, and for television."

As pro-hockey's first century drew to a close, a self-described "third-line player", Craig Patrick, thus found himself where an NHL executive with that surname should be.

On the first line.

Quebec Netminders Inc.

Professional hockey's two most innovative goaltenders were French-speaking Quebeckers who both wore the "flake" label with good humor and pride. The first, of course, was the indomitable Jacques Plante, the Shawinigan native who pioneered angle-play, movement in and around the net, and the goalie mask, in a long and successful career. So what if he liked to knit?

Although Plante never knew his true successor, there can be no doubt that he passed the Canadiens' proverbial torch on to Patrick Roy, the Huck Finn look-alike who joined Montreal in 1985 and stood the National Hockey League on its collective ear while talking to his goalposts.

It started with a chance meeting in the spring of 1985 in Sherbrooke, Quebec, between an academic and a young goalie with a life full of potential.

The young goalie was Roy; the academic was François Allaire, a physical education and human kinetics proponent who had many theories about goaltending to implement.

Roy had joined the Sherbrooke Canadiens that spring for the American Hockey League play-offs after two seasons with the Granby Bisons of the Quebec Major Junior Hockey League where he had goals-against averages of 6.26 and 4.44 on a mediocre team. He led Sherbrooke to the Calder Cup championship.

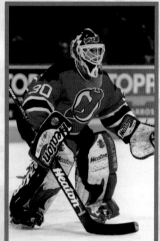

Martin Brodeur

"I didn't have a problem with the goals-against average," Allaire said. *"Patrick was what I was looking for in a goalie to work with; young, tall, very supple, very quick and very athletic."*

Roy had those attributes, and he listened as Allaire introduced his trademark butterfly style to the young netminder. Similar to the style pioneered by Chicago's Glenn Hall in the 1950s, the *papillon* sacrificed some angles play for down-low net protection.

"Studies of where and how goals were scored showed that more than seventy per cent were low shots, below the goalies' knees," Allaire said. *"With big, faster players stuffing the crease or screening the goalie from further out, there were fewer and fewer shots coming unimpeded to the net. The typical Canadian down-the-lane snapshot that angles goalies squared off against was disappearing. A European style of working the puck down low and behind the goalie was in vogue, and this meant that the goaltender would almost have to work inside his posts."*

Stéphane Fiset

Patrick Roy

The butterfly netminder stayed deep in his crease, taking away the bottom of the net and the corners, and learned to stay "tall and under control" when he went to his knees in scrambles.

Roy and Allaire worked together for almost a decade, backstopping two Stanley Cups with the Montreal Canadiens.

That was Allaire's debut, and along with his brother, Benoît, he established the Co-Jean Hockey School, which rapidly became the training ground for a generation of technically proficient, made-in-Quebec netminders.

Among the many young goalies to attend the school, and later serve as instructors in many cases, were such NHL stalwarts as Félix Potvin, Martin Brodeur, Stéphane Fiset, Jocelyn Thibault, Patrick Lalime, Eric Fichaud, Jimmy Waite and Dominic Roussel.

In the five drafts from 1995 to 1999, Quebec-produced goalies were at a premium, with fourteen selected in the first two rounds. In 1995, a record was set when three, Jean-Sébastien Giguère (Halifax), Martin Biron (Beauport) and Marc Denis (Chicoutimi), were first-round choices. Mathieu Garon (Victoriaville) and Francis Larivée (Laval) were second-round picks a year later, and the pinnacle of Quebec Netminders Inc. production was reached in 1997 when Val d'Or's Robert Luongo was selected fourth overall in the draft.

Denis backs up Patrick Roy in Colorado, while Buffalo's Biron is touted to replace Dominik Hasek. Garon and José Théodore are the goalies of the future for the Canadiens, as are Jean-Sébastien Giguère with Calgary and Luongo of the New York Islanders.

And, many more wait in the (butterfly) wings.

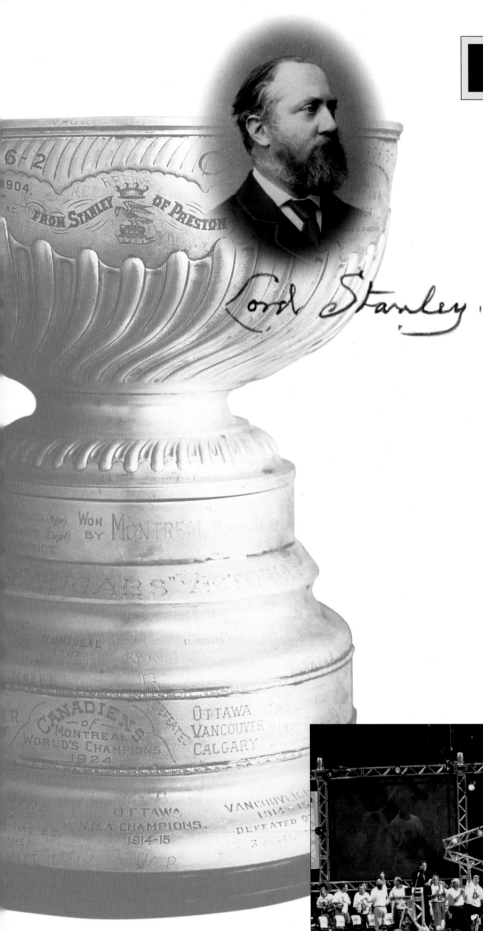

STANLEY CUP

1975-76	MONTREAL CANADIENS
1976-77	MONTREAL CANADIENS
1977-78	MONTREAL CANADIENS
1978-79	MONTREAL CANADIENS
1979-80	NEW YORK ISLANDERS
1980-81	NEW YORK ISLANDERS
1981-82	NEW YORK ISLANDERS
1982-83	NEW YORK ISLANDERS
1983-84	EDMONTON OILERS
1984-85	EDMONTON OILERS
1985-86	MONTREAL CANADIENS
1986-87	EDMONTON OILERS
1987-88	EDMONTON OILERS
1988-89	CALGARY FLAMES
1989-90	EDMONTON OILERS
1990-91	PITTSBURGH PENGUINS
1991-92	PITTSBURGH PENGUINS
1992-93	MONTREAL CANADIENS
1993-94	NEW YORK RANGERS
1994-95	NEW JERSEY DEVILS
1995-96	COLORADO AVALANCHE
1996-97	DETROIT RED WINGS
1997-98	DETROIT RED WINGS
1998-99	DALLAS STARS

1999

DALLAS STARS

Winners

1980

New York Islanders

1984

Edmonton Oilers

1990

1993

Montreal Canadiens

1995

New Jersey Devils

1986

Montreal Canadiens

Change overtook change as the century wore down. By media coverage of the various hot topics alone, 1999 became the hottest news year in a decade for the league. Wayne Gretzky suddenly announced his retirement, and without much more fanfare, and in spite of some cloying, awkward farewells, in late April he was out of the game he had dominated for two decades. An era, and a century, were drawing to an end.

The Sunbelt

The idea that hockey is a game best played in an area with snow and frozen ponds has been scuttled. While cold parts of the North American continent plus Europe and Russia might be the best spots to produce hockey players, the NHL and the pro game has moved slowly southward.

With the Atlanta Thrashers making their debut as an NHL expansion team in the 1999-2000 season, the league had ten teams in the "Sunbelt" area of the U.S. In addition, several minor pro leagues (East Coast, Western and Central leagues plus several International league teams) thrive in the warmer climates.

The Los Angeles Kings, part of the original 1967 expansion, took hockey to the sunshine first. The Atlanta Flames spent most of the 1970s in Georgia before moving to Calgary in 1980. But in the 1990s, six expansion teams (San Jose, Tampa Bay, Anaheim, Florida, Nashville and Atlanta) plus three franchise moves, (Minnesota to Dallas, Winnipeg to Phoenix, Hartford to Raleigh, N.C.) changed the NHL's geography dramatically.

A shark's mouth view in San Jose

Teamu Selanne, Anaheim Mighty Ducks

A large influence on placing teams in those cities was the fact that they represent major U.S. television markets and were a hefty influence on the NHL's increased exposure on national TV.

"Many of the southern areas we now have teams in were the fastest growing on the continent, and we wanted to be there," said NHL Commissioner Gary Bettman.

There is no doubt that the trade of Wayne Gretzky, the NHL's number one star, to the L.A. Kings by the Edmonton Oilers in 1988 had a big influence on the direction of the NHL's growth. San Jose and Anaheim were California areas quick to cash in on the upsurge in the "ice" game in the warmer climates.

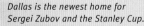

Dallas is the newest home for Sergei Zubov and the Stanley Cup.

Interview

WAYNE GRETZKY

Echoes of a Great One

Wayne Gretzky and a few numbers is all it takes
– 1,487, 894, 1,963, 2,875, plus 208, 122, 250, 382.

OF ALL THE RECORDS YOU SET, WHICH ONE GAVE YOU THE MOST SATISFACTION?

For some reason I can't really explain, scoring fifty goals in thirty-nine games was a favorite moment in my career. Two great natural goal scorers, Rocket Richard and Mike Bossy, had scored fifty in fifty games, and I never thought of myself as a goal scorer at that level. But in a way the Rocket's record still stands. I've never thought that I broke his record. The league was very different when he did it, six teams and maybe stronger and lower scoring. I'm really proud that I did it because it never was something I thought about or ever had as a target. Sometimes, the things that happen sort of unexpectedly are the most satisfying.

YOUR CAREER HAD MANY TIES TO THE CAREER OF GORDIE HOWE, AND YOUR RELATIONSHIP WITH HIM HAS ALWAYS SEEMED SPECIAL TO YOU. SOME RANDOM THOUGHTS ON THE MAN?

I was eleven years old when I met him at a banquet. He had been my

DESPITE HAVING THE CAREER RECORD FOR SCORING GOALS, YOU NEVER THOUGHT OF YOURSELF AS A GOAL SCORER?

If somebody asked me to describe myself, I would say I'm a playmaker. If you name the great goal scorers in history, the list would have Gordie Howe, Rocket Richard, Bobby Hull, Phil Esposito and Mike Bossy. I never felt I was gifted in that area of the game like those guys. I think something that gets overlooked is how hard I worked at scoring goals, the number of shots I took in practice to become an accurate shooter. I'm the first to tell you I was blessed with some great skills, but there's a lot more to my game than people recognize. I'm proud of the fact that I worked as hard as anybody.

hero for as long as I could remember and it was the most nervous I've ever been in my life. I didn't see him again until I was in the WHA in 1978. I know people who have had idols, then when they met the person, they were disappointed. For me with Gordie, it was just the opposite. I had under-estimated him in my hero worship. He was much greater in real life than in my fantasy.

DIDN'T THAT ADD TO THE THRILL OF BREAKING HIS CAREER RECORDS?

Of course, it gave me a tremendous charge to break his points and goal record. But those are also times of reflection for me. It's difficult to compare what Gordie and I did because the game has changed so much since he had his big years. There were no five-man rushes with defensemen involved through much of his career, the way the game has been in the time I've played. But, really, there's no way you can compare anyone to him or even mention them in the same breath as Gordie Howe. He stands alone as a man and as an athlete. He was better for longer than anyone.

Interview   Wayne Gretzky

THE BACKYARD SESSIONS WITH YOUR FATHER AND THE GUIDANCE HE GAVE YOU IN OUR CAREER, EVEN WHEN YOU WERE IN PRO HOCKEY, ARE LEGENDARY. WHAT WERE THE KEY THINGS HE TAUGHT AND TOLD YOU?

My dad always joked that he flooded our backyard to make a rink because he was sick of sitting in cold rinks while I played and practiced, and with ice behind the house, he could stay in where it was warm. What he stressed was repetition, doing things, like making a pass and taking a pass, over and over until it became automatic to do it right. One small thing was that in most of the passing drills I did, he insisted that I pass over something, a stick or pole on the ice, so that I had to lift the puck to get it to where I wanted it to go. It was a big asset in games to be able to loft a pass, say, a foot off the ice and over opponents' sticks, and have the puck come down flat. He had some drills for me to do where I didn't go where the puck was but where it was going to be. Sure, a player must have some instinct to anticipate the play but he helped learn to read situations so that I just knew that if this and this and this were happening on a play, the

puck was likely to go there, then be there when the puck got there. If I showed any kind of arrogance, any sort of sign that I was a 'snotty' kid, my dad corrected it very quickly, and harshly, if that's what it took. He drilled it home to me that I was no better or bigger than anyone else.

HOW DO YOU TRANSLATE THE LESSONS YOU RECEIVED FROM YOUR FATHER TO WHAT YOU TELL KIDS WHEN THEY ASK ABOUT PLAYING NOW?

I loved to play hockey, absolutely loved everything about it, and would have lived my whole life in skates. My dad saw that I had that love for the game, but that I had to work hard to be the best I could at it. My advice to kids is simple. Play because you love to play hockey. Don't ever think about making a lot of money out of hockey. Just love to play, work hard at it, and everything will fall into place.

Wayne plays ball hockey with his brothers.

WHAT DO YOU CONSIDER THE BIGGEST MOTIVATION IN YOUR CAREER?

I suppose because of my size, there was always someone saying or writing that the next level up would be the one where it would be too much for me. It started when I scored a lot of goals as a kid, and I don't ever

remember not having pressure on me somehow from somewhere. It was both external, from the expectations of others, and internal, from wanting to show anyone with doubts about me that they were wrong and that I could do the job. After a time, the pressure just became a fact of life for me.

COULD ANYTHING HAVE BEEN MORE ADVANTAGEOUS FOR A YOUNG PLAYER THAN YOUR TRADE TO THE EDMONTON OILERS IN 1978?

It would be very hard to create a better situation than the Oilers turned out to be for me and all the other guys who played there. I was seventeen when I got there and had most of the last season of the WHA to learn pro hockey on a team with really knowledgeable veterans. I got to play for Glen Sather, who was like a second father to me and, has since been established as one of the best executives the game ever had. He used the skill I had as an asset and didn't try to change me into something I wasn't. Then John Muckler joined as co-coach, and I learned a tremendous amount about the game from him. But what made it such an exceptional experience was that Glen rounded up such a great collection of young talent – Mark Messier, Kevin Lowe, Glenn Anderson, Grant Fuhr, Jari Kurri, Paul Coffey, Charlie Huddy, Esa Tikkanen – and we were able to grow up together into a Stanley Cup team.

HAVING KURRI ON YOUR WING WAS NOT A SETBACK TO YOUR CAREER?

Jari had such great talent and such superior instinct for the game that he made it look easy, and that meant he wasn't as appreciated as he should have been. Was there really a better forward for two hundred feet of ice than him in the 1980s? From the start, he and I just fit together and, very quickly, we knew where the other one was on the ice in all situations. What could be any better than a four-on-four with Jari, Coffey and Huddy as the other three?

Welcome to L.A.

WAS THE TRADE TO THE KINGS (IN 1988) A MIXED EMOTION THING FOR YOU?

Very much so, distinctly good and bad sides to it. The Oilers had won four Stanley Cups in five years and the team still was on the young side so who knows what we might have accomplished? They won another Cup in 1990 without me. A bad side was the many people who just didn't know how things were said that Janet (Gretzky had married Janet Jones in the summer of 1988) had pushed me to get out of Edmonton to California because of her acting career. Nothing could be farther from the truth. It turned out to be a great adventure and a big challenge in L.A., a very positive experience most of the time.

DURING YOUR TIME THERE, WAS THERE ANY THOUGHT OF EDMONTON BEING A SMALL MARKET CANADIAN TEAM THAT MIGHT HAVE PROBLEMS SUPPORTING AN NHL TEAM AS SALARIES INCREASED?

When the Oilers were going great guns in the mid-1980s and the rink was full every night, it was the same group of fans at every game. I would look behind our bench and see familiar faces most nights, and if someone wasn't there, I was tempted to ask if they were sick. First, the same group of fans was very demanding, and you had to do something to satisfy them every night. But the big question then was that when the team declined as all teams do and those fans lost interest, where would we find the new fans to replace them in a city the size of Edmonton, which did not have a large percentage of the population who could afford it?

DID THE ATTENTION AND THE AMOUNT OF MEDIA COVERAGE YOU RECEIVED EVER BOTHER YOU?

Signing autographs for kids never seemed like work, and my dad gave me a lesson there. I developed a signature you could read because my dad told me that if someone thought I was important enough to ask for an autograph, then that person didn't deserve a chicken scratch. I suppose all the media attention, especially the criticism and that I wouldn't be able to play well at the next level, was good for me. I must admit that when I read some of the stories about myself, I would shake my head. One year I reported to camp at one hundred and seventy-five pounds, maybe eight pounds above normal after trying all summer to put on a little beef. There was a story that I came to camp fat and out of shape.

WHAT WAS THE WEIRDEST BIT OF RECOGNITION YOU REMEMBER?

Actually, it was a case of not being recognized. In 1982 after the world championship, I went to Martinique for three weeks to get away from everything. About the third day I was there, I walked on the beach and saw something I couldn't believe. A guy with a Wayne Gretzky Titan hockey stick was shooting a ball at a paper cup. He turned out to be from France, working there, and I never did find out where he got the hockey stick.

WHAT WERE THE BIGGEST DISAPPOINTMENTS ALONG THE WAY?

I think it was when the Kings missed the 1994 playoffs, the first time I had been on a club in my life that wasn't in the playoffs. Losing to the Calgary Flames in the 1986 playoffs was hard to take, too, because it could have meant five consecutive Cup wins to tie the record.

Wayne and Janet

WHAT WAS THE BIGGEST THRILL OF IT ALL?

That's easy. The first Stanley Cup in 1984 by the Oilers. There's no charge like it because it's a team win.

We wish to thank the following for their special participation and contributions: Evelyn Armstrong, Jean Béliveau, Bruce Bennett, Anne Fotheringham, George Gross, Stu Hackel, Frédéric Huard, Dick Irvin, Bernard Lachance, Laurent Marquart and Claire Senneville. Outside special contributors who rallied around the project include Phil Pritchard, Eric Campbell and Jane Rodney of the Hockey Hall of Fame, Dan Diamond, John Morrison, Neil Mainville and Jeff Neiman. As well, a special thank you to Los Angeles' finest, Bob Borgen, The Timeline Man.

Last, and definitely most, this book could not and would not be what it is without the very special contributions of Julie Desilets and Geneviève Desrosiers, two moms who skated faster than The Roadrunner and still made it in time for check-out at the daycare centre each evening.

Bibliography / Sources

Behind the Cheering, by Frank J. Selke with Gordon Green, McLelland & Stewart, Toronto, 1962.

Jean Béliveau, My Life in Hockey, by Jean Béliveau with Chrys Goyens and Allan Turowetz, McLelland & Stewart, Toronto, 1994.

Boss, The Mike Bossy Story, by Mike Bossy and Barry Meisel, McGraw-Hill Ryerson Limited, Scarborough, Ont., 1988

The Boys of Saturday Night, Inside Hockey Night in Canada, by Scott Young, Macmillan of Canada, Toronto, 1990.

Canada Cup of Hockey/76, The Official History, Worldsport Properties, Toronto, 1976.

The Days Canada Stood Still, Canada vs USSR 1972, by Scott Morrison, McGraw-Hill Ryerson, Toronto, 1989.

Firewagon Hockey, The Story of the Montreal Canadiens, by Andy O'Brien, The Ryerson Press, Toronto, 1967.

Forever Rivals, Montreal Canadiens – Toronto Maple Leafs, James Duplacey, Charles Wilkins, edited by Dan Diamond, Dan Diamond and Associates, Inc., Toronto, 1996.

The Game, by Ken Dryden, Macmillan of Canada, Toronto, 1983.

The Game of Our Lives, by Peter Gzowski, McLelland & Stewart, Toronto, 1981.

The Glory Years, Memories of a Decade, 1955-65, by Billy Harris, Prentice-Hall Canada, Scarborough, Ont., 1989.

The Habs, An Oral History of the Montreal Canadiens, 1940-1980, by Dick Irvin, McLelland & Stewart, Toronto, 1991.

Hockey is our Game, by Jim Coleman, Key Porter, Toronto, 1987.

Hockey, The Official Book of the Game, Hamlyn Publishing, London, 1980.

The Leafs, An Anecdotal History of the Toronto Maple Leafs, by Jack Batten, Key-Porter Books, Toronto, 1994.

Lions in Winter, by Chrys Goyens & Allan Turowetz, Prentice-Hall, Toronto, 1986.

Lions in Winter, Revised edition, by Chrys Goyens & Allan Turowetz, McGraw-Hill Ryerson, Toronto, 1993.

Los Angeles Kings, Hockeywood, by Rick Sadowski, Sagamore Publishing, Champaign, Il, 1993.

The Mad Men of Hockey, by Trent Frayne, McLelland & Stewart, Toronto, 1974.

The Montreal Canadiens, An Illustrated History of a Hockey Dynasty, by Claude Mouton, Key Porter, Toronto, 1987.

The Montreal Forum, Forever Proud, by Chrystian Goyens, with Allan Turowetz and Jean-Luc Duguay, Les Éditions Effix Inc., Montreal, 1996.

Howie Morenz, Hockey's First Superstar, by Dean Robinson, Boston Mills Press, Erin, Ont., 1982.

National Hockey League 75th Anniversary Commemorative Book, Edited by Dan Diamond, McLelland & Stewart, Toronto, 1991.

Net Worth, Exploding the Myths of Pro Hockey, by David Cruise & Alison Griffiths, Viking, Toronto, 1991.

The Official National Hockey League Stanley Cup Centennial Book, Edited by Dan Diamond, McLelland & Stewart, Toronto, 1992.

Official Guide & Record Book, 1998-99; 1999-2000; National Hockey League Publications, Toronto & New York, 1998, 1999.

On Fire, The Dramatic Rise of the Calgary Flames, Eric Duhatchek & Steve Simmons, Polestar Press Ltd., Winlaw, B.C. 1986.

100 Great Moments in Hockey, by Brian Kendall, Viking (Penguin Books Canada Ltd.) Toronto, 1994.

The Patricks, Hockey's Royal Family, by Eric Whitehead, Doubleday Canada Limited, Toronto, 1980.

Red's Story, Red Storey with Brodie Snyder, Macmillan of Canada, Toronto, 1994.

Larry Robinson For The Defence, by Larry Robinson with Chrys Goyens, McGraw-Hill Ryerson, Toronto, 1988.

Sittler, by Darryl Sittler & Chrys Goyens, with Allan Turowetz, Macmillan of Canada, 1990.

The Trail of the Stanley Cup, Volume 1, 1893-1926 inc., by Charles S. Coleman, National Hockey League Publications, 1966.

The Trail of the Stanley Cup, Volume 2, 1927-1946 inc., by Charles S. Coleman, National Hockey League Publications, 1969.

The Trail of the Stanley Cup, Volume 3, 1947-1967 inc., by Charles S. Coleman, National Hockey League Publications, 1976.

Years of Glory, 1942-1967, The National Hockey League's Official Book of the Six-Team Era, Edited by Dan Diamond, McLelland & Stewart, Toronto, 1994.

The Miami Herald, Miami, Fla.

Le Journal de Montréal, Montreal.

Documentation La Presse, Montreal.

City of Montreal Public Library

Pittsburgh Post-Gazette, Pittsburgh, Pa.

The Toronto Star, Toronto.

Editor's Note: *We have made every effort to trace the ownership of copyrighted photos. If we have failed to give adequate credit, we will be pleased to make changes in future printings.*

Photos are detailed left to right, top to bottom on the page they appear. Photographer's name is listed in italics. Source of photo, if differing from author or copyright publication, appears in parentheses. Year photo taken is listed, if known.

FOREWORD

Pages 6-7 JEAN BÉLIVEAU'S LAST GAME, 1971, *John Jaqua,* (Collection Jean Béliveau), ©Time Inc. - Sports Illustrated / Collection Jean Béliveau.

INTRODUCTION

Pages 8-9 LESTER PATRICK, ©Hockey Hall of Fame.
FRANK PATRICK, 1934, ©NHL Images.
MURRAY (MUZZ) PATRICK, 1962, ©Bruce Bennett Studios.
LYNN PATRICK, ©Hockey Hall of Fame.
CRAIG PATRICK, 1981, ©John Halligan.

STANLEY CUP WINNERS

Pages 48, 98, 150, 206 STANLEY CUP, ©Hockey Hall of Fame.
LORD STANLEY OF PRESTON, ©Dan Diamond.
Pages 49, 99, 151, 207 STANLEY CUP, ©Hockey Hall of Fame.

FIRST QUARTER – 1901-1925

Pages 10-11 (Montage)
(Background) CHAIR-SWING, 1923, *Hulton Getty,* ©Tony Stone Images.
EXTERIOR ICE RINK, ©Hockey Hall of Fame.
VICTORIA RINK, ©Hockey Hall of Fame.
RENFREW MILLIONAIRES IN SUITS, ©Hockey Hall of Fame.
LESTER PATRICK, ©Hockey Hall of Fame.
Page 12 MCGILL AT VICTORIA RINK, ©Hockey Hall of Fame.
Page 13 SHINNY GAME, ©Hockey Hall of Fame.
PATRICKS' LUMBERMILL, Courtesy of Bill Cunningham and Craig Patrick.
PATRICKS IN SOUTH DURHAM, Courtesy of Bill Cunningham and Craig Patrick.
Page 14 LORD STANLEY OF PRESTON, ©Dan Diamond
SHINNY ON LAKE, ©Hockey Hall of Fame.
Page 15 "HOCKEY ON ICE", 1877, ©The Gazette
MONTREAL VICTORIAS, 1897, ©Hockey Hall of Fame.
Page 16 VICTORIA RINK, ©Hockey Hall of Fame.
FRANK PATRICK, 1900, ©Hockey Hall of Fame.
Page 17 MCGILL HOCKEY CLUB, ©Hockey Hall of Fame.
Page 18 LESTER PATRICK, ©Hockey Hall of Fame.
ART ROSS, *Turofsky,* ©Hockey Hall of Fame.
Page 19 J.L. GIBSON, ©Hockey Hall of Fame.
PORTAGE LAKE HOCKEY TEAM, ©Hockey Hall of Fame.
Page 20 THE SILVER SEVEN, ©Hockey Information Service.
OTTAWA - WANDERERS GAME, 1911, ©Hockey Hall of Fame.
Page 21 OTTAWA SILVER SEVEN, 1911, ©Hockey Hall of Fame.
NEWSY LALONDE, ©Hockey Hall of Fame.
Page 22 GEORGES VÉZINA, ©Hockey Hall of Fame.
Page 23 DICK IRVIN IN DOORWAY, ©Hockey Hall of Fame.
THE MONTREAL WANDERERS, ©Hockey Hall of Fame.
Page 25 THE PATRICK FAMILY, Courtesy of Bill Cunningham and Craig Patrick.
THE PATRICKS' LOGGING CAMP IN NELSON, B.C., Courtesy of Bill Cunningham and Craig Patrick.
Page 26 J. AMBROSE O'BRIEN, ©Hockey Hall of Fame.
THE ORIGINAL STANLEY CUP, ©Hockey Hall of Fame.
HAILEYBURY HOCKEY TEAM, ©Hockey Hall of Fame.
Page 28 FRANK PATRICK, ©Hockey Hall of Fame.
JOE MALONE, *James Rice,* ©Hockey Hall of Fame.
PAGE 29 NHA TROPHY, ©Hockey Hall of Fame.
Page 29 BERT LINDSAY, ©Hockey Information Service.
LALONDE, TAYLOR AND PATRICK, 1910, Courtesy of Bill Cunningham and Craig Patrick.
Page 31 FRED (CYCLONE) TAYLOR, ©Hockey Information Service.
Page 32 FRED TAYLOR, ©Hockey Hall of Fame.
Page 33 PORTAGE LAKE HOCKEY TEAM, 1902, ©Hockey Hall of Fame.
Page 34 MEMBERS OF THE RENFREW MILLIONAIRES, 1910, Courtesy of Bill Cunningham and Craig Patrick.
Page 35 NEWSY LALONDE STANDING, ©CHC.
NEWSY LALONDE SKATING, *Bill Galloway,* ©Hockey Hall of Fame.
THE CANADIENS HOCKEY CLUB, ©Hockey Hall of Fame.
Page 36 NEWSY LALONDE, ©Hockey Hall of Fame.
JACK DARRAGH, ©Hockey Information Service.
CY DENNENY, ©Hockey Information Service.
CYCLONE TAYLOR, ©Hockey Hall of Fame.
ERNIE JOHNSON, ©Hockey Hall of Fame.
GEORGE BOUCHER, ©Hockey Hall of Fame.
GEORGES VÉZINA, *Turofsky,* ©Imperial Oil-Turofsky/Hockey Hall of Fame.
Page 37 DIDIER PITRE, ©Hockey Hall of Fame.
JOE MALONE, ©Hockey Hall of Fame.
FRANK NIGHBOR, ©Hockey Hall of Fame.
FRANK MCGEE, ©Hockey Information Service.
EDDIE GERARD, ©Hockey Information Service.
CLINT BENEDICT, *James Rice,* ©Hockey Hall of Fame.
SPRAGUE CLEGHORN, ©Hockey Information Service.
Page 38 BRUCE RIDPATH, ©Hockey Hall of Fame.
THREE SOLDIERS, ©Hockey Hall of Fame.
Page 39 DENMAN STREET ARENA, VANCOUVER, ©Hockey Hall of Fame.
THE VANCOUVER MILLIONAIRES, 1912, ©Hockey Hall of Fame.
Page 40 JOSEPH CATTARINICH, ©Bruce Bennett Studios.
Page 41 FRANK FREDERICKSON, ©Hockey Hall of Fame.
FREDERICKSON IN REYKJAVIK, ©Hockey Hall of Fame.
COVER OF CANADIAN SPORTS, ©Hockey Hall of Fame.
Page 42 FRANK FOYSTON, ©Hockey Hall of Fame.
JACK WALKER, ©Hockey Hall of Fame.
BABE DYE, ©Hockey Hall of Fame.
Page 43 SEATTLE METROPOLITANS, 1917, ©Hockey Hall of Fame.
Page 44 MUTUAL STREET ARENA, TORONTO, ©Hockey Information Service.
PRESIDENT FRANK CALDER, ©Dan Diamond.
THE TORONTO BLUESHIRTS, ©Hockey Hall of Fame.
Page 45 BILLY BOUCHER, 1925, ©Hockey Information Service.
Page 46 GEORGES VÉZINA, ©Hockey Hall of Fame.
Page 47 REDVERS (RED) GREEN, 1926, ©NHL Images.
WILFRID (SHORTY) GREEN, ©John Halligan.
HAMILTON TIGERS, 1925, ©Hockey Information Service.
Page 48 OTTAWA STANLEY CUP CHAMPIONS, 1905, ©Hockey Hall of Fame.
Page 49 VICTORIA COUGARS STANLEY CUP CHAMPIONS, ©Bruce Bennett Studios.
KENORA THISTLES STANLEY CUP WINNERS, 1907, ©Dan Diamond.
MONTREAL WANDERERS, WINNIPEG, 1907, ©Dan Diamond.
SEATTLE METROPOLITANS CUP CHAMPIONS, 1917, ©Dan Diamond.
TORONTO ARENAS CHAMPIONS, 1919, ©Hockey Hall of Fame.

SECOND QUARTER – 1926-1950

Pages 50-51 (Montage)
(Background) SOLDIERS MARCHING, ©Hockey Hall of Fame.
DETROIT COUGARS, 1927, ©Hockey Information Service.
THREE RANGERS, ©Hockey Hall of Fame.
MAURICE RICHARD IN ACTION, ©Bruce Bennett Studios.
LESTER PATRICK IN OFFICE, 1948, ©John Halligan.
Page 52 DETROIT'S GORDON KEATS, ©Bruce Bennett Studios.
Page 53 CHICAGO BLACKHAWKS, ©Hockey Hall of Fame.
EDDIE SHORE WITH STICK, ©Hockey Hall of Fame.
EDDIE SHORE, ©Dan Diamond.
Page 54 MERVYN (RED) DUTTON, ©John Halligan.
Page 55 PITTSBURGH PIRATES, 1925, ©NHL Images.
MONTREAL MAROONS, ©Hockey Hall of Fame.
BROOKLYN AMERICANS, ©Bruce Bennett Studios.
Page 56 MAJOR FREDERIC MCLAUGHLIN, ©Hockey Hall of Fame.
CHICAGO BLACKHAWKS, 1938, ©Hockey Information Service.
Page 57 IVAN (CHING) JOHNSON, ©John Halligan.
Page 58 BUN COOK, ©Hockey Hall of Fame.
Page 59 PORTLAND ROSEBUDS, ©Hockey Hall of Fame.
DICK IRVIN SR., ©Dan Diamond.
Page 60 HOWIE MORENZ ON ICE, ©Hockey Hall of Fame.
JOHNNY GAGNON, ©Hockey Hall of Fame.
AUREL JOLIAT MOURNING, *Galloway,* ©Hockey Hall of Fame.
HOWIE MORENZ BREAKING HIS LEG, ©Hockey Hall of Fame.
Page 61 CLINT BENEDICT, ©Dan Diamond.
Page 62 TED LINDSAY, ©NHL Images.
MAURICE RICHARD, *Turofsky,*©Imperial Oil-Turofsky/Hockey Hall of Fame.
HOWIE MORENZ, *James Rice,* ©Hockey Hall of Fame.
EDDIE SHORE, ©Hockey Hall of Fame.
TURK BRODA, ©Hockey Hall of Fame.
EARL SEIBERT, ©Dan Diamond.
Page 63 MILT SCHMIDT, ©Bruce Bennett Studios.
CHARLIE CONACHER, ©Hockey Hall of Fame.
AUREL JOLIAT, *Galloway,* ©Hockey Hall of Fame.
DIT CLAPPER, ©Bruce Bennett Studios.
TINY THOMPSON, ©Dan Diamond.
KING CLANCY, 1932, ©Hockey Information Service.
Page 64 ART COULTER, ©John Halligan.
Page 65 JACK ADAMS AS PLAYER, ©Dan Diamond.
JACK ADAMS WITH SAWCHUK, 1952, ©Hockey Information Service.
KING CLANCY OF MAPLE LEAFS, *Turofsky,* ©Imperial Oil-Turofsky /Hockey Hall of Fame.
Page 66 THE SILVER FOX, LESTER PATRICK, ©Bruce Bennett Studios.
Page 67 PHILADELPHIA QUAKERS, ©Hockey Information Service.
Page 68 NELS STEWART, ©Bruce Bennett Studios.
Page 69 CHICAGO BLACKHAWKS, ©Hockey Hall of Fame.
MONTREAL MAROONS, ©Hockey Information Service.
BOSTON BRUINS, 1939, ©Hockey Information Service.
Page 70 CONN SMYTHE, ©Hockey Hall of Fame.
MAPLE LEAF GARDENS, ©NHL Images.
Page 71 CHARLES CONACHER, ©Bruce Bennett Studios.
Page 72 CHUCK GARDINER, ©Bruce Bennett Studios.
Page 73 BUSHER JACKSON, ©Bruce Bennett Studios.
FRANCIS (KING) CLANCY, ©Hockey Hall of Fame.
Page 74 BAILEY AND SHORE SHAKING HANDS, ©Hockey Hall of Fame.
Page 75 FRANK PATRICK, 1934, ©NHL Images.
GM ART ROSS, ©Hockey Hall of Fame.
Page 76 TOE BLAKE, 1937, ©Hockey Information Service.
MAURICE RICHARD, *David Bier,* ©CHC.
Page 77 ACTION, RICHARD, *David Bier,* ©CHC.
Page 78 RICHARD SCORING, *Turofsky,* ©Imperial Oil-Turofsky /Hockey Hall of Fame.
Page 79 MAURICE RICHARD SITTING, *Frank Prazak,* ©Hockey Hall of Fame.
PRESIDENT CLARENCE CAMPBELL, ©Dan Diamond.
MAURICE RICHARD WITH TROPHY, *Bob Fisher,* ©CHC.
Page 80 JAMES NORRIS, ©Hockey Hall of Fame.
DETROIT'S OLYMPIA STADIUM, ©Hockey Hall of Fame.
MAAA WINGED WHEELERS, ©Hockey Hall of Fame.
Page 81 THE LONGEST GAME, ©Hockey Information Service.
Page 83 LYNN, LESTER AND MURRAY PATRICK, ©Bruce Bennett Studios.
BOXER MUZZ PATRICK, ©John Halligan.
Page 84 RANGERS HEXTALL, WATSON, PATRICK, ©John Halligan.
Page 85 MEL HILL, ©John Halligan.
CECIL THOMPSON, ©Bruce Bennett Studios.
Page 86 THE KRAUT LINE, 1942, ©Bruce Bennett Studios.
DOUG AND MAX BENTLEY, 1948, ©Dan Diamond.
Page 87 HAP DAY & CLARENCE CAMPBELL, 1949, ©Bruce Bennett Studios.
ACTION, TURK BRODA IN GOAL, 1949, ©Bruce Bennett Studios.
Page 88 BAUER, SCHMIDT & DUMART, ©Hockey Hall of Fame.
BAUER, SCHMIDT & DUMART ACTION ©Hockey Hall of Fame.
Page 89 DICK IRVIN SR. & JR., ©NHL Images.
REG, MAX AND DOUG BENTLEY, 1942, ©Bruce Bennett Studios.
Page 90 FRANK SELKE, ©Hockey Hall of Fame.
THE KID LINE, ©Hockey Hall of Fame.
Page 91 BÉLIVEAU SIGNING CONTRACT, 1953, *David Bier,* ©Collection Jean Béliveau.
Page 92 THE RENFREW MILLIONAIRES, ©John Halligan.
Page 93 SYD HOWE, 1936, ©Hockey Information Service.
Page 94 SYL APPS, 1940, ©Hockey Information Service.
Page 95 LESTER PATRICK NIGHT, 1947, ©John Halligan.
Page 96 NY RANGERS VS NY AMERICANS, ©John Halligan.
CARL VOSS, ©NHL Images.
KING CLANCY, ©Hockey Hall of Fame.
Page 98 DETROIT RED WINGS, ©NHL Images.
Page 99 MONTREAL CANADIENS, ©Hockey Information Service.
NEW YORK RANGERS, 1933, ©John Halligan.
BOSTON BRUINS, 1939, ©Bruce Bennett Studios.
OTTAWA SENATORS, ©Hockey Information Service.
TORONTO MAPLE LEAFS, 1949, ©Dan Diamond.

THIRD QUARTER – 1951-1975

Pages 100-101 (Montage)
(Background) RUSH HOUR, 1950, *Hulton Getty,* ©Tony Stone Images.
OLYMPIC CROWD, *Mel DiGiacomo,* ©Bruce Bennett Studios.
CCCP – CANADA BANNER, ©Bruce Bennett Studios.
JEAN BÉLIVEAU'S LAST GAME, 1971, *John Jaqua* (Collection Jean Béliveau), ©Time Inc. - Sports Illustrated / Collection Jean Béliveau.
LYNN PATRICK & SYD SALOMON III, 1966, ©Bruce Bennett Studios.
MURRAY PATRICK GM/COACH, 1962, ©Bruce Bennett Studios.
Page 102 MURRAY PATRICK, ©John Halligan.
Page 103 MUZZ PATRICK WITH PLAYERS, ©John Halligan.
BILL MOSIENKO, 1952, ©Bruce Bennett Studios.
Page 104 WHALERS' GORDIE HOWE, *Bruce Bennett,* ©Bruce Bennett Studios.
GORDIE HOWE 544TH GOAL, 1963, ©Bruce Bennett Studios.
Page 105 HOWE OF DETROIT RED WINGS, 1970, *Graphic Artists,* ©Hockey Hall of Fame.
YOUNG GORDIE HOWE, ©Bruce Bennett Studios.
GORDIE HOWE WITH SONS, ©Hockey Hall of Fame.
Page 106 GORDIE HOWE'S 600TH GOAL, 1965, ©Bruce Bennett Studios.
GORDIE HOWE SITTING, *Frank Prazak,* ©Hockey Hall of Fame.
Page 107 GORDIE HOWE SKATING, *Mel DiGiacomo,* ©Bruce Bennett Studios.
ACTION MARK & GORDIE HOWE, *Mel DiGiacomo,* ©Bruce Bennett Studios.
ACTION GORDIE HOWE, ©Hockey Hall of Fame.
Page 108 GLENN HALL LOOKING FOR PUCK, *Kilpatrick,* ©Collection Jean Béliveau.
Page 109 ALEX DELVECCHIO, ©Hockey Hall of Fame.
RAYNER VS LINDSAY, ©Dan Diamond.
Page 110 (Background) STANLEY CUP PARADE IN MONTREAL, *René Picard,* ©La Presse.
ACTION HENRI RICHARD, *Mel DiGiacomo,* ©Bruce Bennett Studios.
GOALIE KEN DRYDEN, *Mel DiGiacomo,* ©Bruce Bennett Studios.
Page 111 ACTION, GORDIE HOWE & MAURICE RICHARD, ©Bruce Bennett Studios.
ACTION CANADIENS – BLACKHAWKS, ©Bruce Bennett Studios.
Page 112 MAURICE RICHARD SHAKING HANDS, 1952, ©Dan Diamond.
MAURICE RICHARD ACTION, 1953, *Roger St-Jean,* ©La Presse.
Page 113 CRAIG AND LYNN PATRICK, ©Hockey Hall of Fame.
Page 114 FRANK MAHOVLICH, *Graphic Artists,* ©Hockey Hall of Fame.
BOBBY HULL VS HENRI RICHARD, 1960, ©Bruce Bennett Studios.
BOBBY HULL'S 28TH BIRTHDAY, 1966, ©Bruce Bennett Studios.
Page 115 THE TACOMA ROCKETS, ©John Halligan.
ACTION MAHOVLICH, ©Dan Diamond.
Page 116 SIGNING OF JEAN BÉLIVEAU'S CONTRACT ©Collection Jean Béliveau.
D. MOLSON, S.POLLOCK & J. BÉLIVEAU, ©Collection Jean Béliveau.
Page 117 JACK ADAMS, ©Hockey Hall of Fame.
Page 118 BOBBY ORR, ©Bruce Bennett Studios.
DOUG HARVEY, *David Bier,* ©David Bier/CHC.
TERRY SAWCHUK, *Frank Prazak,* ©Hockey Hall of Fame.
G. HOWE, J. BÉLIVEAU & B. HULL, *David Bier*, ©Collection Jean Béliveau.
Page 119 FRANK MAHOVLICH, ©Hockey Hall of Fame.
PIERRE PILOTE, *Graphic Artists,* ©Hockey Hall of Fame.
BERNARD GEOFFRION, *Frank Prazak,* ©Hockey Hall of Fame.
JACQUES PLANTE, ©John Halligan.
PHIL ESPOSITO, ©Bruce Bennett Studios.
TIM HORTON, *Graphic Artists,* ©Hockey Hall of Fame.
Page 120 BRAD PARK, *Mel DiGiacomo,* ©Bruce Bennett Studios.
ACTION, GUMP WORSLEY & BOBBY HULL, ©Bruce Bennett Studios.
DAVE KEON, ©Hockey Hall of Fame.
Page 121 PUNCH IMLACH, *Graphic Artists,* ©Hockey Hall of Fame.
PUNCH IMLACH WITH LEAFS, ©Bruce Bennett Studios.
DAVE KEON, ©Dan Diamond.

BOB BAUN WITH STANLEY CUP, ©Dan Diamond.
Page 122 PIERRE PILOTE, *Frank Prazak,*
©Hockey Hall of Fame.
JEAN BÉLIVEAU & YVAN COURNOYER,
©Collection Jean Béliveau.
Page 123 ACTION, JEAN BÉLIVEAU, *Aussie
Whiting,* ©Collection Jean Béliveau.
Page 124 JEAN BÉLIVEAU, *Denis Brodeur,*
©Collection Jean Béliveau.
BOBBY ORR, *Mel DiGiacomo,*
©Bruce Bennett Studios.
Page 125 ACTION BOBBY ORR &
BOBBY ROUSSEAU, *Mel DiGiacomo,*
©Bruce Bennett Studios.
BOBBY ORR & HENRI RICHARD,
©Hockey Hall of Fame.
Page 126 TERRY SAWCHUK IN NET,
©Dan Diamond.
ACTION, ALEX DELVECCHIO,
©NHL Images.
Page 127 STAN MIKITA, *Bruce Bennett,*
©Bruce Bennett Studios.
CHICAGO BLACKHAWKS, 1965,
©Hockey Hall of Fame.
Page 128 G. HOWE & B. GADSBY, 1965,
©Bruce Bennett Studios.
Page 129 MUZZ PATRICK,
©Bruce Bennett Studios.
Page 130 GLENN HALL, 1962,
©Bruce Bennett Studios.
TERRY SAWCHUK & JOHNNY BOWER, 1965,
Graphic Artists, ©Hockey Hall of Fame.
JACQUES PLANTE, *David Bier,* ©David Bier/CHC.
TERRY SAWCHUK, ©Dan Diamond.
Page 131 NEW YORK RANGERS VS TORONTO
MAPLE LEAFS, ©Hockey Hall of Fame.
BILL MASTERTON, ©Bruce Bennett Studios.
Page 132 CALIFORNIA SEALS ACTION,
©NHL Images.
Page 133 L.A. VS ST. LOUIS, ©London Life-
Portnoy/Hockey Hall of Fame.
LYNN PATRICK & SYD SOLOMON III, 1966,
©Bruce Bennett Studios.
CLARENCE CAMPBELL, ©Bruce Bennett Studios.
Page 134 LOS ANGELES KINGS VS MINNESOTA
NORTH STARS, 1968, ©Bruce Bennett Studios.
MONTREAL VS TORONTO ACTION, *David Bier,*
©Collection Jean Béliveau.
Page 135 RED KELLY, ©Hockey Hall of Fame.
TONY ESPOSITO ACTION, ©Hockey Hall of Fame.
Page 136 BUFFALO VS VANCOUVER, 1970,
©NHL Images.
GIL PERREAULT & PUNCH IMLACH,
©Hockey Hall of Fame.
YOUNG BOBBY ORR, ©Bruce Bennett Studios.
Page 137 ALAN EAGLESON, *Graphic Artists,*
©Hockey Hall of Fame.
JIM NEILSON & BOB PULFORD, 1967,
©Bruce Bennett Studios.
Page 138 BOSTON'S BOBBY ORR,
©London Life-Portnoy/Hockey Hall of Fame.
YOUNG BOBBY ORR, ©Bruce Bennett Studios.
Page 139 TEAM CANADA'S BOBBY ORR, 1976,
©Bruce Bennett Studios.
BOBBY ORR IN SUIT, ©Bruce Bennett Studios.
Page 140 CANADA–RUSSIA SUMMIT BANNER,
1972, *Mel DiGiacomo,* ©Bruce Bennett Studios.
VLADISLAV TRETIAK, 1972, *Mel DiGiacomo,*
©Bruce Bennett Studios.
RUSSIAN TEAM, 1972, *Mel DiGiacomo,*
©Bruce Bennett Studios.
Page 141 PHIL ESPOSITO, 1972, *Mel DiGiacomo,*
©Bruce Bennett Studios.
VALERI KHARLAMOV, 1972, *Mel DiGiacomo,*
©Bruce Bennett Studios.
VLADIMIR PETROV, 1972, *Mel DiGiacomo,*
©Bruce Bennett Studios.
CANADIAN TEAM, 1972, *Mel DiGiacomo,*
©Bruce Bennett Studios.
Page 142 GUY LAFLEUR WITH CUP,
©Hockey Hall of Fame.
MARCEL DIONNE, *Rod Hanna,*
©Bruce Bennett Studio.
ACTION, DAVE SCHULTZ, *Mel DiGiacomo,*
©Bruce Bennett Studios.
BRAWL NORTH STARS VS FLYERS, *Mel DiGiacomo,*
©Bruce Bennett Studios.
ACTION, BERNIE PARENT, *Mel DiGiacomo,*
©Bruce Bennett Studios.
Page 143 LYNN PATRICK, ©Bruce Bennett Studios.
CRAIG PATRICK, ©NHL Images.
Page 144 1972 SUMMIT POSTER,
©Hockey Hall of Fame.
ACTION TOMMY WILLIAMS, ©John Halligan.
Page 145 ULF STERNER, ©John Halligan.
BORJE SALMING, ©Bruce Bennett Studios.
Page 146 MUZZ, LESTER & LYNN PATRICK,
©Hockey Hall of Fame.

Page 147 TRETIAK, 1972, *Mel DiGiacomo,*
©Bruce Bennett Studios.
YVAN COURNOYER, *Bruce Bennett,*
©Bruce Bennett Studios.
Page 148 BOBBY HULL & GORDIE HOWE,
Mel DiGiacomo, ©Bruce Bennett Studios.
BOBBY HULL, *Chuck Solomon,*
©Bruce Bennett Studios.
TED GREEN, *Mel DiGiacomo,*
©Bruce Bennett Studios.
Page 149 BERNIE PARENT, *Mel DiGiacomo,*
©Bruce Bennett Studios.
Page 150 DETROIT RED WINGS, 1952,
©Hockey Information Service.
Page 151 DETROIT RED WINGS,
©Hockey Hall of Fame.
MONTREAL CANADIENS, 1956,
©Collection Jean Béliveau.
MONTREAL CANADIENS, 1969,
©Collection Jean Béliveau.
GEORGE ARMSTRONG, ©Dan Diamond.
ACTION BOSTON BRUINS, 1970, ©John Halligan.

───────────────────────

FOURTH QUARTER – 1976-2000

Pages 152-153 (Montage)
(Background) TERRY SAWCHUK IN TV STUDIO,
Graphic Artists, ©Hockey Hall of Fame.
MARIO LEMIEUX WITH JOURNALISTS, 1997,
Dave Sandford, ©Hockey Hall of Fame.
STAPLES CENTER, 1999, Courtesy of the
Los Angeles Kings.
THE MIGHTY DUCKS STATUE, 1997, *Bruce Bennett,*
©Bruce Bennett Studios.
WAYNE GRETZKY (REAR VIEW),
©Bruce Bennett Studios.
CRAIG PATRICK, ©John Halligan.
Page 154 DOUG JARVIS, ©Bruce Bennett Studios.
DARRYL SITTLER, *Mel DiGiacomo,*
©Bruce Bennett Studios.
Page 155 STAPLES CENTER, 1999, Courtesy of the
Los Angeles Kings.
JUMBOTRON, *B. McCormick,*
©Bruce Bennett Studios.
Page 156 LANNY MCDONALD, 1980,
©Bruce Bennett Studios.
OILERS CUP WINNERS, 1988,
©Bruce Bennett Studios.
Page 157 AL ARBOUR, ©Hockey Hall of Fame.
ACTION, TONELLI, *Bruce Bennett,*
©Bruce Bennett Studios.
MONTREAL CANADIENS, *Mel DiGiacomo,*
©Bruce Bennett Studios.
CANADIENS BANNERS, 1996, *Robert Laberge,*
©Bruce Bennett Studios.
Page 158 ESA TIKKANEN, 1988,
©Bruce Bennett Studios.
SERGE SAVARD ON BENCH,
©Bruce Bennett Studios.
ROGATIEN VACHON, *Denis Brodeur,*
©Denis Brodeur.
Page 159 CRAIG PATRICK,
©Bruce Bennett Studios.
GUY LAFLEUR, *Mel DiGiacomo,*
©Bruce Bennett Studios.
Page 160 GLENN PATRICK, 1976,
©John Halligan.
CRAIG PATRICK, WASHINGTON CAPITALS,
©John Halligan.
Page 161 MUZZ AND LYNN PATRICK WITH
GORDIE HOWE, ©NHL Images.
Page 162 JASON BOWEN, 1997, *Brian Winkler,*
©Bruce Bennett Studios.
BRYAN HELMER, ALBANY RIVER RATS, ACTION,
J. McIsaac, ©Bruce Bennett Studios.
Page 163 MIKE BOSSY,
©Bruce Bennett Studios.
DENIS CHASSE, 1996, *Paul Angers,*
©Bruce Bennett Studios.
JEAN BÉLIVEAU OF THE QUEBEC ACES,
Courtesy of Collection Jean Béliveau.
ACTION SYLVAIN BLOUIN, 1997, *Paul Angers,*
©Bruce Bennett Studios.
Page 164 CRAIG PATRICK, ©Hockey Hall of Fame.
Page 165 U.S. OLYMPIC HOCKEY TEAM, 1980,
©Hockey Hall of Fame.
PHIL ESPOSITO & CRAIG PATRICK, 1981,
©John Halligan.
Page 166 JAROMIR JAGR, 1998, *Bruce Bennett,*
©Bruce Bennett Studios.
DOMINIK HASEK, 1998, *Bruce Bennett,*
©Bruce Bennett Studios.
ACTION SAKU KOIVU, 1998, *Bruce Bennett,*
©Bruce Bennett Studios.
Page 167 VACHON AND DZURILLA, 1976, *Denis
Brodeur,* ©Denis Brodeur.
TEAM SWEDEN, 1998, *Bruce Bennett,*
©Bruce Bennett Studios.

TEAM CANADA, 1976, *Denis Brodeur,*
©Denis Brodeur.
Page 168 MIRACLE ON ICE TEAM, 1980,
©Bruce Bennett Studios.
RICH SUTTER, 1987,
©Bruce Bennett Studios.
Page169 LAFLEUR AND BOSSY, *Denis Brodeur,*
©Denis Brodeur.
GUY LAFLEUR, *S. Levy,* ©Bruce Bennett Studios.
MIKE BOSSY, 1984, ©Bruce Bennett Studios.
ACTION LAFLEUR, 1983, ©Bruce Bennett Studios.
ACTION BOSSY, ©Bruce Bennett Studios.
Page 170 TIKKANEN, GREGG, FUHR,
©Bruce Bennett Studios.
Page 171 JOEY MULLEN, ©Hockey Hall of Fame.
PETER STASTNY, *Miles Nadal,*
©Hockey Hall of Fame.
BORJE SALMING, ©Bruce Bennett Studios.
Page 172 ERIC LINDROS, 1997, *J. Giamundo,*
©Bruce Bennett Studios.
Page 173 ACTION ERIC LINDROS, 1998,
John Tremmel, ©Bruce Bennett Studios.
PAUL KARIYA, 1999, *H. DiRocco,*
©Bruce Bennett Studios.
Page 174 HERB BROOKS AND CRAIG PATRICK,
1981, ©John Halligan.
CRAIG PATRICK BEHIND THE BENCH,
©John Halligan.
Page176 LEMIEUX, PATRICK & COFFEY, *Bruce
Bennett,* ©Bruce Bennett Studios.
LANNY MCDONALD WITH CUP, *Bruce Bennett,*
©Bruce Bennett Studios.
Page 177 RICH AND RON SUTTER,
©Bruce Bennett Studios.
BRENT AND BRIAN SUTTER,
©Bruce Bennett Studios.
COACH DARRYL AND BROTHER DUANE SUTTER,
©Bruce Bennett Studios.
MATS SUNDIN, *J. Giamundo,*
©Bruce Bennett Studios.
Page 178 MARIO LEMIEUX,
©Bruce Bennett Studios.
Page 180 MARIO LEMIEUX,
©Bruce Bennett Studios.
FETISOV AND STARIKOV, ©Bruce Bennett Studios.
Page 181 MIKE GARTNER, *Bruce Bennett,*
©Bruce Bennett Studios.
Page 182 ALEXEI YASHIN, 1999,
A. Pichette, ©Bruce Bennett Studios.
SAKU KOIVU, 1999, *Robert Laberge,* ©CHC.
TEEMU SELANNE, *A. Foxall,*
©Bruce Bennett Studios.
ACTION MATS SUNDIN, 1997, *C. Andersen,*
©Bruce Bennett Studios.
GOALIE ARTURS IRBE, 1998,
J. Giamundo, ©Bruce Bennett Studios.
Page 183 DOMINIK HASEK, *Jim McIsaac,*
©Bruce Bennett Studios.
ACTION DOMINIK HASEK, 1998, *J. Leary,*
©Bruce Bennett Studios.
Page 184 MARIO LEMIEUX & WAYNE GRETZKY,
Denis Brodeur, ©Denis Brodeur.
Page 185 YOUNG WAYNE GRETZKY,
©Hockey Hall of Fame.
SOO GREYHOUND WAYNE GRETZKY, 1978,
Ottawa Citizen, ©Hockey Hall of Fame.
ACTION GRETZKY, *Miles Nadal,*
©Hockey Hall of Fame.
GRETZKY ON BENCH, 1996, *M. Hicks,*
©Bruce Bennett Studios.
Page 186 SCOTTY BOWMAN, *Scott Levy,*
©Bruce Bennett Studios.
Page 187 IGOR LARIONOV, 1999,
J. Giamundo, ©Bruce Bennett Studios.
SLAVA FETISOV, 1998, *John Tremel,*
©Bruce Bennett Studios.
WAYNE GRETZKY, ©Bruce Bennett Studios.
Page 188 WAYNE GRETZKY,
©Bruce Bennett Studios.
Page 189 KINGS' GRETZKY, 1995, *R. Laberge,*
©Bruce Bennett Studios.
GRETZKY AND HOWE, *Bruce Bennett,*
©Bruce Bennett Studios.
GRETZKY & HULL, 1996, *M. Desjardins,*
©Bruce Bennett Studios.
WAYNE GRETZKY AS RANGER,
©Bruce Bennett Studios.
Page 190 MARIO TREMBLAY VS DALE HUNTER,
Armand Trottier, ©La Presse.
MONTREAL VS QUEBEC, ACTION,
©Bruce Bennett Studios.
Page 191 LANNY MCDONALD, *Bruce Bennett,*
©Bruce Bennett Studios.
WAYNE GRETZKY & JARI KURRI,
©Bruce Bennett Studios.
PAVEL BURE VS MARK MESSIER,
©Hockey Hall of Fame.

Page 192 MONTREAL'S MOLSON CENTRE, 1996,
Robert Laberge, ©Bruce Bennett Studios.
BUFFALO'S MARINE MIDLAND ARENA, 1998,
C. Andersen, ©Bruce Bennett Studios.
ST. LOUIS KIEL CENTER, 1996, *J. Giamundo,*
©Bruce Bennett Studios.
Page 193 GARY BETTMAN, 1996, *Dave Sandford,*
©Hockey Hall of Fame.
BOB GOODENOW, 1996, *Dave Sandford,*
©Hockey Hall of Fame.
Page 194 ALEXEI YASHIN, 1995, *Robert Laberge,*
©Bruce Bennett Studios.
Page 195 GAYLORD ENTERTAINMENT CENTER,
1999, *J. Russell,* ©Bruce Bennett Studios.
ACTION BOB BOUGHNER, 1999, *J. Russell,*
©Bruce Bennett Studios.
ROD BRYDEN, *Bruce Bennett,*
©Bruce Bennett Studios.
OTTAWA PALLADIUM, 1996, *Robert Laberge,*
©Bruce Bennett Studios.
Page 196 GIANT OCTOPUS,
©Hockey Hall of Fame.
BERNIE PARENT AND BAT, 1975, ©NHL Images.
COLORADO AVALANCHE WITH CUP AND RATS,
©Hockey Hall of Fame.
Page 197 RONALD COREY, 1998, *Bob Fisher,*
©CHC/Bob Fisher.
ARTURS IRBE, 1998, *Jim McIsaac,*
©Bruce Bennett Studios.
Page 198 WAYNE GRETZKY,
Denis Brodeur, ©Denis Brodeur.
GUY LAFLEUR, ©Bruce Bennett Studios.
BOB GAINEY, *Chuck Solomon,*
©Bruce Bennett Studios.
RAY BOURQUE, *Bruce Bennett,*
©Bruce Bennett Studios.
DENIS POTVIN, 1980, ©Bruce Bennett Studios.
PATRICK ROY, *Denis Brodeur,* ©Denis Brodeur.
Page 199 STEVE SHUTT, ©Bruce Bennett Studios.
MARIO LEMIEUX, *Anthony Neste,*
©Bruce Bennett Studios.
JAROMIR JAGR, ©Bruce Bennett Studios.
PAUL COFFEY, *Bruce Bennett,*
©Bruce Bennett Studios.
DOMINIK HASEK, 1995, *H. Scull Jr.,*
©Bruce Bennett Studios.
LARRY ROBINSON, 1981, ©Bruce Bennett Studios.
Page 200 JAROMIR JAGR, 1996, *Jim McIsaac,*
©Bruce Bennett Studios.
MARIO LEMIEUX SALUTING,
©Bruce Bennett Studios.
Page 201 PATRICK ROY, 1999, *J. Russell,*
©Bruce Bennett Studios.
Page 202-203 MARIO LEMIEUX WITH JOURNAL-
ISTS, 1997, *Dave Sandford,* ©Hockey Hall of Fame.
Page 204 MARIO LEMIEUX, 1997, *Dave Sandford,*
©Hockey Hall of Fame.
CRAIG PATRICK, ©John Halligan.
Page 205 PATRICK ROY, 1998, *H. DiRocco,*
©Bruce Bennett Studios.
MARTIN BRODEUR, *Denis Brodeur,* ©Denis Brodeur.
STÉPHANE FISET, 1998, *Bruce Bennett,*
©Bruce Bennett Studios.
Page 206 DALLAS STARS, 1999,
©Bruce Bennett Studios.
Page 207 GRETZKY WITH CUP, 1984,
Bruce Bennett, ©Bruce Bennett Studios.
NEW YORK ISLANDERS, *Bruce Bennett,*
©Bruce Bennett Studios.
EDMONTON OILERS, 1990, *Bruce Bennett,*
©Bruce Bennett Studios.
MONTREAL CANADIENS, 1993, *André Pichette,*
©CHC.
BOB GAINEY WITH CUP, 1979, *Bruce Bennett,*
©Bruce Bennett Studios.
Page 208 ARROWHEAD POND, *Scott Levy,*
©Bruce Bennett Studios.
A SHARK'S MOUTH VIEW, 1996, *A. Foxall,*
©Bruce Bennett Studios.
TEEMU SELANNE, *Brian Winkler,*
©Bruce Bennett Studios.
SERGEI ZUBOV, ©Bruce Bennett Studios.
Page 209 GRETZKY RETIREMENT, *Bruce Bennett,*
©Bruce Bennett Studios.
GRETZKY & RICHARD WITH HART TROPHY, *Denis
Brodeur,* ©Denis Brodeur.
Page 210 EDMONTON OILERS' WAYNE GRETZKY,
Bruce Bennett, ©Bruce Bennett Studios.
WAYNE PLAYING WITH BROTHERS,
©Hockey Hall of Fame.
Page 211 WAYNE GRETZKY WITH KINGS
SWEATER, *Bruce Bennett,* ©Bruce Bennett Studios.
WAYNE GRETZKY AND JANET JONES, *Bruce
Bennett,* ©Bruce Bennett Studios.
Page 212-213 GRETZKY'S FAREWELL, 1999,
Bruce Bennett, ©Bruce Bennett Studios.